# HIGH SCHOOL PREPGENIUS

## AN ACADEMIC GUIDE TO EXCELLENCE

*I would like to acknowledge several people who helped to make this book exceptional: Karen Rudolph, Cari Bounds, Kelly Cantrell, Elizabeth Hartley and Monica Solis-Hoefl. I am truly thankful for your expertise and insight that you so willingly shared because of your love and dedication to see all high school students succeed.*

## THOUGHTS FROM JEAN

When I first began teaching my college test prep program in 2003, I started out with the intentions of helping students learn how to ace standardized tests. My goal was for them to become confident, earn high scores, and receive scholarships as my own children did. Although this has become a reality, with numerous students of mine raising their SAT score by as much as 600 points, and many becoming National Merit scholars, I found an even greater need for guidance in *other* areas in high school. Many students over the years have expressed a loss of direction when navigating their way through these important four years. This book is intended for use as a student roadmap for high school success. It covers information for all academic paths (public, private, charter, and homeschool), so find what applies to your particular situation. My daughter, Judah, has added her own input and experience to enhance this effort, as well as extensive research into the key areas that students face when traversing this uncharted territory known as high school.

## THOUGHTS FROM JUDAH

As coauthor of *High School Prep Genius: A Guide to Academic Excellence*, it is my sincere wish to give all the students who read this book information they need to succeed not only in high school, but also in all their academic endeavors. Looking back over my own educational journey, I have come to realize the narrow-mindedness of my focus and the opportunities I missed because of it. Throughout high school and college, I focused my attention on getting the grades, but not gaining the knowledge from my classes. I turned in all my homework, seriously studied for all my tests, and worried tremendously about each grade. I wasted a lot of time fussing over the wrong aspect of education. Consequently, I graduated from high school, college, and graduate school with a 4.0 GPA, but without really enjoying my studies. It was not until my senior year of college that I realized all the effort put into school was meaningless if I walked away without learning anything. The purpose of education is not simply making grades. It is to gain knowledge about the world and practical applications of such knowledge. It is from this perspective that I write this book.

# Table of Contents

I.  **Introduction** . . . . . . . . . . . . . . . . . . . . . . . . . . . . 11
   - How to Use This Book . . . . . . . . . . . . . . . . . . . . 13
   - College and Career Notebook . . . . . . . . . . . . . . . . 15
   - Student Timeline: Before High School Begins . . . . . . . . . . . 45
   - 9th-12th Grade Student Timelines . . . . . . . . . . . . . . . 55

II.  **Foundation For Personal Success** . . . . . . . . . . . . . . . . 89
   - Chapter One:  Personal Development . . . . . . . . . . . . . . 91
   - Chapter Two: Interests That Make You Interesting . . . . . . . . 107
   - Chapter Three: Own Your Beliefs . . . . . . . . . . . . . . . 123
   - Chapter Four:  Building a Healthy You . . . . . . . . . . . . 135
   - Chapter Five: Your Financial Independence . . . . . . . . . . . 149
   - Chapter Six: Building a Strong Support System . . . . . . . . . 161

III.  **Foundation For Academic Success** . . . . . . . . . . . . . . . 165
   - Chapter Seven: Academic Development . . . . . . . . . . . . 177
   - Chapter Eight: Effective Studying . . . . . . . . . . . . . . . 187
   - Chapter Nine: Tests and Papers . . . . . . . . . . . . . . . 201
   - Chapter Ten: Getting Organized . . . . . . . . . . . . . . . 217
   - Chapter Eleven: High School Mechanics . . . . . . . . . . . 233
   - Chapter Twelve: Going Beyond the Basics . . . . . . . . . . 249

IV.  **Foundation for Future Success** . . . . . . . . . . . . . . . . 273
   - Chapter Thirteen: Future Development . . . . . . . . . . . . 275
   - Chapter Fourteen: Choosing a School . . . . . . . . . . . . 293
   - Chapter Fifteen: Standardized Test Prep . . . . . . . . . . . 311
   - Chapter Sixteen: College Applications . . . . . . . . . . . . 328
   - Chapter Seventeen: Paying for school . . . . . . . . . . . . 347
   - Chapter Eighteen: College Essentials . . . . . . . . . . . . 367

Appendix A: How to Build a Homeschool Transcript . . . . . . . . . . 399

Appendix B: Talent Searches . . . . . . . . . . . . . . . . . . . . 409

Appendix C: Great Books to Get You Started . . . . . . . . . . . . 415

Appendix D: Reduce Test Anxiety Through Relaxation Techniques  425

Appendix E: Admissions Terminology . . . . . . . . . . . . . . . 431

Author Biographies . . . . . . . . . . . . . . . . . . . . . . . . 439

# PART I:

# Introduction

# Introduction

BEFORE CONTINUING with this guide, readers must understand two underlying principles of this book. First, academic success, by any measure, requires dedication. Most obstacles can be overcome by hard work and determination. When it comes to breaking down barriers, the issue is not if it can be done, but whether the person is willing to put in the time and effort in order to accomplish it.

Second, prepared students make good citizens. The purpose of this guide is not simply to help students do well in school and ultimately get into the colleges of their dreams. While we hope this book helps every student accomplish those goals, the real purpose of this book is to help shape students' personal and academic development by giving each student the tools needed to succeed. It is not enough to be students who look good on paper and get into college; instead, students should be the types of people who will use their talents and abilities to enrich not only their individual lives, but also the world as a whole.

Education is a wonderful tool; it is a blessing to have so many opportunities to learn. In no other time in history has the wealth of knowledge been so readily available to anyone who has the desire to learn. Sadly, many students take the privilege of higher education for granted. In many ways, high school and college have become self-evident rights—something students are entitled to. This mentality is troubling because students who succumb to it run the risk of missing the full potential of their academic journey.

In the United States, students spend an average of forty hours a week attending classes and completing homework during the school year, for twelve mandatory years. To complete the bare minimum requirement of schoolwork, a student will put in roughly seventeen thousand hours in the classroom. That is a lot of time to devote to any endeavor. Why not make the most of these efforts?

## WHO CAN USE THIS BOOK?

This book is full of important information for both parents and students alike. Parents or guardians should try to make one hour available each week to review this information with their students. Some may choose to treat it like a book club and discuss their thoughts and impressions on a chapter-by-chapter basis.

This book will highlight four sets of people (parents, high school guidance counselors, private college planning representatives, and college admissions counselors) all of whom can help students succeed in high school and beyond. Students should be open to sharing this book and their questions with them. These people are there to support and encourage.

Parents: They are a student's cheering section! They want the best possible future and have wisdom and experience on their side. They can help students with deadlines, motivation, and emotional support.

High School Guidance Counselors: Almost every high school has one or more, but it will ultimately be a student's job to make appointments with them, ask for their advice, and talk about appropriate class scheduling. They can also help when it comes to post-high school plans, but students will need to do any follow-up work needed to apply to colleges as well as scholarships. *The parents of homeschooled children take on the role of guidance counselor for their students.*

Private College Planning Representatives: For a fee, these independent consultants can help students with college essays, applications, timelines, extracurricular activities, tutors, scholarships, test prep, etc.

College Admission Counselors: Many admissions counselors travel to recruit prospective students and work to fulfill their school's enrollment goal for that year. Getting to know them personally can go a long way in helping to get an acceptance letter, so students should keep in contact with them during the college application journey.

Not everyone will have or need all four of these people to help them get through high school. This book was created to fill any gaps in a student's preparation for high school and beyond. Even if a student is fortunate enough to have many of these people in his or her life, the information in this book can be used as a supplementary guide. Students may also choose to use this book as a substitution for one or more of these resources if they are unavailable.

# How to Use This Book

The chapters are written with the students in mind and have thought-provoking exercises. At the end of each chapter, there is a section specifically for parents. Although students shouldn't have to worry about reading these sections, it is imperative that parents consistently keep up with their student's reading and follow the instructions for parents contained within each chapter. Adult readers should expect to find chapter-specific homework for them as well!

**For optimal reading and understanding, parents and students should read the student sections together.** Alternatively, if parents or guardians are unable to maintain a consistent reading schedule with their students, students may read the entire book first, and then pass the book on to parents who need to read the rest to ensure they get all of the important information.

Parents: This book emphasizes many times the importance of keeping good records. Before getting started, take a moment to look over the College and Career Notebook section preceding the first chapter. It should give you a good preview of what to watch for.

This book is designed to help every high school student chart his or her course for success. *Since education can be achieved through public, private, charter, and homeschool settings, feel free to ignore or adjust accordingly if any part of this guide does not apply to you.*

## HOW THE BOOK IS ARRANGED

The first section is the Foundation for Personal Success. This section includes Chapters 1-6. These chapters include information on fostering personal growth, developing interests, establishing belief systems, promoting mental and physical health, creating financial independence, and building a strong support system. The key to success in life begins with a strong sense of self.

The second section is the Foundation for Academic Success. This section includes Chapters 7-12. These chapters include information on academic essentials, effective study skills, organization techniques, the basics of high school, and tips for the high school experience. The core of high school is not only the curriculum in the classroom, but also the student's ability to learn and adapt the information to everyday life.

The third section is the Foundation for Future Success. This section includes Chapters 13-18. These chapters include information on planning for the future, picking a path after high school, studying for important entrance exams, applying to college, paying for higher education, and understanding college essentials. High school is only a stepping stone to greater things; therefore, having a solid high school experience can lead to a productive future.

At the end of the book are five appendixes that expand upon information addressed in some of the chapters. Students should use these appendixes to help build strong foundations.

## WHY THIS BOOK IS IMPORTANT

The high school journey is one of personal struggles and growth. During the adolescent years, students face the transition from childhood to adulthood. These changes are both exciting and terrifying for many students as well as their parents. It is our company's goal, through the addition of *High School Prep Genius: A Guide to Academic Excellence*, to equip each student for the journey ahead.

As each semester starts, students receive a list of school supplies to purchase—tools to help them in their courses. This guide is another tool to help you through the next several years of school. High school comprises four important years of a student's academic life. Students can take several different routes during these years and end up in very different places. Whether you are just starting your high school journey or nearing the end of the voyage, this book can be your compass. Navigating through the waters of high school can be tricky, but with the right guidance, you can reach your desired destination.

# COLLEGE AND CAREER NOTEBOOK

The first thing you should do with this program is create a college and career notebook. Preparation and organization are skills that make the high school years and college application process infinitely easier. If you start the planning process now, working little by little as you go, you will eliminate the extra stress of trying to get everything done all at once as high school graduation nears. The college and career notebook should contain all the necessary information for applying to a school or a job in one place.

Even if you are unsure about your future plans, make the notebook. Plans change. Don't let unpreparedness force you to rush to get this information together when you need it. This will give you the freedom to explore different options after high school without shutting the door to any particular avenue. If this notebook is not used for college, it will make a great high school portfolio, keepsake, or résumé builder.

## GETTING STARTED

Purchase a large, three-ring notebook. Get some pocketed dividers (at least seven) and label the tabs as follows:

- Four-Year Degree Plan and Four-Year Summer Plan
- Student Profile
- High School Classes and Transcript Information
- Test Prep Chart
- College Search and Career Choices
- Scholarship Information and Financial Aid
- Volunteer Work and Extracurricular Activities
- Awards and Honors.

For each tab in your folder, there is a sample chart or table in this section to get you started. These should give you an idea of the spreadsheet or chart you can make on your computer to organize your notebook; or feel free to make a copy of the ones in this book. Simply copy each table, and fill the cells with the necessary information.

Each year you should fill out the table or chart for each tab. This allows you to keep a track record of your high school progress, and more importantly, it all stays organized! A record of curriculum is especially important for a homeschooled student, but all students can benefit from doing this, especially if the colleges you apply to ask you about what you accomplished during high school. Impress the schools by being able to provide a detailed list of everything you studied.

Do not put off creating this notebook until your junior or senior year. Start now to make the whole process a lot easier.

# Four-Year Degree Plan and Four-Year Summer Plan

## MAP OUT YOUR HIGH SCHOOL PLAN

Many people think there is only one path to finishing high school. This simply isn't true. Depending on your goals and motivations, you can take one of three typical avenues toward high school graduation. There are average, accelerated, and exceptional high school career tracks. Check out the following three-tier guide to high school and see what academic path might be right for you. You can use the following information to help build your high school degree plan.

# THREE-TIER GUIDE TO HIGH SCHOOL

| Discipline | Distinguished (Exceptional) Program (+4 AP Courses) | Recommended (Accelerated) Program (+2 AP Courses) | Minimum Program* (Average) |
|---|---|---|---|
| English | 4 Credits | 4 Credits | 4 Credits |
| Mathematics | 4 Credits (algebra 1, algebra 2, geometry, pre-calculus or pre-college math) | 4 Credits (including algebra 1, algebra 2, geometry) | 3 Credits (including algebra 1, geometry) |
| Science | 4 Credits (including biology, chemistry, physics) | 4 Credits (biology, chemistry, physics) | 3 Credits (including biology, chemistry) |
| Social Studies | 4 Credits (world history, geography, U.S. history, government, or economics) | 4 Credits (world history, geography, U.S. history, government, economics) | 4 Credits (world history, geography, U.S. history, government, economics) |
| Physical Education | 1 ½ Credits | 1 ½ Credits | 1 ½ Credits |
| Health | ½ Credit | ½ Credit | ½ Credit |
| Foreign Language | 3 Credits (all in the same language) | 2 Credits (both in the same language) | 0 Credits |
| **Fine Arts | 1 Credit | 1 Credit | 1 Credit |
| Technology Applications | 1 Credit | 1 Credit | 1 Credit |
| Electives | 4 ½ Credits | 3 ½ Credits | 6 Credits |
| Speech | ½ Credit | ½ Credit | 0 Credits |
| **TOTAL** | **28 Credits** | **26 Credits** | **24 Credits** |

Note: These three plans are meant to serve as a guideline only. Your personal plan may vary due to personal curriculum as well as area and school requirements. Bible and religious studies may be added and counted as one credit each year.

*As of 2012, the minimum/average program is used primarily in schools for students in special education.
**Classes covered in the Fine Arts category are painting, sculpting, drawing, printmaking, computer graphics, jewelry making, ceramics, etc. Drama, theatre and music classes are considered performing arts and could be categorized as an elective.

# Your High School Degree Plan

Creating a four-year high school degree plan is a great way to keep track of the classes you need to take to graduate. Once you have decided which path you will take in high school (average, accelerated, or exceptional), sit down with your parents and guidance counselors and find out what classes you will need to take to achieve your goals. If you are homeschooled, then you need to make a plan that corresponds with your state's requirements (if applicable). Planning ahead will allow you to get the most from your academic experiences; it also ensures that you stay on course and take a balanced load of high school classes.

## TYPICAL MINIMUM REQUIREMENTS FOR GRADUATION

4 credits of English
4 credits of history/social studies/government
4 credits of math
4 credits of science
1 credit of fine arts
1 credit of physical education
1 credit of foreign language
½ credit of health
Electives will vary and are not required

## SUGGESTED CLASSES

Logic
Latin
Economics
Speech and debate
SAT and ACT preparation course

## IMPORTANT SKILLS

Self-directed learning
Critical Thinking
Self-discipline

| High School Graduation Checklist (Sample 1) | | | |
|---|---|---|---|
| **Subject** | **Credit** | **Grade Completed** | **Year Completed** |
| English | 1. _____ | | |
| | 2. _____ | | |
| | 3. _____ | | |
| | 4. _____ | | |
| **Subject** | **Credit** | **Grade Completed** | **Year Completed** |
| History | 1. _____ | | |
| | 2. _____ | | |
| | 3. _____ | | |
| | 4. _____ | | |
| **Subject** | **Credit** | **Grade Completed** | **Year Completed** |
| Math | 1. _____ | | |
| | 2. _____ | | |
| | 3. _____ | | |
| | 4. _____ | | |
| **Subject** | **Credit** | **Grade Completed** | **Year Completed** |
| Science | 1. _____ | | |
| | 2. _____ | | |
| | 3. _____ | | |
| | 4. _____ | | |
| **Subject** | **Credit** | **Grade Completed** | **Year Completed** |
| Fine Arts | 1. _____ | | |
| Physical Ed | 2. _____ | | |
| Health | 3. _____ | | |
| Foreign Lang | 4. _____ | | |
| **Subject** | **Credit** | **Grade Completed** | **Year Completed** |
| Electives | 1. _____ | | |
| | 2. _____ | | |
| | 3. _____ | | |
| | 4. _____ | | |

| Suggested Classes | | | |
|---|---|---|---|
| **Subject** | **Credit** | **Grade Completed** | **Year Completed** |
| Logic | 1. _____ | | |
| Latin | 1. _____ | | |
| Economics | 1. _____ | | |
| Speech | 1. _____ | | |
| Test Prep | 1. _____ | | |

## Recommended Plan (RHSP) & Distinguished Achievement Plan (DAP)
## For Grade 9 Students Entering in 2010-2011 and Thereafter

| Curriculum | Course | H/Pre-AP | Sem A | Sem B | Alternative Course | H/Pre-AP | Sem A | Sem B |
|---|---|---|---|---|---|---|---|---|
| English (4.0) | Eng. Lang. Arts I | | | | | | | |
| | Eng. Lang. Arts II | | | | | | | |
| | Eng. Lang. Arts III | | | | | | | |
| | Eng. Lang. Arts IV | | | | | | | |
| | Eng. Lang Arts V | AP | | | | | | |
| Mathematics (4.0) | Algebra I | | | | | | | |
| | Geometry | | | | | | | |
| | Algebra II | | | | | | | |
| | Pre-Calculus | | | | | | | |
| | Calculus | AP | | | | | | |
| Science (4.0) | Biology | | | | | | | |
| | Chemistry | | | | | | | |
| | Physics | | | | | | | |
| | Human Anatomy | | | | | | | |
| Social Studies (3.5) | World Geography | | | | | | | |
| | World History | | | | | | | |
| | U.S. History | | | | | | | |
| | Government | | | ■ | | | | |
| Economics (0.5) | Economics | | | ■ | | | | |
| Health (0.5) | Health | | | ■ | | | | |
| Physical Education (1.0) | | | | | | | | |
| | | | | | | | | |
| World Lang. (2.0) *[DAP—3.0] | | | | | | | | |
| | | | | | | | | |
| Fine Arts (1.0) | | | | | | | | |
| Speech (0.5) | Communication App.(0.5) | | | | | | | |
| Electives (5.0) *[DAP—4.0] | | | | | | | | |
| Elective | | | | | | | | |
| Elective | | | | | | | | |
| Elective | | | | | | | | |
| Elective | | | | | | | | |
| Elective | | | | | | | | |
| Tests | | | | | | | | |
| PSAT | | | | | | | | |
| SAT | | | | | | | | |
| ACT | | | | | | | | |

*DAP-Distinguished Achievement Program

_____ DOB _____ PEIMS ID _____ SID _____

**GRADUATION DATE** _____

| Goals | | |
|---|---|---|
| **Gr** | **Total Credits** | |
| 8th | | |
| | | |
| 9th | | |
| | | |
| 10th | | |
| | | |
| 11th | | |
| | | |
| 12th | | |
| | | |

| Comments |
|---|
| |
| |
| |
| |
| |
| |
| |

## YOUR FOUR-YEAR SUMMER PLAN

Summers provide a great chance to gain an edge for the next year as well as do something that will look good on your college applications. Don't waste your summers being lazy; get out there and do something good for yourself and your community. If you are having trouble coming up with ideas of what to do this summer, check out Chapter 12.

## Four-Year Summer Plan

### Summer Before Freshman Year

| Program Name | Description | Dates | Hours Partici-pated | Achievements | Contact Info |
|---|---|---|---|---|---|
|  |  |  |  |  |  |
|  |  |  |  |  |  |
|  |  |  |  |  |  |
|  |  |  |  |  |  |
|  |  |  |  |  |  |
|  |  |  |  |  |  |
|  |  |  |  |  |  |
|  |  |  |  |  |  |
|  |  |  |  |  |  |
|  |  |  |  |  |  |

**Four-Year Summer Plan**

**Summer Before Sophomore Year**

| Program Name | Description | Dates | Hours Partici-pated | Achievements | Contact Info |
|---|---|---|---|---|---|
| | | | | | |
| | | | | | |
| | | | | | |
| | | | | | |
| | | | | | |
| | | | | | |
| | | | | | |
| | | | | | |
| | | | | | |

## Four-Year Summer Plan

### Summer Before Junior Year

| Program Name | Description | Dates | Hours Partici-pated | Achievements | Contact Info |
|---|---|---|---|---|---|
| | | | | | |
| | | | | | |
| | | | | | |
| | | | | | |
| | | | | | |
| | | | | | |
| | | | | | |
| | | | | | |
| | | | | | |
| | | | | | |

**Four-Year Summer Plan**

**Summer Before Senior Year**

| Program Name | Description | Dates | Hours Partici-pated | Achievements | Contact Info |
|---|---|---|---|---|---|
| | | | | | |
| | | | | | |
| | | | | | |
| | | | | | |
| | | | | | |
| | | | | | |
| | | | | | |
| | | | | | |
| | | | | | |

## Student Profile

You can use a student profile for college résumés and applications, for internships, and work. It is a way to show administrators and future employers the things that motivate you, to form your goals, and to figure out how you can achieve those goals. For each year, include the following information as it applies to you specifically. When applying to college, this information can help you write your college essay or prepare for any interviews you might have.

Write down your current learning goals as well as long-term aspirations. Include some samples of class work that you are really proud of next in your folder with this page. This can include links to video or audio recordings of activities, such as speech and debate. You can also include the results of any projects that required complex thinking and interdisciplinary problem-solving skills. Put whatever you think is important and expresses your skills and talents as a student. Remember the purpose of this section is to sell your strong points, so emphasize the positives. (*You can even enhance your résumé by adding in your traveling experience.*)

STUDENT PROFILE

| YEAR | | | |
|------|--|--|--|
| 9TH | | | |
| 10TH | | | |
| 11TH | | | |
| 12TH | | | |

# Test Prep Examination Inventory

Your test prep examination inventory helps you keep track of how well you are doing on each type of exam. Make sure to write down how much you prepared for each exam and the results of extra preparation. This way you can gauge whether your test prep is effective. Always learn how to take the test and use appropriate study materials to get the most out of your studying.

## TEST PREP EXAMINATION INVENTORY

| TEST | GRADE | DATE | SCORE |
|------|-------|------|-------|
| **PSAT/NMSQT** | FRESHMAN_____ <br> SOPHOMORE_____ <br> JUNIOR_____ | _____ <br> _____ <br> _____ | _____ <br> _____ <br> _____ |
| **PSSS** | _____ <br> _____ <br> _____ | _____ <br> _____ <br> _____ | _____ <br> _____ <br> _____ |
| **SAT** | _____ <br> _____ <br> _____ <br> _____ <br> _____ <br> _____ | _____ <br> _____ <br> _____ <br> _____ <br> _____ <br> _____ | _____ <br> _____ <br> _____ <br> _____ <br> _____ <br> _____ |
| **\*SAT II** | _____ <br> _____ <br> _____ <br> _____ <br> _____ <br> _____ | _____ <br> _____ <br> _____ <br> _____ <br> _____ <br> _____ | _____ <br> _____ <br> _____ <br> _____ <br> _____ <br> _____ |
| **EXPLORE** | EIGHTH GRADE_____ <br> FRESHMAN_____ | _____ <br> _____ | _____ <br> _____ |
| **PLAN** | SOPHOMORE_____ | _____ | _____ |
| **ACT** | _____ <br> _____ <br> _____ <br> _____ <br> _____ <br> _____ | _____ <br> _____ <br> _____ <br> _____ <br> _____ <br> _____ | _____ <br> _____ <br> _____ <br> _____ <br> _____ <br> _____ |
| Accuplacer (dual-credit test) | _____ | _____ | _____ |

*SAT II tests are subject tests (i.e., math, history, English) and should only be taken if the college of your choice requires one or more of them.

# College Comparison Worksheet and Application Checklist

When it comes time to pick a college, chances are you will be wavering between a few different options. One of the best ways to evaluate the best college for you is by seeing the different colleges side by side. Every time you find a college that you are interested in, add it to the chart below. This way, when it is time to apply to different colleges, you can evaluate which colleges make the best matches. You can also refer back to this chart when it comes time to either accept or reject college offers.

Don't worry about filling out all of the information at first. Just concentrate on keeping an accurate list of schools that interest you. Later on, you can fill in the boxes for admissions and financial aid deadlines for your top picks. Check the colleges' websites to see what statistics they have available regarding returning students, percentage of applicants accepted, dorm life, and Greek life.

| COLLEGE NAME: | | | |
|---|---|---|---|
| Location<br>· distance from home | | | |
| Size<br>· enrollment<br>· physical size of college | | | |
| Cost of School<br>· tuition and fees<br>· room and board<br>· transportation<br>· estimated total budget<br>· application fee, deposits | | | |
| Affiliation<br>(public, private, proprietary) | | | |
| Environment<br>· type of school (two-year, four-year)<br>· school setting (urban, rural)<br>· location/size of nearest town<br>· religious affiliation | | | |
| Admissions Requirements<br>· deadline<br>· tests required<br>· average test scores, GPA, rank<br>· special requirements<br>· notification | | | |

| COLLEGE NAME: | | | |
|---|---|---|---|
| Academics<br>· potential major(s) offered<br>· special requirements<br>· accreditation<br>· student-faculty ratio<br>· typical class size<br>· study abroad<br>· internships<br>· professor or teaching assistants | | | |
| Financial Aid<br>· deadline<br>· required forms<br>· percentage receiving aid<br>· scholarships<br>· loans<br>· work-study | | | |
| Housing<br>· residence hall requirement<br>· availability<br>· types and sizes<br>· food plan | | | |
| Student Body<br>· male, female, co-ed<br>· part-time, full-time, commuter<br>· four-year graduation rate | | | |
| Facilities<br>· academic<br>· recreational<br>· other<br>· personal counseling<br>· career placement<br>· clinic<br>· campus security | | | |
| Activities<br>· clubs, organizations<br>· Greek life<br>· athletics (division I,II,III)<br>· intramurals<br>· other | | | |
| Specialty Programs<br>· honors<br>· disability | | | |
| Campus Visits<br>· when<br>· special opportunities | | | |

# College Application Checklist

Keep track of when all your college applications are due using your application checklist. To review the information on applying for colleges, check out Chapter 16.

| COLLEGE NAME | | | |
|---|---|---|---|
| Campus Visit | | | |
| Date | | | |
| Date | | | |
| Interview | | | |
| Date/Interviewer | | | |
| First Letter of Recommendation | | | |
| NAME: | | | |
| Date requested | | | |
| Date sent | | | |
| Second Letter of Recommendation | | | |
| NAME: | | | |
| Date requested | | | |
| Date sent | | | |
| Third Letter of Recommendation | | | |
| NAME: | | | |
| Date requested | | | |
| Date sent | | | |
| Counselor Letter of Recommendation (if applicable) | | | |
| NAME: | | | |
| Date requested | | | |
| Date sent | | | |
| Application Elements (use proper postage/ return address) | | | |
| Application (if not completed online) | | | |
| Essay | | | |
| Test scores | | | |
| Transcript | | | |
| Financial aid forms | | | |

| COLLEGE NAME | | | |
|---|---|---|---|
| Application fee or waiver request | | | |
| *Make copies for your records | | | |
| Received reply | | | |
| Accepted | | | |
| Denied | | | |
| Waiting list | | | |
| Notification of Decision Sent to College (date) | | | |
| Tuition deposit (date sent) | | | |
| Send Housing Info | | | |
| Application | | | |
| Date requested | | | |
| Date sent | | | |
| Deposit | | | |
| Date requested | | | |
| Date sent | | | |
| Schedule Orientation | | | |
| Shop for School (see list) | | | |
| Buy Books (shop early for best price and selection) | | | |

## Scholarships and Financial Aid

This checklist keeps you on track for scholarship deadlines and requirements. Sometimes applying for scholarships can be overwhelming. Take time to write down the ones you want to apply for and what is needed for those applications. This will help you prioritize your applications.

Don't miss out on a great scholarship opportunity because you forget to write down the deadline. Don't forget to apply for small scholarships since there may be less competition. Also, brainstorm questions that you may have next to each scholarship contest. There are tons of scholarships out there; (24 billion dollars a year) all you need to do is find them and apply!

## SCHOLARSHIP CHECKLIST

| Scholarship Website | Log-in name password | Contest Requirements | Deadline | Award Money | Essay | App. Mailed | Results |
|---|---|---|---|---|---|---|---|
| | | | | | | | |
| | | | | | | | |
| | | | | | | | |
| | | | | | | | |
| | | | | | | | |
| | | | | | | | |
| | | | | | | | |
| | | | | | | | |

## Volunteering and Extracurricular Activities

Colleges are looking for "well-rounded" students who have been involved in their community. Keep records of all activities, community service, and athletic participation. An Excel spreadsheet is an easy way to update the times and dates.

Make sure to log volunteer time. You should record a minimum of twenty-five hours each year and start in ninth grade, if not earlier. You can log time for the hours you spent working, and often organizations let you count the driving time to and from the job.

Don't forget about getting letters of recommendation from each supervisor (on organization letterhead) so you can use them for future referrals. Keep those letters in the pockets of the divider so you don't lose them.

You should be building your interests in high school by exploring a variety of extracurricular activities. This will help you learn important life skills outside of the classroom and help you narrow down potential career choices. Keep a record of different activities to reference in college applications and job résumés.

Volunteer/Community Service Log _____ Grade

| LOCATION | POSITION | DETAILS/ACTIVITY | DATES/TIME | CONTACT/ Supervisor | LETTER OF REC. |
|---|---|---|---|---|---|
| | | | | | |
| | | | | | |
| | | | | | |
| | | | | | |
| | | | | | |
| | | | | | |
| | | | | | |
| | | | | | |
| | | | | | |

Extracurricular Activities Log _____ Grade

| ACTIVITY/JOB | POSITIONS HELD | LEADERSHIP SKILLS | CONTACT INFO | LETTER OF REC. |
|---|---|---|---|---|
| | | | | |
| | | | | |
| | | | | |
| | | | | |
| | | | | |
| | | | | |
| | | | | |
| | | | | |
| | | | | |
| | | | | |

# Awards

Keeping track of awards and honors is a great way to catalog your high school achievements. It will also come in handy when applying for colleges, scholarships, or jobs. If you are going to apply to colleges, the awards and honors log will also serve as a "brag-sheet" to give to potential letter-of-recommendation writers.

Do not be ashamed to write down even the smallest achievements. You may not think a community award is important now, but your future admissions board might.

Keep a copy of awards in your notebook. If you won or completed something that won't fit in your notebook, write down a description and take a picture or create a DVD to highlight that award.

**Awards/Honors Log** _____ **Grade**

| AWARD RECEIVED | DETAILS | DATE | INCLUDED/ PICTURE |
|---|---|---|---|
| | | | |
| | | | |
| | | | |
| | | | |
| | | | |
| | | | |
| | | | |
| | | | |
| | | | |
| | | | |
| | | | |

## Sample Résumé/Bragsheet

The Résumé/Brag-sheet is a concise compilation of the pertinent information that you have been recording in your college and career notebook. It summarizes extra-curricular activities, volunteer work, awards received, job experience, travel experience, club associations, etc., which can be used for college entrance, scholarship contests, and internship opportunities. Since the paper will be skimmed quickly, make it noteworthy and appealing to the reader.

**Name**
Street, City, State
Phone

**DOB:**
**GPA:**
**Class Rank/Percentile:**
**Best Combined SAT/ACT Score:**
**PSAT Score:**

**Current Classes**
1.
2.
3.
4.
5.
6.

**Extra-Curricular Activities**

| Grade | 9 | 10 | 11 | 12 |
|---|---|---|---|---|

**Clubs:**
A.
B.
C.
**Community Service**
1.
2.
3.
4.
**Awards/Honors/Achievements**
•
•
•
**Sports**
X.
Y.
Z.
**Work Experience**
1.
2.
3.
**Travel Experience**
1.
2.
3.

## ENHANCEMENT IDEAS

Your college and career notebook is almost complete. Before you close the book on planning for your future, here are a few ideas and examples you can include to help you enrich the contents highlighting your high school experience, transcript, student profile, and also your uniqueness.

1. Create a blog
2. Run a fundraiser
3. Get media coverage
4. Develop an instructional manual
5. Attend a local workshop
6. Learn computer programming
7. Study a critical foreign language
8. Travel outside your home country
9. Study to become a ventriloquist
10. Join a circus for a summer
11. Join a local class at the community center
12. Get a membership in an association that interests you
13. Review a documentary for the local paper
14. Attend a residential summer program
15. Make an informational video/DVD
16. Develop software
17. Get nominated for awards/scholarship
18. Enter competitions
19. Invent something and create a prototype
20. Audition for a part

# 7-8

## Student Timeline: Before High School Begins

If you are currently in seventh or eighth grade, high school is just around the corner. You may be excited or apprehensive (or both!). No matter what, you'll have to face it. Realize that high school is not the end goal. It is a stepping stone on the pathway to your best future. Utilize your opportunities as means to get you to your ideal destination, whether that is personal, academic, or professional. It's never too early to start thinking about college and career aspirations, so start now.

## SCHOLARSHIPS

The college scholarship search can actually start as early as seventh grade. With time on your side, you can now get ahead of the game by searching for scholarships. Not only will this show you the application requirements for upcoming scholarships in high school, but also give you opportunities to start applying to scholarships designed for middle school students! Read more in Chapter 17.

## ACADEMIC PROGRAMS

A wide variety of academic programs exists to enhance your educational experience. From summer science camps to classes at your local community center, see if you can find opportunities that are both fun and intellectually stimulating. Have your parents help you look for extracurricular activities that will help you reach the goal of academic achievement.

Destination Imagination has great opportunities for middle school students to learn and experience creativity, teamwork and problem solving. It is an educational program in which student teams solve open-ended challenges and present their solutions at tournaments. For more info, visit www.idodi.org.

## TALENT SEARCHES

Talent searches are a great way to show off your abilities. These programs are designed to assess and foster the natural talents you possess. They will also enrich your academic experience by offering challenging coursework. Students who are involved in a talent search become eligible to attend specialized academic programs such as prestigious summer camps at high-level universities and supplemental online classes.

Participating in a talent search during middle school can help you with college admissions. Often college admission counselors are looking for students who exhibited maturity and focus at an early age. The purpose of talent searches is to recognize these qualities; having a talent search on your application is very prestigious. See more detailed information in Appendix B.

## FUN TIP

Seventh graders should consider visiting college campuses and meeting with admissions counselors. By taking early initiative, admissions counselors are more likely to remember students when they apply a few years later and give them priority for acceptance.

## PREPARING FOR HIGH SCHOOL

A student's high school experience can be as diverse as the students who attend high school. While no student will experience the exact same thing during high school, there are common recurring myths almost all incoming high school freshmen believe. Take time to read over these myths and make sure you understand why they are not true.

**Myth # 1: Take all the hard courses early so you can blow off your senior year.**
**Truth:** Colleges look at students' entire transcripts to evaluate their candidacy. Therefore, every semester counts. It is important to learn as

much as possible throughout all four years of high school. Admissions counselors want to see a continuous progression of harder coursework, including the final semester. Even if students are not planning on going to college, the classes they take during high school will prepare them for the future. Also, if students take advanced courses early, they can usually incorporate college course work their last couple of years in high school!

**Myth #2: Upperclassmen are scary.**
**Truth:** Every student in high school has been a freshman before. Therefore, they all understand the fears felt by the incoming freshmen. While some upperclassmen might be bullies—there are usually mean kids in every class—most upperclassmen are too busy with their own academic journeys to worry about the new students. Students should spend their time making friends with other students regardless of their age or class rank.

**Myth #3: You'll probably fail.**
**Truth:** Although high school is harder than middle school, freshmen have grown and are capable of handling the new workload. Teachers are there to help each student understand the new materials, and students have a wealth of resources like tutors to help them succeed. It will take more effort on your part to do well in your classes, but if you work hard and seek outside help when needed, you should have no trouble passing the classes.

**Myth #4: High school is only about academics.**
**Truth:** Although the academic aspect is the most important portion of high school, it is only one piece of a student's high school experience. High school is a combination of academics, social interactions, and future planning. Students use their high school years to learn, grow, and establish plans for the rest of their lives. If students focuses solely on the academic aspect of high school, they miss out on a wealth of opportunities to grow outside of the classroom.

**Myth #5: High school is *all* that matters.**

**Truth:** While high school is generally only four short years of a student's life, the habits and mindsets students develop during these years establish a foundation for their future interactions with people and studies. Students begin to develop into adults during these years; therefore, they should establish healthy habits early on. How students treat their responsibilities, peers, authority figures, and future plans all affect the choices they make now and later on in life. Conversely, some students make the mistake of not looking beyond high school. The four years spent in high school go by very quickly, but the choices students make during high school may very well have lifelong consequences. Do not make the mistake of settling for a momentary pleasure that comes with a lifelong price tag.

# Five Essential Tips for Incoming Freshmen

While navigating through these next few years, be sure to keep this list in mind.

1. Students need to build confidence during their high school years. Find activities that show off your strengths, and realize that nobody is good at everything. Cut yourself some slack when faced with failure, and congratulate yourself for trying. Believing you are capable will do a lot to increase your success rate. Success starts with believing that you can be successful!

2. Show up to class. Students can't succeed if they do not show up for class. Realize that every grade counts starting from freshman year. If you pay attention from the beginning, you will have the tools you need to move forward. Keep absences and tardies to a minimum.

3. Teachers are there to help you, so take advantage of the opportunity. They also need to get to know you so they can write your letters of recommendation in the future.

4. Do something with your time, like getting involved in clubs, teams, band, church groups, etc. By joining early, students can set themselves up for leadership positions later in high school. This motivates you and teaches time management.

5. Develop a strong support system. The changes faced in high school and beyond can be really challenging. Having a strong network of support will help students overcome the challenges ahead.

# GUIDE FOR PARENTS
## Tips for Seventh and Eighth Grade

Although this book is primarily for ninth through twelfth grades, getting a jumpstart on preparing for high school and college can give your student an edge. Seventh grade may seem a bit early to start thinking about college admissions; there is a difference between starting to prepare and obsessing about your student's future. No student at this age should be worrying about college or even worrying about high school since it is still far in the future. However, parents can set their students up for success later on by preparing early. If a student develops lofty goals for college and beyond at a young age, he or she won't be spending the majority of high school playing catch-up. It is better to divide preparation into little bits of work over a long period than saving the majority of the work until the end. Education is like building a house; students need a firm foundation, and it takes time to build. During this stage, parents should be doing the majority of work to help prepare their students for the future. This can include early test prep to help identify a younger student's weaknesses. If your middle-schooler is taking advanced classes, he or she may be eligible to take AP courses as early as ninth or tenth grade (see Chapter 12). *Also, remember that the Four-Year Summer Plan (inside your college and career notebook) starts the summer before ninth grade.*

## COMMON STRUGGLES FOR HIGH SCHOOL STUDENTS

High school students face two kinds of struggles: personal and academic. Students use their time in high school to figure out how they respond to their circumstances and themselves. As students strive to establish their own identities, peer relationships become increasingly important and family relationships tend to become tense while students grapple to establish independence. No student knows the most healthy response to every situation. Freshmen and sophomores in high school tend to wrestle more with peer relationships and stress about the increased workload of high school from middle school. Juniors and seniors in high school start to feel the weight of impending college and career choices and begin to struggle with making decisions about the future and worrying over standardized test scores.

Recognizing common struggles can help students evaluate whether they need to seek outside help. Remember: If you are having a hard time, you are not alone. It is typical for students to face some type of personal or academic struggle during high school. Never be afraid to seek help when you need it. Parents, teachers, and counselors are all willing to sit down and assist students through difficult times.

## COMMON PERSONAL STRUGGLES FACED BY HIGH SCHOOL STUDENTS

1. Eating disorders
2. Cutting, self-injuring
3. Divorce of parents
4. Girlfriend/boyfriend relationships
5. Relationships with their parents
6. Peer relationships, fitting in
7. Depression
8. Bullying, at school and online
9. Drug and alcohol temptations
10. Physical relations, pressure to engage in sexual activities

## COMMON ACADEMIC STRUGGLES

1. Learning disabilities like dyslexia and ADD/ADHD
2. Worries about college admissions
3. Financial stressors
4. Increased amount of homework and reading assignments
5. Overextension between academic and other activities
6. Personality clashes with teachers
7. Standardized test and state scores
8. Lack of interest in subjects
9. Distractions by technology, cell phones, tablets, social media
10. Fear of failure

## PRE-HIGH SCHOOL PARENT'S HOMEWORK

**Introduce logic games/curriculum into the student's agenda:** Choose books, courses and games that strengthen your student's critical thinking skills and help him or her to reason logically. Developing logic skills is important to the development of a student's brain. Knowing how to think and reason will help a student tackle the educational challenges of high school and college as well as standardized tests. Outside of the classroom, the student will be able to think for himself or herself, learn to develop cohesive arguments, and nurture the ability to find the flaws in the arguments of other people. Some logic resources are The Critical Thinking Company, The Fallacy Detective, and The Thinker's Toolbox.

**Have your students read many classic books:** Reading good books strengthens students' reading and writing ability, increases vocabulary, and opens their minds to new ideas. Classic books are well known, increase a students' knowledge, have lasting value, and are unabridged. For book ideas, see Appendix C.

**Check into talent searches:** It is a good idea to have all seventh-grade students take the SAT-I, the general college admission SAT, regardless of whether you think they are gifted. Your child might surprise you. Having your student take the SAT-I in seventh grade will possibly open the doors to a host of educational opportunities, including educational programs, scholarships, and educational counseling. It might help you be able to recognize special abilities he or she possesses.

During the fall semester of seventh grade, have your child take a good test prep class. This way the student can prepare for the December or January SAT or December or February ACT. If your student missed the talent searches in seventh grade, Duke University offers one for eighth graders. For more information, see Appendix B.

**Incorporate test prep into the curriculum:** Students should spend at least 20 minutes a day on SAT or ACT prep to get familiar with the test. Use the shortcuts, strategies, and test-taking techniques that can make best use of that time. (For example, pull a few questions from each section of *The Official SAT Study Guide* by the College Board to use as practice every day.) See which tests your students are more inclined to do well on and focus on your students' strengths. If your students do better with the SAT, make sure to find a course that teaches the logic behind the test questions and doesn't waste time on information that is irrelevant to the actual test. Sign up for a daily question at http://sat.collegeboard.org/practice/sat-question-of-the-day or www.actstudent.org/qotd. For information on how to ace standardized tests such as the SAT and PSAT/NMSQT, visit www.collegeprepgenius. com. You can also sign up there for "The No Brainer Way to Scholarships E-Newsletter," which contains scholarship information, college prep tips, success stories, etc.

**Check out the grammar program:** Knowing the rules and structures of the English language is very important. Sadly, many students come out of middle school without a firm grasp of the basic grammar of their language. Not having a firm foundation before entering high school can cause a lot of trouble down the road. Grammar is important for speaking eloquently, writing well and learning foreign languages, and it even comes in handy on the dreaded standardized tests. Students must understand the basic rules before they can move on to the more complex grammar of high school and college.

**Review our Three-Tiered High School Program Plan:** High school is just around the corner. Talk with your students about what type of goals they have for the future. Talk about interests and what types of activities they would like to be involved in when in high school.

**Optional testing:** Check to see if your school/co-op administers the PSSS for the younger students and the PLAN for eighth- and ninth-graders. These tests help identify early a younger student's weaknesses on tests like the PSAT/ NMSQT, SAT, and ACT. (Find more information in Chapter 15.)

**Scholarship search:** Make college a reality by obtaining scholarships now and learning the particulars about the financial aspect of college. Some scholarships are available for younger students; you don't want to miss out! Read Chapter 17 on how to pay for college.

## Student Timeline: Ninth Grade

High school is an opportunity to prepare yourself for a successful future. It may not seem like it, but you have the rest of your life to be an adult. Make the best use of your time as a teenager. Learning to choose the right steps now will help lead you down a path of excellence for the rest of your life.

High school can be a scary time. The stakes are higher and your choices have bigger consequences. No matter what type of school you attend (public, private, charter, or home school), you will face decisions and situations that could change your life: College, classes, friends, romantic relationships, cigarettes, driving, and alcohol, to name a few.

Don't freak out. Not every choice has life-altering consequences. Your job is to do the best you can, so don't agonize over temporary setbacks. Things that are so important today will seem inconsequential in just a few short years. However, this is not the time to blow off your responsibilities. Classes are harder, grades more important, and you will have to start thinking about your future. On top of all of that, ninth-graders today face a highly competitive academic environment.

If you are starting to feel overwhelmed or stressed, you should know that high school can be really fun. You will meet new friends, learn to drive, and go to parties, football games, and dances. You will be challenged and discover your ability to overcome those challenges. You will have many opportunities to learn and to play. You will participate in youth groups, extracurricular activities, and maybe even go on a few dates. You may develop lifelong friends and mentors, as well as figure out who you want to be when you grow up. Ultimately, your high school experience is up to you. You can allow yourself to drown in the distractions, worries, or temptations. Or you can rise above them through hard work, determination, and a nonchalant attitude towards the bumps in the road.

Remember, high school is only one brief stop on your life's journey. Even if everything goes wrong for you during these years, you can always start fresh in college.

**THINK ABOUT IT FOR FRESHMEN**

Freshman year is the perfect time to get involved and explore your interests through clubs, extracurriculars, and electives. Joining clubs early can set you up for leadership positions later in high school. Also think about visiting school-hosted career day programs to see what is out there. Take a moment to explore the types of extracurricular activities that are available to you, and decide where you want to get involved. Set aside time each week to start searching for scholarships.

I want to join:

_____

_____

_____

_____

_____

_____

_____

_____

## MONTH-BY-MONTH TIMELINE

**May:** Start your college and career notebook to not only chart your course for success, but also stay organized through the high school years. Establish an email address solely for college and career information. This way when you register for college information or apply for schools and scholarships you will be able to keep everything in one place. It's a good idea to make the email address simple and tied to you. It's best to stick with something professional, like your name (Example: jane.smith@ myname.com).

**College & Career Notebook:** If you are likely to forget your password, write it down in your notebook.

**June:** Check with your school district to see if they are accepting registrations for the October PSAT/NMSQT. If so, register now to reserve your place. Get a copy of the Official Student Guide to the PSAT/NMSQT from your guidance counselor and go to www.collegeboard.com/student/testing/psat/about/bulletin.html to get familiar with the test. Set up a profile at www.collegeboard.com, sign up for the free SAT "Official Question of the Day," and have it sent to your new email address. Don't delete them; store them in a folder for later practice. Spend at least an hour a week practicing with the PSAT/NMSQT test questions. Look into enriching activities for your four-year summer plan. Also, set up a similar profile at www.ACTstudent.org for the ACT.

**College & Career Notebook:** Store your username and password to your collegeboard.com account inside your notebook.

**July:** Make a list of short- and long-term goals. For short-term goals, think about the things you wish to accomplish during ninth grade. For long-term goals, think about the things you wish to accomplish during high school. Record your goals in the student profile section of your college and career notebook. If your school does not have a group freshman orientation, then make an appointment with the school to tour the campus and find out where all your classes will be. If possible, introduce yourself to your guidance counselor and teachers and ask any unanswered questions.

**College & Career Notebook:** Put your list of goals inside the notebook. This will help you stay motivated. Quicker than you realize, you will see these accomplished!

**August:** Review the three-tier high school plan before you register for classes. Decide which courses are right for you and your personal academic and future goals. Don't be afraid to challenge yourself.

**College & Career Notebook:** Record your new classes along with your summer activities in your notebook.

**September:** If you did not do so in June, sign up for the October PSAT/NMSQT at the counselor's office. Also, sign-up for the EXPLORE test if available at your school.

**College & Career Notebook:** Keep a record of dates/times for any upcoming standardized tests.

**October:** The PSAT/NMSQT is usually the third week of October; go in prepared with pencils and a calculator. Keep in mind: There is no pressure on this test now so you can relax and get familiar with the format. However, in your junior year the PSAT/NMSQT counts for scholarships.

**College & Career Notebook:** Log any extracurricular activities or volunteer hours that you have accumulated this semester.

**November:** Start looking around on college websites. Establish categories to look at—large/small, public/private, near/far from home, etc. Make a list of things you like and dislike about colleges to help you narrow down your choices in the future. Do not assume that the big-name universities will be the best fit for you.  Store your PSAT test booklet away until you get your scores in a few weeks.

**College & Career Notebook:** Put your college research in your notebook to come back to later.

**December:** Once you get your PSAT/NMSQT results, review  it along with the booklet to determine what areas need improvement. Use the holiday break to review your first semester and keep yourself on the ball. Sign up for the PSSS if available at your school (see Chapter 15 for more information).

**College & Career Notebook:** Store your PSAT/NMSQT scores in a pocket of your college and career notebook for later review. Keep track of your grades for the semester.

**January:** Consider signing up for the prestigious Congressional Award (see Chapter 12) or a similar award program.

**College & Career Notebook:** Use your notebook to create a plan to reach your new awards goal.

**February:** Start searching and applying for scholarships now (see Chapter 17). You can start by creating an account at www.fastweb.com.

**College & Career Notebook:** Keep track of scholarships opportunities that you find and write down the steps to apply to them.

**March:** Spend at least a couple of hours a week practicing with actual PSAT/NMSQT and/or SAT questions.
**College & Career Notebook:** Keep track of all the practice problems that you missed, correct them, and go over them frequently.

**April:** Start researching your summer reading list. Try to find classic works that interest you and will keep your bookshelf in use. See Appendix C for a list of great books to get you started.
**College & Career Notebook:** Write down the books that interest you the most to check out from the library or download them on your e-reader.

**May:** At the end of the year, review your transcript to make sure everything is correct. Research and register for interesting summer opportunities.

# GUIDE FOR PARENTS TIPS FOR NINTH GRADE

Regardless of your child's academic institution, it is important for you to make a game plan early to ensure a successful high school experience. Parents need to be proactive. Do not expect guidance counselors or teachers to helm the ship pointing your child to success. It's your job. Sit down with your daughter before she enters high school and make a plan. Discover what your son wants to accomplish during his high school years and decide how to help him achieve it.

The information in this timeline is for every student regardless of grade level. If you daughter is in 9th grade, then she should concentrate on the section covering 9th grade. If your son is in 11th grade, he should concentrate on the 11th grade section as well as the information for the preceding grade levels. The timeline for each grade begins with the summer before school starts. If you read this book during the semester, try to find time to incorporate some of the summer suggestions into the regular school year.

## PARENTS' PRE-HIGH SCHOOL CHECKLIST

Make sure any honors courses from middle school have transferred to your child's high school transcript. Help create the College and Career Notebook and log in summer activities for the Four-Year summer plan.

## PARENT TIPS FOR NINTH GRADE

Children need encouragement from their parents to follow their dreams. It can be hard to stick to goals. Be a cheerleader, a coach, and an active player in the game of success. Let your daughter know you support her and keep her accountable.

High school does not need to be a stressful time in the parent-child relationship. Proper planning and patience can ward off any unnecessary amounts of tension or anxiety. As your daughter proves herself mature, reward those positive character traits with freedom and independence. Your son will make mistakes. Just make sure you are there to offer help, guidance, and discipline when necessary. If you are having trouble communicating with your child, seek out a counselor for helpful advice.

Doing things early puts your child in the position to succeed. Feel free to start the college search by browsing the Internet and collecting college literature. Your son could start saving money for college right now, and your daughter can start researching scholarship contests and opportunities (See Chapter 17). Encourage learning outside the classroom as much as possible.

If your student is interested in playing sports in college, learn about the NCAA (National Collegiate Athletic Association) and check out its requirements.

## PARENTS' NINTH-GRADE CHECKLIST

- ☐ Talk to your student about classes and make a degree plan. Spur him or her to take the most challenging classes they can handle.
- ☐ Encourage good study habits.
- ☐ Help your student set high school goals. (academically, spiritually and socially)
- ☐ Stress the importance of volunteering in your community.
- ☐ Discuss his or her interests for possible career choices.
- ☐ Look into summer jobs to start saving money, or internships to get experience.
- ☐ Add studying for the PSAT/NMSQT into his or her schedule/curriculum. Visit www.collegeprepgenius.com for information on acing standardized tests.
- ☐ Get your student involved in extracurricular activities and make sure he or she records details in the college and career notebook.
- ☐ Set up profiles of your student at scholarship websites. (Use a separate email address from his or her personal one.)
- ☐ Be supportive and understanding.
- ☐ Mark your calendar to review your student's transcript at the end of

the year for accuracy.

☐ Sign your student up for the Preliminary SAT Scoring Service and EXPLORE test if available at your school.

☐ Check into Destination Imagination (www.idodi.org).

☐ Set aside some time each week for you/your student to search/apply for scholarships.

☐ Apply for the Congressional Award. (See Chapter 12.)

☐ Sign up for "The No Brainer Way to Scholarships E-Newsletter" at www.collegeprepgenius.com.

---

## PARENTS' HOMEWORK

Talk with your ninth-grader about the possibility of doing something really special and rewarding after graduation. This could be planning a trip to Europe or going on a summer-long mission trip to the heart of Asia. Making this plan now will allow your student to begin to earn and save money and be motivated to work hard throughout the next four years.

# Student Timeline: Tenth Grade

Classes get a little bit harder sophomore year. Many of them will build on the material learned from previous semesters. If you are still struggling with certain concepts from last year, you should get help as soon as possible. It will be worth your time to solidify the fundamentals, so you can enter tenth grade ready to meet the challenges.

With a full year under your belt, you should be more familiar with your school, its staff, and your peers. As you feel more comfortable in your surroundings, allow yourself to get more involved in the extracurricular activities that you might have missed your first year. Branch out from your comfort zone and have some fun.

Now that you are no longer the new kid, remember what it was like not knowing what was going on, trying to find your way, and maybe even feeling a little bit scared. So have sympathy for the new freshman class. Be patient and helpful, and perhaps even find someone whom you can mentor, but don't be condescending.

Continue to work on your long-term goals and some new short-term ones. Make sure to review the classes you are going to take and double-check your degree plan to see if you are staying on track.

Start thinking about the future, but remember to enjoy the present. One of the best resources to help you in this goal is the PLAN test. This test is offered by the makers of the ACT and is designed to assess college readiness, career interests, and ACT preparedness. Unlike the ACT, the PLAN test is not a nationally based test and is administered at the individual school's discretion. Not every school will offer it so you will need to check with your school. Even if your school does not offer it or if you are a homeschooled student, you can check nearby school districts and take it at a different school (fees will vary from school to school).

**THINK ABOUT IT FOR SOPHOMORES**

Graduation is closer than you may realize. Soon you will have to make a decision about what you will do after high school. Although you are only a sophomore, thinking about this now will help you make the decision when it comes. The Internet is also a great resource for researching potential colleges or careers.

Here are a couple websites to get you started.
www.careerpath.com
www.careertech.org
www.bls.gov/ooh/
My career interests are:

_____

_____

_____

_____

_____

_____

_____

_____

## Month-By-Month Timeline

**June:** Find a place to volunteer. Start or continue with the list of great books in Appendix C for your summer reading. Consider going to a college fair or visiting some local colleges.

**College & Career Notebook:** Remember to record your volunteer hours in your College and Career Notebook.

**July:** Take a prep course for the PSAT/NMSQT. Find one that focuses on the logic behind the test and the recurring patterns. Visit a college campus. Visit the campus bookstore and maybe buy a t-shirt or memorabilia to commemorate your visit.

**College & Career Notebook:** Record your preliminary PSAT/NMSQT score to see if they improve later. (If you haven't taken a real PSAT before the prep class, take a practice one to give you a baseline score so you will know how much you improve.)

**August:** Make sure your college and career notebook is updated with extracurricular activities, volunteer hours, and all your class information from freshman year.

Strongly consider including geometry in your sophomore year, since it is on both the PSAT/NMSQT and the SAT exams. Consider taking classes outside your high school; decide if you can or want to handle the extra course load. Continue to use this time to develop your interests, or work on some academic weaknesses.

**College & Career Notebook:** Look at last year's goals and reevaluate. Celebrate the successes and figure out reasons for lack of achievement. Think about why you want to reach certain goals and make a plan for how you will accomplish them this year.

**September:** Sign up (if you have not done so already) and continue preparing for the PSAT/NMSQT that you will take in October. Look for your local college fair and sign up to attend. Sign up for the PLAN test, if available at your school.

If you don't already know how to cook and do laundry, have your parents teach you now. Learn how to make a grocery list, read a recipe, and put it all together. Have a dialogue with your parents about increasing your allowance because of your newly added responsibilities.

**College & Career Notebook:** Keep track of all upcoming PSAT/NMSQT or PLAN dates.

**October:** Take the PSAT/NMSQT for practice. Sign up, if you have not done so already, for extracurricular activities that interest you.

Set up a profile at www.cappex.com, where you can enter your GPA, class rank, test scores, etc., and it will create a graph showing how you compare to all the other students who were admitted or denied acceptance at the schools you are looking into.

**College & Career Notebook:** Keep a record of your extracurricular involvement, volunteer work, and employment.

**November:** Make sure you are doing well in all your classes. Save your best papers and projects for your college and career notebook. Apply for awards.
**College & Career Notebook:** When you get your PSAT/NMSQT test booklet back, put it away until you receive your scores.

 **December:** You will receive the results for the PLAN and/or the PSAT/NMSQT. Read materials sent with your score report. Look at the areas that need improvement and plan accordingly.

Take personality and career tests. If you find a potential job that really interests you, tailor your extracurricular activities, volunteer opportunities, and part-time jobs to match. Look into military career options. Consider a college ROTC program or speak with a local military recruiter with your specific questions.
**College & Career Notebook:** Check your PSAT/NMSQT score and note improvement from your freshman score. Store your scores in a pocket of your college and career notebook.

**January:** Keep studying! Continue to look for volunteer opportunities. Visit a local college night and meet with admissions counselors from across the country. Sign up for the February ACT at www.act.org.
**College & Career Notebook:** Make sure to keep track of your upcoming ACT. Don't forget it!

**February:** Kick up your college and universities search. Spend some time narrowing down your options. Identify the entrance requirements of your possible choices. Some schools require extra tests like SAT II subject tests or extra classes for particular majors. Take the ACT.
**College & Career Notebook:** Keep all your college brochures and literature in your notebook and sort through it. Eliminate schools that no longer interest you.

**March:** Register for the June SAT.
**College & Career Notebook:** Keep track of upcoming test dates!

**April:** Work on increasing your vocabulary with classic literature and word-of-the-day (WOTD) calendars. Also, check out the College Prep Genius VocabCafé Book Series to help increase your vocabulary skills at www.vocabcafe.com.

**College & Career Notebook:** Make a section of your notebook for learning new vocabulary words where you can store WOTDs.

**May:** Review your transcript to make sure it is correct. Ensure that you have summer plans that work toward your long-term goals, whether through dual credit courses, part-time work, volunteer internships, or extracurricular programs.

Ask your guidance counselor about AP class opportunities for next year. Sign up for the June ACT. Check with your school district to see if they are signing up for the October PSAT/NMSQT this month. If so, then register now to reserve your place.

**College & Career Notebook:** Remember to record your extracurricular hours in your college and career notebook.

# GUIDE FOR PARENTS
# TIPS FOR
# TENTH GRADE

Because of all the preparation done in ninth grade, the high school journey should be becoming a little easier to manage. If your child did not start the preparation in ninth grade, it is not too late to start. Go back to the tips for ninth grade and follow the steps to help prepare any tenth-grader for the next few years. Make sure you check your student's transcripts from ninth grade to make sure everything is complete.

Again, parents need to make sure their students are taking the most difficult classes they can handle. Students need to take courses that focus on language, mathematics, and critical thinking skills. Stress the importance of studying hard and getting good grades. Have them work on their vocabulary by reading good books.

Test prep should also be more of a focus this year to help students prepare for the important PSAT/NMSQT. Start spending at least an hour a week working on testing strategies. If a student hasn't taken a good prep course yet, find one that focuses on test structure rather than test content. Remember the SAT is a reasoning test and the ACT is a knowledge test. See Chapter 15 for more information on testing.

Throughout tenth grade, future college plans should be a more important topic of discussion. Parents, don't overwhelm your students with worries about the future. Just start talking to them about what they want to do after high school. Since there is still plenty of time to think about post-graduation plans, the college search can be fun and stress-free. Browse the Internet for colleges and send off requests for brochures. By the end of sophomore year, students should start thinking about what type of college is right for them. Have them consider the college size, atmosphere, and price. If your student is not keen on going to college, talk about other post-graduation options.

Make a point to discuss goals and plans for the next three years. Your child will still need encouragement. Create a reward system for him to help encourage him to accomplish his goals. Try to keep him accountable.

This is also a time to teach practical life lessons. Speak to your daughter about how to avoid unwanted sexual attention and what to do if someone tries to kidnap her or sexually assault her. Speak to your son about when he should fight or flee from dangerous situations. Make sure to instruct both children of both genders to be alert and aware of their surroundings at all times.

Teach them about car insurance, since your child will soon be driving on his or her own. Be understanding and patient. Be sure to encourage your student to call you no matter what.

## FUN TIP

Car insurance companies often give discounts for "good students" in high school and college.

### PARENTS' TENTH-GRADE CHECKLIST

- ☐ Review classes and double-check the degree plan. Make sure students are taking the most difficult classes they can handle.
- ☐ Inspire them to elevate their high school goals.
- ☐ Continue to encourage good study habits.
- ☐ Check to see if their interests in possible career choices have grown or changed.
- ☐ Teach them to find more volunteer work in the community.
- ☐ Expand their involvement in extracurricular activities to help foster interests.
- ☐ Reinforce the importance of a summer job and the need to save money for college.
- ☐ Start working on their résumés.
- ☐ Continue to make sure they are still studying for the PSAT/NMSQT. Visit www.collegeprepgenius.com.
- ☐ Sign them up for the October PSAT/NMSQT (do it early to help ensure a spot) and the fall PLAN if available at your school.

- ☐ Review the Common Application to see if there are any gaps to fill in.
- ☐ Sign up at more scholarship websites.
- ☐ Set aside time each week for you or your student to search and apply for scholarships.
- ☐ Start the college search by creating a graph at www.cappex.com (Using your student's GPA, class rank, SAT score, etc., students can see how they compare to others who were accepted or denied at a particular college.)
- ☐ Mark your calendar to review your student's transcript at the end of the year.
- ☐ If you haven't done so, read about the Congressional Award in Chapter 12.
- ☐ If you haven't done so, sign up for "The No Brainer Way to Scholarships E-Newsletter" at www.collegeprepgenius.com.

---

## SOPHOMORE PARENTS' HOMEWORK

Download a common application (at www.commonap.com) and begin filling out the information for your child. Use the common application as a tool to help you guide your child through his or her degree plan. You will be able to see what gaps need to be filled, as well as ensure that you are on the right track. Do not send this application anywhere; merely print it off, fill it out, and store it in your student's college and career notebook. Later on, your son or daughter can use the information for real applications.

# Student Timeline: Eleventh Grade

Now that you're halfway through your high school adventure, it is definitely not the time to slack off, but rather time to step up your preparation. Colleges really focus on the grades of juniors, so you need to keep those grades high.

Studying for the PSAT/NMSQT should be at its most intense this summer. Practice for the PSAT/NMSQT at least six to eight hours per week over the summer, and take several full-length, timed practice tests on the weekends. During the third week in October, you'll take the PSAT/NMSQT, which counts toward the National Merit Scholarship Program. Since you should be at the top of your test-taking game, it is a good idea to take the SAT in October as well. You also have several opportunities to take the SAT again in the spring if you want (or need) a higher score.

Many students want to try to get the SAT out of the way in their junior year so they do not have to worry about it during senior year. Decide if you are ready to take the ACT and see how well you do on that test too. Sometimes students do better on one test or another. By taking both the SAT and the ACT, you can decide which test you should focus your attention on.

Hopefully you followed the advice for the previous grades and are now involved in some sort of extracurricular activity. Find a way to prioritize the activities in your life and be willing to let some frivolous, but fun, things go.

 **THINK ABOUT IT FOR SOPHOMORES**

Your decision for post-graduation is just around the corner. Now is the time to settle on your criteria for making future plans. Do you want to go to college? If so, where are you thinking about going? If college does not appeal to you, what are you going to do after high school? Before the year is over, give some serious thought to your future. Chapter 13 is dedicated to helping you make your future plans.

After graduation I want to:

_____

_____

_____

_____

_____

_____

_____

_____

_____

_____

_____

_____

# Month-By-Month Timeline

**June:** If needed, retake a PSAT/NMSQT prep course to help refresh your memory. Spend at least six to eight hours each week during the summer practicing for this important test—treat it like a part-time job. Talk to your parents about the financial reality of going to school; see what needs to be done to make college a reality. Take the June ACT.
**College & Career Notebook:** Keep track of all your practicing for the PSAT/NMSQT and your practice test scores to monitor improvement.

**July:** Prioritize quality family time. Try to spend at least one night a week eating dinner with your family. Maybe try a game night!
**College & Career Notebook:** Be sure to record all your summer activities.

**August:** Make sure your college and career notebook is up-to-date. Evaluate your short-term and long-term goals. Review your four-year degree plan before registering for classes.
**College & Career Notebook:** Review the three-tier high school plan to make sure you are on the right track.

**September:** Register early to take the PSAT/NMSQT and October SAT. Maintain your extracurricular activities. If you are thinking about playing college sports, talk to your guidance counselor about the academic requirements for playing sports in college (Division I or II). Start the NCAA certification process. For rules and regulations, visit www.eligibilitycenter.org. It takes a long time to complete this process, so start now if not earlier.

**College & Career Notebook:** Save samples of your best work for your portfolio.

**October:** Take the October SAT and then the PSAT/NMSQT. On the PSAT/NMSQT answer sheet, sign up for Student Search Service (SSS), which gives participating colleges the chance to send you information regarding college and scholarship opportunities. Register for the November SAT.

**College & Career Notebook:** As you receive literature and information from schools (from SSS), place any scholarship information inside your notebook.

**November:** Keep your grades high. Take the SAT again to see if you can raise your score. Sign up for the December ACT.

**College & Career Notebook:** Make note of any leadership positions you have attained in your extracurricular activities. See if you can get letters of recommendations from the adults in charge who speak about your leadership potential.

**December:** Review your PSAT/NMSQT results. Register for the January SAT. Consider taking it a couple more times in the spring if you need a higher score. (There are still March, May, and June tests.) Take the December ACT.

**College & Career Notebook:** Be sure to be recording your volunteer and extracurricular hours.

**January:** If you plan to take the ACT again, register now for the one in February. Take the SAT again this month. When you explore different college and universities, double-check which test they prefer and if they have any SAT II requirements. Memorize your social security number (if you haven't already) because it is required on most college applications.

Visit a local college night and speak with admissions counselors from colleges that interest you.

**College & Career Notebook:** Really go through your college information. Organize and carefully examine your different options.

**February:** Narrow down your criteria and look for schools that match your preferences as a whole. Once you have done your college search, make a list of your top ten schools to explore more thoroughly. Use your college comparison sheet in your college and career notebook to help you evaluate your favorites. With your parents, discuss whether your preliminary list meets your needs and interests and whether you are considering realistic colleges for your goals, financial position, and academic background. Make plans to visit the schools where you have a strong interest.

Register for the March SAT if you still need to raise your score. Make sure you have completed the relevant math courses (algebra 2 and geometry for the SAT; trigonometry for the ACT). Take a prep course (if you haven't already). Maintain your extracurricular involvement.

**College & Career Notebook:** Make a list of colleges that you would like to check out.

**March:** Talk to people who have your "dream job" and see what you need to do to get there. Pay special attention to their advice about school choice and study emphasis. Speak with employers about potential part-time positions, summer jobs, and possible internship opportunities. Talk to friends and family who have served in the military and see if it is a good option for you.

**College & Career Notebook:** Keep a list of everyone who took the time to give you advice and send each one a hand-written thank you note.

**April:** Contact your top schools to request admissions and financial aid literature, so you can better evaluate your choices. Write down the admissions application requirements and the financial aid requirements for each school and the application deadlines. Register for the May SAT I and SAT II if needed. Continue to evaluate your list of colleges and be sure to eliminate the ones that don't fit your criteria. Look into summer jobs or apply for special summer academic or enrichment programs. Register for the May and/or June SAT.

**College & Career Notebook:** Keep track of upcoming SAT I and SAT II dates.

**May:** Take your AP exams this month. Take the May SAT if you are signed up for it. If you still want a higher SAT score, sign up for the June SAT.

Attend college weekends to get a feel for the university atmosphere and check out schools that might not be on your list. Use your summer wisely: internships, summer courses, etc. If you can't find something you like to do, try starting your own business.

**College & Career Notebook:** Check to make sure your notebook is well-organized.

# ▌GUIDE FOR PARENTS
# TIPS FOR
# ELEVENTH GRADE

This is the year of standardized tests! With enough preparation, students can not only do well on tests like the PSAT/NMSQT, SAT, and ACT, but they can also receive great rewards for their efforts in the form of college admissions and substantial financial aid. Keep students from feeling overwhelmed by helping them study for these tests early.

Again, review the tenth-grade transcript to make sure that everything is correct. Continue to enroll your student in challenging courses. Make sure your child saves samples of his best work for his portfolio and continues to keep good records of extracurricular activities and volunteer work.

Continue to discuss their goals and plans for the next two years. High school is halfway over, and junior year needs to concentrate on post-graduation plans. Discuss your student's choices. If your daughter wants to go to college, have her make a list of her top schools. If she wants to go into the military, schedule a meeting with the local branch recruiters.

On a practical side, teach your child about automobiles. Teach him how to check the oil and other car fluids. You also want to teach your daughter how to change a tire in a safe place so she can get familiar with how to take a tire on and off. If she has her own car, put together an emergency car packet to put in her trunk with some essential tools like a thermal blanket, gas tank, jumper cables, and flares.

## PARENTS' ELEVENTH-GRADE CHECKLIST

- ☐ Review class schedules and double-check degree plans. Are any necessary classes missing? Use the three-tier plan as a guideline.
- ☐ Search local colleges for dual-credit opportunities.
- ☐ Add AP classes if appropriate.
- ☐ Prepare a college preparatory schedule for the next two years.
- ☐ Review the Common Application to find any gaps.
- ☐ Continue encouraging self-motivation and good study habits.

- ☐ Review and update college and career notebooks.
- ☐ Support involvement in extracurricular activities.
- ☐ Check on volunteer work résumés.
- ☐ Help students reexamine their possible career choices.
- ☐ Encourage summer jobs to help save money for college.
- ☐ Discuss what aspects of college are important to students (i.e., size, public/private, diversity of student body).
- ☐ Encourage students to attend college and career fairs.
- ☐ Visit colleges that interest students. (Be careful not to visit during a school holiday, as many campuses will be closed or empty.)
- ☐ Make sure students are studying heavily for the PSAT/NMSQT since the junior year is when it counts toward the National Merit Scholarship Program.
- ☐ Sign students up early for the PSAT/NMSQT at a local school.
- ☐ Have students study for and take the October and November SATs. Check out www.collegeboard.com for official deadlines.
- ☐ Have students study for the ACT.
- ☐ Look for scholarship contests.
- ☐ Set aside time each week to search and apply for scholarships.
- ☐ Ensure students have a social security number for college applications and financial aid.
- ☐ If homeschooling, start thinking about homeschool graduation plans for next year.
- ☐ Mark your calendar to review the transcript at the end of the year to make sure it is correct.
- ☐ Keep encouraging students to work toward the Congressional Award (Chapter 12).
- ☐ If you haven't done so, sign up for "The No Brainer Way to Scholarships E-Newsletter" at www.collegeprepgenius.com.

## JUNIOR PARENTS' HOMEWORK

Before your son ends his junior year, check his high school degree plan and make sure he is on track for graduation next year. Double-check transcripts to see if the school's administration has recorded everything correctly. It is easier to fix it now than next year. If you are homeschooling your daughter, begin working on her homeschool transcript. Your student will need these early next year when she starts to apply for colleges. *For more information on making a homeschool transcript, see Appendix A.*

# 12

## Student Timeline: Twelfth Grade

The tassel is worth the hassle! It has taken a long three years to get here, but all the hard work and preparation you have done should make this the easiest year yet. This can, however, be a very stressful time because it's filled with finalizing college and career plans. Even if uncertainty still clouds your final decision, relax and realize that you have plenty of time to make a good choice.

If you have not achieved your desired scores on the standardized tests, then keep them as a priority. Do not worry; you have at least four more chances to improve your score. If necessary, practice three to four hours per week. Schedule the SAT in October and November, and if you still need a higher score, take the December and January tests as well.

Tie up any loose ends regarding college applications and financial aid decisions. As a general rule, students should apply to the most competitive colleges as early as possible—even in the fall months. (Consider the Early Decision option if it will motivate you to get your applications done early!) Applying takes a lot longer than you think and can be very stressful if you wait until the last minute. Find out if the college of your choice allows early decision, early action, or some other special process. (For terms such as these, see Appendix E.)

Keep your grades up and do not drop off here on the final lap. Do not give in to senioritis! Your college admission acceptance is conditional on your successful completion of high school. Do not blow off your last year just to find out that it ruined your chances of going to the school of your dreams or knocked you out of the rankings for a great scholarship.

Searching for scholarships and financial aid should also be a major focus. Continue searching and applying for scholarships. If applicable, students should apply for "Early Award" because if their grades drop, it won't affect it. The deadline is around the middle of December.

Be serious in your approach to college; otherwise it's a long and expensive continuation of high school. If you do not think college is right for you and your goals, consider your alternatives. There are routes to success that do not involve college. Even if you do not go to college, the hard work you have put into school and preparing for college has not been in vain. You undoubtedly developed skills that will benefit you.

The following timeline is offered largely for the college-bound. If that is no longer your goal, simply adapt the schedule to fit your post-graduation plans. Choosing not to go to college is not an excuse to be lazy. If anything, it requires additional responsibilities and preparation.

 ## THINK ABOUT IT FOR SENIORS

Once you are finally finished with high school, you can breathe a deep sigh of relief. Use this summer to take a break and relax before your next set of responsibilities begins. You may not have the luxury of taking the entire summer off, but be sure to schedule times to rest and relax. You can also use this time to do something that you have always wanted but never had the time to do. This could mean taking a trip to Europe, spending the summer on a humanitarian mission, or taking an internship in an appealing occupation. This is your summer; make the most out of it.

The summer after graduation I want to:

_____

_____

_____

_____

_____

_____

_____

_____

_____

_____

_____

_____

_____

_____

# Month-By-Month Timeline

*Remember: Different schools have different application deadlines. Be sure that you understand when everything is due for each school. Some schools have earlier deadlines, and this general timeline will not fit for those schools. Also, make sure you read the following chapter on choosing the right path after high school.*

**June:** Take the SAT if you are signed up for it. Check your score online, and if you still need or want a higher SAT score, spend time during your summer studying for it. Make sure you study with actual College Board material and take full-length tests. By now you should know where your strengths and weaknesses are on this test. Take a review prep course if necessary and focus on increasing your scores. For more information on how to ace the SAT, go to www.collegeprepgenius.com.
**College & Career Notebook:** Look over your standardized test scores and decide if getting a higher score is a practical goal.

**July:** As you continue to volunteer, take on leadership roles. Enroll in outside classes (academic or extracurricular) to boost your college admissions chances.
**College & Career Notebook:** Keep records of all your summer activities. Make sure to accurately log hours of volunteering.

**August:** If you haven't already done so, make plans to visit all your favorite schools. While there, meet with current students and the faculty in your prospective departments.

Make a list of things you want to accomplish before you graduate. Evaluate your long-term college and career goals, but also make time to do the fun things that are part of high school. Look over your high school degree plan and meet with your guidance counselor to make sure everything is on track. If you have an easy year because you have finished all your requirements, add some extra AP classes or other challenging courses. You can also take dual-credit courses to get some college basics out of the way and reduce later college expenses. Look into CLEP courses to see if they will help you achieve your future goals.

**College & Career Notebook:** Make sure your college and career notebook is up to date.

**September:** Put together a college admissions deadline folder. On the Internet, go through each college and university's website to find application requirements and deadlines. Write a checklist, or print one from the website, for everything that is required for your admissions application. Do this for the financial aid applications too. If you have any questions, contact the school's admissions department. Once you have a list of everything you need for your application, write out a timeline that sets deadlines for getting it all done.

Review your transcript and extracurricular records. Decide who you want to write your letters of recommendation, and ask them to do it. Be sure to give your letter-writers plenty of time to write—three to four weeks at a minimum. Also, if someone is too busy to write a letter, finding out early will help give you time to find someone else. If you need a higher SAT score, sign up for the October and possibly the November SAT at www.collegeboard.com.

**College & Career Notebook:** Collect all your application information, deadlines, and letters in an organized spot in your notebook.

**October:** Mail your college applications on time. See if your first-choice school has an early decision option and decide if that option is right for you (See Appendix E for more information on early decision). Sign up for the November SAT if needed. Also, check to see if your prospective colleges offer the Early Award option, which allows you to find out your financial aid package early!

**College & Career Notebook:** Use the college application checklist to update your records.

**November:** Make sure your grades continue to stay high. Complete any additional college applications. Make copies of all applications for your portfolio before mailing them. Start obtaining all information needed for the

FAFSA. Make sure to complete all financial aid information for your schools. Talk to your parents about the financial realities of your education and make a financial game plan. Look at what scholarships the universities offer and see how much money you will need to come up with on your own. Since you haven't received any acceptance letters or official financial aid packets yet, you cannot make a final plan, but you can at least get an idea of the upcoming costs of school.

**College & Career Notebook:** Compare costs of different colleges and decide how much of a factor this will be in making your final decision.

**December:** Have official SAT and/or ACT scores sent to your colleges. (Many colleges allow you to turn in an initial score but also a higher one later, so check with them to know if you should take the test again. They often don't review the information until January.) Make a final list of schools that you are considering. File your last college applications. Register for your FAFSA pin number at www.pin.ed.gov. Have everything ready to apply for the FAFSA as early as January 1. (The sooner you apply, the more money is available.) Don't forget to ask your school for a transcript in a sealed envelope for each school or, if you are homeschooled, have your parents send one in.

**College & Career Notebook:** Continue keeping records. Your volunteer hours still count, even after you apply to colleges.

**January:** Keep working on your classes. Have your parents or guidance counselor send the transcript, after double-checking that everything is right, of your first-semester grades to your prospective schools. Complete your FASFA and taxes for schools. Make sure you have all the paperwork done for your schools. Attend a local college night if you have not made a final decision or have more questions for your prospective college(s).

**College & Career Notebook:** If you applied for early action or early decision, you may start expecting decision letters from your prospective schools.

**February:** Monitor your applications, making sure that all materials are sent and received on time. (Don't assume they have reached the right person. Always follow up!) Keep up with everything you have sent in: FAFSA, financial aid applications, etc. Complete more scholarship applications if needed.

**College & Career Notebook:** Review your notebook and use the information to put together a portfolio that can be used for college or internship interviews. Be proud of your work so far!

**March:** Stay focused on studying! Acceptance letters generally arrive between March 1 and April 1. Review housing options and submit applications for on-campus residence halls because dorm rooms often fill up fast. Ask your admission counselors about housing; some schools won't let you pick housing until you have paid a deposit. Some may allow paying a deposit early and then asking for a refund later, yet some deposits are nonrefundable.

**College & Career Notebook:** As you receive your letters, put them in your college and career notebook. This way you can compare offers from each college.

**April:** Your financial aid packets should arrive between April 1 and May 1. Review your college acceptance and financial aid award letters. Weigh your options and decide on the best school for you in all aspects. Most colleges require you to make your decision by May 1, so use this month to decide on the school that is best for you. Once you have decided, send in your deposit and inform the other schools of your decision. If you haven't done so yet, send your college your FAFSA information and complete final paperwork.

**College & Career Notebook:** As you receive your letters, put them in your college and career notebook for easy review.

**May:** Take any AP exams that correspond with your classes. Send in your health records to the registrar's office with your measles/mumps/rubella (MMR) and TB test records. Remember: Your TB test must be within the past twelve months and from a U.S. doctor. If you have decided to go into the military instead of college, talk with your local recruiter about the forms and documents needed for enlistment. Find out when you will go to basic training.

**College & Career Notebook:** Get a copy of your final transcript and add it to the rest of your information to complete the notebook.

**June/July:** Inform your chosen college's financial aid department about any outside scholarships, grants, or other kinds of student aid from any private sources that you will receive. Make any final housing payments. Sign up for any new student orientation programs that will be offered at your school. Mail your final high school transcript that shows your graduation date. You should receive your Stafford Loan information this summer if you applied. Register for your college classes if you haven't done so already, and get your orientation schedule. Make sure your housing assignment is secured.

Spend the summer enjoying your family. They have been your support in the past school years and will continue to be so in the future. Don't forget to hug your family members at least ten times a day until you leave for college.

**College & Career Notebook:** Congratulations, you're done!

## IF YOU MISS AN APPLICATION DEADLINE

Call the school to explain the situation. Ask what options are available to you and see if there are any grace periods. Always double-check that your information arrived at the school on time. If you submit a common application or any supplemental information through the common application website, the website will send an email, so make sure it is the separate one you created. This email will inform you when the application or supplemental information has gone through. Remember, some colleges will accept applications after the deadline if they have not yet filled their incoming class. However, financial aid may be much harder to obtain late in the application process.

# GUIDE FOR PARENTS TIPS FOR TWELFTH GRADE

Parents need to keep in mind this may be the last year to impart wisdom and knowledge to their children on a daily basis. Depending on what your daughter decides to do after high school, this may also be the last year she lives under your roof. Therefore, it is imperative that you have adequately prepared her to live and thrive in the outside world. Help your son understand how to make wise choices for himself, and encourage him to make the most of every day. Remember, although high school may be ending, education is a lifelong endeavor.

Before this year begins, think about any lasting lessons that you want to pass on to your student. Do you need to encourage him to be more financially responsible? Have you taught her about the dangers of texting and driving? Take an honest look at your child's maturity and identify the areas that need improvement. Don't forget to recognize the areas in which your student has improved and reward those improvements adequately.

Remember to review the eleventh-grade transcript to make sure everything is correct. Continue to discuss their goals and plans for their final year. Make sure they understand grades are especially important in the twelfth grade as some schools count the grades every six weeks for the class rank and GPA. Make sure you understand all the college admissions terminology found in Appendix E.

Tell your child you are proud of him or her. All too often parents make sure their children know when they are upset, but they fail to tell them when they are proud. Even if your son has not been the ideal student during these last few years, reaching senior year is an important accomplishment. Make sure you take the time to let him know that you are proud of how hard he has worked and of his many accomplishments. Your daughter may never say it, but hearing that her parents are proud of her is one of the best compliments she can receive.

Be understanding and patient. This is probably going to be one of the hardest years in your relationship with your students. It can be very difficult to watch them make plans and get excited about moving out of the house. It is also extremely stressful to finalize post-graduation plans and get everything taken care of before May. Try not to let the mix of emotions interfere with enjoying this time with your child.

Make family time a priority and don't withdraw from your relationship. While it might be a good idea to give your son space as he tries to figure some things out, don't let him push you out completely. Although he might not vocalize it, he is probably scared and needs to know that you support him.

## PARENTS' TWELFTH-GRADE CHECKLIST

- ☐ Make sure students have all their necessary credits.
- ☐ Look over their college notebooks and review the colleges that interest them.
- ☐ Help your students fill out applications for their college choices.
- ☐ Have their SAT or ACT scores sent to the colleges.
- ☐ Set up the FAFSA pin number at www.pin.ed.gov.
- ☐ Fill out the FAFSA in January at www.fafsa.ed.gov.
- ☐ Encourage continual volunteering in the community.
- ☐ Inspire students to work in the summer and to keep saving money.
- ☐ Add studying for the SAT if they need to raise their scores. For more information visit www.collegeprepgenius.com.
- ☐ Look for any gaps in their extracurricular activities.
- ☐ Visit colleges and universities with your student.
- ☐ Make a list of college application deadlines and fees (waivers are available).
- ☐ Check into dual-credit opportunities for your student.
- ☐ Look into adding more AP classes to enhance transcripts.
- ☐ If homeschooling, decide on graduation plans (group vs. individual).
- ☐ Take senior pictures in the fall.
- ☐ If you haven't done so, sign up for "The No Brainer Way to Scholarships E-Newsletter" at www.collegeprepgenius.com.
- ☐ Think about the guidelines, responsibility, and consequences of prom

and discuss these with your teen.

☐ Look into senior rings, and order caps and gowns.

☐ Mark your calendar to review the transcript after each semester.

☐ Set aside time each week to search/apply for scholarships.

☐ It is not too late to start/continue with the Congressional Award requirements.

☐ Get a power of attorney in case of medical emergencies, educational decisions, legal problems, renewing passports, traffic incidents, study abroad obligations, etc.

---

### SENIOR PARENTS' HOMEWORK

If ever there was a time for staying on top of deadlines, senior year would be it. Find out when everything (applications, financial aid, etc.) is due, then put it on your calendar. Students need to be responsible; however, with everything going on, it is possible for them to miss critical dates. Review the college application checklist in the college and career notebook section.

# PART II:

# Foundation for Personal Success

# CHAPTER ONE:
# PERSONAL DEVELOPMENT

H IGH SCHOOL is about more than just learning some cool stuff. This period in your life is about taking responsibility—responsibility at school, responsibility at home, and, most importantly, responsibility at a personal level. In exchange for greater freedom, students must meet greater expectations for their behaviors. These next four years will prepare you to enter into the adult world, and so will this first section in *High School Prep Genius*.

## DEVELOPING INTO AN ADULT

Effectively, society recognizes eighteen-year-olds as adults. At the age of eighteen, you have the right to vote, enlist in the military, and move out—all of which are very important decisions that seriously affect your life path. You must be prepared to evaluate your decisions and the consequences of those decisions. While some parents might protest that teenagers are not ready for these types of responsibilities, the truth is, you will face these decisions sooner rather than later. Whether your parents like it or not, during high school you become an adult. You meet adult challenges that you will have to face alone and decisions that you will have to make for yourself. It is hard for parents to look at their fifteen-year-old adolescent and recognize their "baby" will soon be out in the real world.

Adolescence can be a tumultuous time for both parents and their students. The tug of war between the parents' right to control and the student's right for independence begins soon after puberty. However, this fact does not mean your parents' or guardians' job ends once you enter high school. On the contrary, the most critical part of their job is just beginning. Your parents now have the responsibility of teaching you how to become an adult, and you have the responsibility of listening to them and trying to learn from their example. Your goal should be to become *self-governed* (one who is not controlled or swayed by others; characterized by self-discipline or self-control).

## MAKING YOUR OWN CHOICES

Independence is invaluable to adulthood. Getting parental advice is often beneficial, but always relying on them to make life decisions for you is detrimental. Ultimately, your life and the choices you make all fall back on you. Once you reach adulthood, your life is your own responsibility. Do not take the easy route and sell your freedom for laziness. While it can be tempting to let others decide the hard stuff for you, it will not be fulfilling.

Do not be a passive observer of your life. Actively take charge and acknowledge that every choice is up to you. There is no shame in trying to reach a goal and failing. This happens to people all the time; life is full of successes and failures. The only shameful choice is to choose not to do anything. If you never reach for anything, how can you expect to grasp your dreams? Life rarely drops opportunities into a person's lap. More often, a good opportunity is the result of hard work and dedication. Do not let yourself miss a chance for success because it requires sacrifice and sweat.

You have the choice to be lazy or diligent. You can choose to go to class, or you can choose to skip your class. You can do your homework, or you can ignore your homework. Parents, teachers, and friends can all influence your decisions, but you are solely responsible for your choices and actions.

## TAKE PERSONAL RESPONSIBILITY

Once you have made a choice, the responsibility of that choice belongs to you. Responsibility is a two-sided coin—for every choice there is a consequence. On one side, you get to make a decision, which is fun. If you want to stay up late the night before a big test, then you have the power to do so. On the other side, you have to deal with the consequences of that decision. If you fail the test because you were too tired to concentrate, it's nobody's fault but your own.

It can be both exciting and terrifying to take responsibility for your decisions. Sometimes you will make wise decisions; sometimes you will make foolish ones. Nobody makes the right choice every time. Therefore, it is important to accept the consequences—both good and bad. Remember choosing not to do something is still a choice, and choosing not to do something has a consequence too.

## OVERCOMING BAD DECISIONS

An important part of maturity is learning from the past. After all, if you never learn from your mistakes, what makes you think you will avoid them in the future? This is often easier said than done. You may be furious, embarrassed, or sad, and the last thing you want to do is be positive. Give yourself some time to be upset, then take a deep breath and force yourself to let those feelings subside. It will then be possible for you to turn a bad choice into a positive life lesson.

Once you have made a mistake, the first thing you need to do is admit your guilt and accept the consequences. Next, you should seek out ways to reverse the negative consequences your choice may have caused others. Then you should turn the consequence into something constructive, a learning experience. Look back at the situation; decide why you made that decision and what you can do differently the next time.

## OWNING YOUR MISTAKES

It can be embarrassing to acknowledge you were wrong. You might feel that others will look down on you for your mistake. However, other people's opinions do not matter nearly as much as your response to a mistake. You are not perfect, and you cannot expect to be perfect. The only thing you can expect from you is the effort to make things right when things go wrong. This means that if your choice has hurt someone else, it is now your responsibility to make up for that hurt. This may not be pleasant for you to do, especially if the person wronged is not generally deserving of your apology. Likewise, you may run into someone who will not forgive you. It is not your responsibility to make others forget your mistake, and some may not. Work to do what is right by that person and let his or her response be his or her responsibility.

Taking personal responsibility also means confessing to mistakes even if nobody else knows you made them. Do not be satisfied with getting away with not being caught. You never know when past choices will come back to haunt you. It is far easier to deal with any immediate consequence than to make matters worse by hiding your shame. After confronting the problem, you will be glad you did.

Learning to take responsibility for your mistakes—even those that are hidden—is far easier as a teenager than when you are an adult. It only takes a quick look at the newspaper to see what happens when business leaders, politicians, and professionals fail to learn this lesson and make matters worse by trying to hide their guilt. At the end of the day, your word and honor are the only things you own. They are the most valuable possessions you will ever find.

## GAINING TRUST

Trust is not a right you get when you reach a certain age, but a gift you receive for proving yourself trustworthy. If you do not abuse trust, people will have no reason to doubt you, your intentions, or your word. For parents to give students complete independence, they must trust them to make the right decisions.

This release of control can be especially difficult for parents if they feel their students will make poor choices. Parents want to protect their children from making mistakes. At the first sign of danger, they are likely to jump back in and try to take over. If you ever feel like your parents are out of line by stepping in, sit down and talk with them about it. Explain your feelings about their interference and explain why you feel that you are making the right decision.

Trust from your peers is not something to take for granted either. When your friends or siblings offer you their trust, take it seriously. If you betray the trust of a peer, regaining it again is almost impossible, for good reason. You may ruin a friendship or relationship if you don't guard the trust effectively.

## BE PROUD OF YOUR DECISIONS

Responsibility doesn't mean only dealing with bad things, but also learning to take credit for the good too. Always focusing on the negative will only lead to frustration and sadness. Let the positive moments encourage you to do more. It is better to focus on your positive qualities—the things you do well (the opportunities you have to help others, and so on)—than to focus only on your faults and chastise yourself for not being better.

You don't have to do something extraordinary in order to be proud of yourself. After all, history is full of people who were not terribly talented but became heroes because they looked past themselves and toward the needs of others. Studying hard to get a good grade, working on your musical ability, or counseling a friend are all good choices you can be proud of.

Do not be ashamed to feel good about yourself when you accomplish your goals. Take time to celebrate your successes and your strengths. Whether anyone notices it, doing the right thing is always a reward in and of itself.

## THINK ABOUT IT

Start today by taking responsibility for your choices. Be honest and ask yourself these questions. Give examples to support your answers.

1. Do I take responsibility for my actions, or do I tend to blame others for what happens to me?

   _____

   _____

   _____

   _____

   _____

   _____

   _____

2. When I make a mistake, do I admit to it or try to find other ways to get out of trouble?

   _____

   _____

   _____

   _____

   _____

   _____

   _____

3. When I get myself into trouble, do I expect others to come to my rescue?

   _____

   _____

   _____

   _____

   _____

   _____

   _____

4. What positive choices have I made that I can be proud of?
   Today:_____
   Last Week:_____
   Last Month:_____
   This Year:_____

5. Do I focus more on the positive or the negative choices I make?
   _____
   _____
   _____
   _____
   _____
   _____
   _____

6. How can I find a balance between learning from my mistakes, and not letting those mistakes dictate the rest of my life?
   _____
   _____
   _____
   _____
   _____
   _____
   _____

7. When others wrong me, am I quick to forgive, or do I hold a grudge?
   _____
   _____
   _____
   _____
   _____
   _____
   _____

## WHAT WOULD YOU DO?

It's time to take the idea of personal responsibility a little bit further. Take time to think through these scenarios and ask yourself, "What would I do?" Be honest and think about the consequences of your decisions. Are they good or bad? If they are bad, how can you move toward good choices? How can you build the courage to do the right thing?

1. Your school is hosting a talent show that you want to be in, but you are afraid your friends will make fun of you.

_____

_____

_____

_____

_____

_____

_____

2. You cheat on a test, but nobody knows.

_____

_____

_____

_____

_____

_____

_____

3. Your best friend finds out you betrayed a secret.

_____

_____

_____

_____

_____

_____

4.  Someone told you a secret and your best friend wants to know it.

_____

_____

_____

_____

_____

_____

5.  You have a test tomorrow, but your friends want you to go to the movies.

_____

_____

_____

_____

_____

_____

6.  You grandmother gives you $100 for your birthday. Do you spend or save?

_____

_____

_____

_____

_____

_____

7.  You want to be a police officer but your mother thinks you should be a doctor.

_____

_____

_____

_____

_____

_____

8. You get your class schedule from your guidance counselor. Do you bother to check it over?

_____

_____

_____

_____

_____

_____

9. You forget to do last night's homework and your teacher does not accept late work.

_____

_____

_____

_____

_____

_____

## GUIDED RESPONSES

1. It is easy to let the fear of what other people might say stop you from doing something, especially if they are your friends. Nobody likes to be embarrassed or thought of as a loser. However, you should not let what people *might* say stop you from doing something that you really enjoy. Your friends should support you in your decision to do the talent show and encourage you to do your best. Good friends laugh with you and not at you. If you are seriously worried about what your friends would say, you should be more concerned about the friends you have than the show.

2. Even if you got away with cheating, you need to come clean and accept the consequences of your actions. Go to your teacher and tell him or her that you cheated and you would like to make it right. Even if you have to take a zero on the test, it will be better than having to live with the

guilt. Coming clean will also save you from bigger consequences later on. Either someone will find out and you will get into trouble anyway, or you will be more tempted to cheat the next time around. Maybe nobody caught you this time, but that does not mean no one will catch you the next time. You might get away with cheating for a while, but odds are you'll eventually get caught. Consequences for cheating are far worse than getting a bad grade on a test.

3.  Honesty is the only thing that will get you out of this one. Breaking trust with a friend is a serious offense. Trust is one of those things that is very difficult to get back once it is lost, though not impossible. The first thing you need to do is apologize to your friend for sharing information that was not yours to share. Ask for forgiveness and tell your friend you understand if he or she does not trust you. Now you have to work on gaining that trust back. Do not be upset if your friend is hesitant to tell you things; it will take time to rebuild that friendship. You also need to apologize to the person you told because sharing that information has also hurt that person's reputation with your friend. If either person has a hard time forgiving you, it's OK. You are only responsible for your reaction to the situation. Continue to try to make things right, and let the others worry about themselves.

4.  It can be hard to keep things from your best friend. After all, you probably share everything. However, it is not your place to share somebody else's information. If that person wanted to share with your best friend, then your best friend would already know. Explain to your friend that you are keeping the other person's trust. Your friend should respect that because if the situation were reversed, your friend would want you to do the same thing.

5.  Your responsibility in this situation can vary depending on how much material you have already studied for your test, and how hard you need to study for it. If you have been studying and know the material, then go have some fun. You deserve it! However, if you have been blowing off studying all week and tonight is the last night you have, then you better skip the movies and hit the books. When trying to evaluate what you should do, be honest with yourself.

Do you know the material? Have you put in the effort to know the material? Would studying more help or be pointless?

6. You have to appreciate a grandmother who gives her grandchild $100 for a birthday present. Anytime you get some extra money, it is always a wise idea to put at least some of it in savings. How much of it should go to savings is up to you. If you are the type of person who loves to spend money, then keep enough to buy yourself something nice and put a little more than normal in savings. Chances are, your savings account could probably use some extra cash. If you are the type of person who always saves, you might want to think about finding something you really want and indulge yourself. After all, it is your birthday. The best idea is to try to find a balance between wasting your money and never enjoying it. And be sure to send Grandma a handwritten thank you note; she'll appreciate that.

7. It can be tricky when your future aspirations do not line up with your parents' aspirations for you. You need to remember that your parents love you and ultimately want the best for you. Think about the reasons why you want to be a police officer. Then sit down with your mom and ask why she thinks you should be a doctor. Explain your reasons and listen to hers. She might see a talent in you that you have not recognized. Or you might explain a desire that she does not understand. Who knows; after talking with her you might decide a career that combines the two jobs is perfect for you. For example, one combination of these two careers is a forensic scientist.

8. You should always look over your class schedule once you get it. Counselors do their best to meet your needs, but even they make mistakes. You care more about your schedule than anyone else does, so it is your job to make sure it is right. It would be a shame to realize after school has started that you are enrolled in the wrong class.

9. If you get to class and realize you have forgotten to do your homework, then you should sit down and start working on it before class starts. If you can get even a little bit of the work done before class begins, a partial grade is better than no grade at all. If you do not have time before class, or the assignment is too complex,

then you need to talk to your teacher. Do not make excuses. Tell your teacher you forgot and acknowledge the fact your teacher does not take late assignments. Ask if there is any extra credit you can do to make up for your lost points. If there is not, or your teacher won't let you turn something in, you are no worse off than you were in the first place. Your teacher will respect the fact you took responsibility for forgetting your assignment. To keep this mistake from happening in the future, you might want to consider working on your note-taking skills and planning time for your assignments.

# GUIDE FOR PARENTS HELPING YOUR CHILD ESTABLISH INDEPENDENCE

Pre-adolescence and adolescence are critical times in your child's life. Up until this point, children had little responsibility in making choices for themselves. Now it is time to let them start making choices on their own. How much freedom should you give your child? As in most things, balance between extremes is an important goal. You will need to ask questions and listen intently. Take an honest look at his or her environment. Students and environments change. A good academic record doesn't preclude your son from having academic struggles in the future. A troublemaking past may not develop into a rebellious future for your daughter. Do not give undue weight to the past, which leads to either a hands-off or suffocating approach.

At eighteen years, it is too late to give your daughter her independence. If she has not learned how to make good decisions by this time, it is almost impossible to teach her after she leaves your house for college, work, family, or military service. Right now the prefrontal cortex in the brain is still developing, causing teens to act more rashly and less logically. Help her start thinking through her impulses, so she can make good decisions later on.

"Helicopter parents" have become a trend in today's society. These parents make every decision for their children in high school, and they continue the practice after their students are well into their twenties and early thirties. Helicopter parenting is neither healthy for the students nor for the parents. Children never learn how to overcome obstacles, solve problems, or communicate with others effectively. Therefore, it is important for parents of teenagers to monitor not only how well your children are doing with responsibilities, but also how you react to their newfound independence. In many ways, a child's failure to become an independent citizen is the product of parents' failure to lead and let go.

## HELPING YOUR STUDENT DEVELOP PERSONAL RESPONSIBILITY

As you begin to give your daughter more freedom, you need to give her more responsibility. As the parent, it is your job to help her foster good habits and help her learn about the consequences of her decisions. Always trying to rescue your daughter from consequences of her actions will not teach her to avoid mistakes in the future. This may mean watching her suffer for her mistakes, which may not be fun, but it is necessary. Remember, teaching her to make wise decisions now saves you the pain of watching her make bigger, more costly mistakes in the future.

A successful strategy for teaching responsibility is allowing small amounts of freedom when your child is as young as possible, and then gauging how he or she does with the new responsibility. For example, allow your preteen son to set his own bedtime, but give him the responsibility to be awake and ready for school at a certain time in the morning. If he fails to achieve his morning ritual, hold him at this level of accountability and offer instructions on how he can improve his performance. If he completely and disastrously fails, then remove the responsibility until he can handle it.

Don't be reactionary when mistakes happen! A parent who provides some freedom only to immediately revoke it at the first sign of trouble does not give the child a chance to solve the problem or learn from the consequences of a poor choice. It is better to monitor the situations your son gets involved in and to step in only when your presence is an absolute necessity. You might be surprised and proud of how your child handles some tricky situations (e.g., fights with friends, bullies at school, teenage temptations). Of course, if at any time you feel your child is in danger, it is your responsibility to intervene.

Be careful not to overreact when your "good" daughter does something wrong. Overbearing responses can bring resentment as she may feel she is being held to a higher standard because of her past achievements. Try to avoid the phrase "you know better than this." Remember every child is different, so be careful not to compare siblings to one another. What works for one student may not work for another.

Reactions and punishments should always be proportional to the offenses committed. Be careful not to treat small offenses as if they are major mistakes. For example, if your son doesn't get into typical teenage trouble yet occasionally forgets to do his chores, it is probably not a sign of rebellion but of absentmindedness.

Conversely, your son needs to be reminded that you are his biggest advocate. This means praising him when he succeeds in both big and small areas. Every accomplishment is noteworthy, even if he has succeeded in that area repeatedly. Don't take his good qualities for granted! Regardless of whether success is rare or commonplace, always recognize it.

Vigilant parents will know when their child is ready for responsibility, confident ones will allow more responsibility, and wise ones will know how much.

---

### PARENTS' HOMEWORK

Allow your student to do one new thing that he or she has been begging to do (e.g., cook a meal, care for a family pet, babysit a younger sibling, spend the night at a friend's house, drive to the store). Let your student know that this is a test run and the outcome will determine future responsibilities and freedoms. Carefully monitor his or her decision-making process, execution, and completion of the task and give him or her a grade on responsibility.

# CHAPTER TWO: INTERESTS THAT MAKE YOU INTERESTING

IMAGINE A world where nobody had any passions whatsoever. People go through life every day doing the same things—work, school, homework—never moving beyond the mandatory. Now try having a conversation. Do you think it is very enjoyable? Of course not! After some small talk, the conversation abruptly hits a dead end. There's nothing to say.

Now think about people with passion. It doesn't matter what they talk about, their enthusiasm ignites the conversation. You learn something new and intriguing about these people, about their conversation topics, or both. Their interests make them interesting people. Interesting people make the world an exciting place. Don't settle for the mandatory; develop your personal interests.

Your interests can manifest themselves in a variety of ways. Your favorite school subjects, the books you read, your spiritual journey, and your hobbies express your interests. You might be saying to yourself, "I don't have a favorite subject. I never read anything that isn't school related, and I certainly don't have any hobbies." While those might be true statements, it does not mean you do not have interests. It just means you have not discovered your interests yet, or you haven't nurtured them properly. More likely than not, you express your interests every day and don't even realize it.

## DISCOVERING YOUR INTERESTS

The first step in developing your passions is developing your curiosity. Curiosity is the fuel of innovation and discovery. People who lack curiosity are more likely to suffer from boredom. Those satisfied with the status quo are more likely to live a mundane life. They passively go through life missing rewarding experiences and opportunities.

How do you develop a sense of curiosity? The answer is simple: learn to ask questions. Questions often inspire other questions, which lead to a quest for knowledge. The more you learn about something, the more likely you are to want to learn more about it. You don't have to be curious about everything; just don't let yourself be curious about nothing. And you never know; people have created careers out of interests.

Self-awareness and openness are other critical components of discovering your interests when it comes to both school and your future career. Pay attention to the types of things you enjoy or don't enjoy. Make sure to be open to new interests. If you believe everything you learn in school is boring, then you will treat new school subjects as boring. However, if you let yourself be intrigued by your classes, you will learn some fascinating stuff.

Try to think of different ways you can use what you are learning. Being able to connect a history lesson to your life will help build an interest. For example, learning that the United States' eighth president, Martin Van Buren, learned English as his second language (his first language was Dutch) might inspire you to learn a second language. After all, President Van Buren overcame a language barrier and was able to rise to the highest government office in the land.

One quick note is in order: do not try to force academic practicality into a professional practicality. If you narrowly define usefulness in terms of what can get you a job, then you will miss a great deal of what school can offer. Even though you may not want to be a math teacher in the future, that does not mean you won't use basic math in everyday life. Learn to see school as a way to open your mind to a new way of thinking. Being open-minded to the usefulness of all information is a hugely valuable skill in life.

## TRY A HOBBY

One of the best ways to develop your interests is through hobbies. Hobbies are more than the things you do in your free time. They are active adventures into the subjects that interest you. Almost anything can be a hobby, so think about things you might like to learn about or get better at. Hobbies allow you to break away from the norm and help you develop your curiosity.

Try to think of hobbies as a way to make you a better person, not simply a way to pass the time. Talking with friends or playing video games are fine activities that can even develop skills. However, they should not be the extent of your hobbies. The key to a good hobby is that it should expand your world and cultivate your growth.

Hobbies come in all shapes and sizes and can develop out of any type of subject. Hobbies can combine two or more activities. Be creative and make up your own, or do some research and participate in somebody else's creation. If typical hobbies don't interest you, search for something unique; there are too many interesting things in this world for you to settle for something you don't enjoy. Your hobbies do not need to lead you to a job or some financial gain. They just need to be activities that inspire you.

Below is a list of possible hobbies and the interests they stem from. If you are having trouble getting started on your own, local community colleges or centers usually provide a wide range of classes to teach you a new hobby. If you do not find anything interesting through these sources, a simple Internet search for hobbies yields a wealth of ideas and tips to get started. Go to your favorite search engine and type in whichever topics interest you.

**Interest in Science**
1. Archaeology
2. Astronomy
3. Building gadgets, rockets, or robots
4. Computer programming
5. Psychology

**Interest in Nature**

1. Bird-watching
2. Gardening
3. Mountain bike riding
4. Dog training
5. Hunting

**Interest in Arts**

1. Filmmaking
2. Painting
3. Playing an instrument
4. Scrapbooking
5. Photography

**Interest in Strategy**

1. Chess
2. Poker
3. Junior Reserve Officers' Training Corp
4. Sudoku
5. Go (Chinese board game)

**Interest in Culinary Arts**

1. Cooking
2. Baking
3. Food blogging
4. Cake decorating
5. Gardening

**Interest in Literature**

1. Short story writer
2. Poetry club
3. Book club
4. Film critiques
5. Blogger

**Interest in Sports**

1. Local sports club
2. Little league team coach
3. Sports from other cultures
4. Martial arts/self-defense
5. Weightlifting

**Interest in Cultures**

1. Foreign languages
2. Foreign films
3. Ethnic cooking
4. Pen pal
5. Travel

**Interest in Faith**

1. Bible study
2. Church or mission volunteering
3. Religious literature
4. Fellowship of Christian Athletes
5. Church/synagogue/mosque youth group

**Interest in Politics**

1. Local campaign volunteering
2. Local party office work
3. Current affairs
4. Internship at the office of your local congressperson
5. Foreign relations journals

**Interest in Money**
1. Economics-related literature
2. Econ-Talk podcasts
3. Stock market
4. Local chamber of commerce volunteer work
5. Financial current affairs

## MAKING THE MOST OF HOBBIES AND EXTRACURRICULAR ACTIVITIES

The most important things to keep in mind when picking extracurricular activities are:

1. Maintain balance: Don't get overloaded with too many activities. Do not neglect what you have to do in order to do what you want to do.
2. Be serious: Don't get involved just to pad a college application; get involved because it is interesting and there is something to learn. Devote enough time to really experience the hobby and continue with it only as long as you enjoy it.
3. Have fun: Don't take this so seriously that it's not fun anymore.
4. Get started: Do not let the fear of failure keep you from starting a hobby.

## TAKE A LEADING ROLE...OR NOT

It is a good idea to assume some leadership responsibilities. Not only will taking the role of a leader increase your problem-solving abilities, but it will also foster other critical skills necessary to succeed in college and the work force.

Likewise, you should also not always be the person in charge; learning how to follow is another important skill. Make sure you are willing to try different positions in your organizations. The variety of job descriptions will be a huge benefit later in life.

## KEEP A RECORD

Once you are involved in different activities, make sure to keep a log of what you are doing and in what role. Many hobbies translate into extracurricular and co-curricular activities, which are very appealing to college admission counselors. Having a list of everything you were involved in during high school will make your high school résumé more impressive and the college application process easier.

Once you have learned some new things, do something that shows off those skills. If you gain a new interest in the classroom, take on a project that allows you to put your knowledge into action. For example, if you studied the Civil War during your freshman year, try participating in (or organizing your own) reenactment. This will be a great way to get hands-on experience, and your efforts can be added to your résumé and college admission applications. Plus, using knowledge in the real world is the best way to stay motivated towards learning.

Keep track of all your different activities using a spreadsheet or simple text document. Divide the activities log by school year. Once you have finished a grade, print off the extracurricular activities log and place it in a folder dedicated to college and career planning. (For additional information on keeping a detailed log, see the college and career notebook.) This way, when it comes time to start applying to colleges, scholarships, or jobs after high school, all the information will be in one spot.

## DOING THE MOST WITH SUMMER

Summer programs are another great way to help follow your interests. Colleges all across the nation offer a variety of summer programs that fit your particular hobbies. Before the summer starts, do some research online. Find programs you want to be a part of and apply. Many summer programs offer scholarships and financial aid, if necessary. Even if the program offered is not at a college you would consider going to, that's OK! You are not obligated to apply, nor will you necessarily get accepted, just because you went to that college's summer program.

Imagine combining your civic-mindedness with cultural experience by taking a volunteer vacation. Teenagers can travel abroad to help people all over the world with programs such as Global Works. These programs can consist of environmental conservation projects, working with endangered animals, renovating schools, building water wells and irrigation systems, and even teaching English. Students may expose themselves to a new culture, learn a new language, and visit new countries. Keep in mind that these programs can be expensive, so be sure to check with each agency regarding cost, airfare, and housing.

## MASTERING YOUR MOTIVATION

When you daydream, what do you dream about? Do you dream about becoming the CEO of a large corporation? Do you fantasize about making a dramatic closing argument in court? Perhaps you imagine yourself working for a humanitarian organization overseas. Or maybe you want to start a family and be a parent. Your daydreams reveal a lot about the things that mean the most to you. By taking some time to analyze what specifically inspires those dreams, you can discover your motivating factors.

Behind every action, there is some kind of motivation. When you decide to do something, you hope to gain something from it. When you make a decision, no matter how big or small, something drives you toward that decision. That something is your motivation. There are both internal and external motivating factors, and most people are motivated by a combination of the two. External motivation comes from an external reward, such as material possessions or the praise of others. Internal motivation comes from an internal reward, such as improving your health or learning a new skill.

When you set a goal for yourself, why do you hope to accomplish that goal? Perhaps your goal is to get an A in biology class. What motivates you to get an A? Is it so your parents, teachers, or friends will be impressed? If so, you are motivated by what others think about you. If it is to understand the material as much as you can, then you are motivated by learning. If it is to get a good grade so you can go to your top college, then you are motivated by the future. Next time you sit down to make a goal, ask yourself why it is important for you to accomplish it. Can you come up with some of your own external and internal motivations?

Remember that things that inspire you will not necessarily inspire your parents, siblings, or best friends. People's environments can also affect their motivations. Some people like to work in large groups while others like to work alone. Some people enjoy sitting at a desk and others need to be outdoors. It is not wrong to be inspired by things that don't motivate others, and it's OK to do the same thing as a friend for completely different reasons. It just means you have a different personality and goals.

## MOTIVATION MATTERS

Motivation guides the decisions you make and helps you accomplish your goals. Without the motivation to do something, chances are you won't do it. Pretend your parents really want you to get an A, but impressing them (or others) doesn't motivate you. In fact, let's say that neither learning nor going to college motivates you. How are you going to be motivated to accomplish this goal?

This is where some creative thinking comes in on your part. Maybe you *are* motivated by money; you would work all day and night at a job just to earn the extra cash. Perhaps you can work out a deal with your parents in which they pay you five dollars for every A. This way when you don't want to do your homework, you can be inspired by the idea of earning some cash.

There are many ways to merge your goals with your motivating factors even if they don't obviously go together. For example, if you are motivated by your friends and their approval, it would be a good idea for you to find a friend who wants to accomplish some shared goal, especially if you aren't too confident. The two of you could provide motivation by encouraging each other to reach that goal.

## WORD OF CAUTION

Generally speaking, most motivating factors are valid—whatever works for you. However, it is entirely possible to be motivated by dangerous, evil, or worthless things. The excuse, "This is just the way I am!" does not make it OK for you to manipulate others.

Even good motivations can become negative if they become consuming. It is fine for desserts to motivate you. If having a scoop of ice cream motivates you to practice a musical instrument, then by all means, scoop away. This does not mean that you practice for 30 minutes and then reward yourself with three bowls. In the same way, being encouraged by parents, friends, and teachers is a good thing; it helps you build meaningful relationships. However, if you let others' opinions completely dominate you, or you let those opinions drive you to do something harmful, then you have let that motivation get out of hand.

It is important to direct your motivations into healthy outlets. It is also important to be honest with yourself and talk with someone older and wiser if you feel that your motivations are bad or you don't know how to balance your motivations and your goals.

## MOTIVATIONS CAN LEAD TO WISE DECISIONS

Knowing what is important to you can also help you evaluate your decisions. Perhaps you really like personal time, you study best in a quiet space, and you hate spending the night anywhere except your own bed. You also might really like soccer. A traveling soccer team that has you studying on a crowded bus and sharing sleeping quarters with other people may be a poor fit. On the other hand, helping run a summer soccer day camp for kids might be perfect!

Knowing these motivators will also help with long-term decisions. What if seeing your friends is the reason you enjoy going to school every day. You also love biology and really want to work in the medical field. If that's true, do you think it would be wise in the future for you to take a job that requires you to spend most of your time alone in a lab? Or would it be better for you to pick a job that does mostly team work or interacts with patients? Knowing that you need other people can save you a lot of job dissatisfaction in the future.

## ⬤ THINK ABOUT IT

Here are some questions to get you thinking about motivation. Remember there are no right or wrong answers. Answer the questions truthfully according to your own personal preference. Do not get caught in the trap of thinking that only "selfless" answers are best. It is OK that you really enjoy making money.

1.  I feel happiest when I _____.
2.  I am more comfortable working in a group. TRUE/FALSE
3.  The thought of spending time or money on others makes me feel
    _____.

4.  The thought of spending time or money on myself makes me feel
    _____.

5.  I spend _____ hours a week working to improve myself.
6.  I spend _____hours a week working to help others.
7.  When asked about my strengths, people say I am really good
    at_____.
8.  When asked about my weaknesses, people say I am really bad at

    _____.
9.  $_____ is a lot of money to me.
10. It is important for me to have_____ dollars
    because_____.
11. I prefer the idea of living a simple life. I want to have just enough
    money to get by and do not need to add additional luxuries.
    ☐ TRUE    ☐ FALSE

12. I prefer the idea of living a luxurious life. I want to make plenty of
    money so I can purchase as many additional luxuries as possible.
    ☐ TRUE    ☐ FALSE

13. I prefer the idea of living a moderate life. I want to make enough
    money to meet my needs and have some left over for additional
    splurges.
    ☐ TRUE    ☐ FALSE

14. It is important for me to travel to new places and to learn about
    new cultures.

☐ TRUE ☐ FALSE

15. It is important for me to stay in a place that I know and where I am comfortable.
☐ TRUE ☐ FALSE

16. I am excited about learning new things.
☐ TRUE ☐ FALSE

17. I am excited about getting to know one thing really well and focusing on it.
☐ TRUE ☐ FALSE

18. My primary concern is helping others outside of my immediate friends and family.
☐ TRUE ☐ FALSE

19. My primary concern is helping my immediate friends and family.
☐ TRUE ☐ FALSE

20. It is important to me that other people know about my successes.
☐ TRUE ☐ FALSE

## MOTIVATIONAL RESULTS

Look at your above answers and think about your responses. Are there any insights that can affect your future planning and decisions? Come up with other scenarios and see if you come up with similar answers. If you are still having trouble identifying your motivational factors, you can find more detailed motivational tests online. A simple Web search for "motivation quiz" will turn up a good amount of results. _____

_____

_____

_____

_____

_____

_____

_____

_____

_____

# GUIDE FOR PARENTS
# HELPING YOUR CHILD DISCOVER THEIR
# INTERESTS FOR POTENTIAL CAREERS

"What do you want to do after high school?" is a scary question. As teenagers grow up, questions about the future become more and more serious. Your daughter may have no idea what she wants to do or where she wants to go after high school. She may have some dreams, but nothing that she is 100 percent set on.

Before she can pick a career path that she will be passionate about, she must discover her passions. Being passionate, or at least enjoying her job, has a two-fold benefit. First, she will likely be happier at work, which means she will most likely be happier in life. Second, happier workers are typically more productive, which enhances job security and encourages a stronger economy.

Perhaps your son knows exactly what he wants to be when he grows up. He may discover, nonetheless, that his "ideal" major in college is not exactly what he expected. How do you prevent a total meltdown? Encourage him during high school to try a variety of activities. He might be surprised to find a previously unknown passion, which can serve as a backup if his initial plans fall through. Students do not need to be involved in everything, but hopefully some new hobbies can broaden their minds to be open to future possibilities.

Experiencing actual work scenarios (through jobs, internships, and volunteer work) is good advice for both the student who knows exactly what he wants to do and the student who is still confused about which direction she will take. Although many careers sound exciting, most jobs have mundane aspects that children may not account for.

Your daughter might think she wants to be a world-renowned violinist until she takes an internship at the local concert hall where she learns that she will have to practice eight to ten hours a day. Although this may sound unsuitable to her, she also learns she really enjoys organizing special events and decides to become a party planner.

Perhaps your son dreams of becoming a veterinarian because he loves caring for pets. A volunteer opportunity at a local animal hospital may reveal he likes caring only for healthy pets and he dislikes dealing with sick animals. Another opportunity in an entrepreneur club could spark an interest in business. He could decide to combine his passions and open a pet store. Other great ways to explore interests are through books, professional mentors, community organizations, family, and friends.

There are three outcomes of actively pursuing interests, and all are good! One, your daughter will decide her interest is no longer a passion and drop it. Two, your son may decide his interest is a potential hobby, but nothing more. Or three, he or she will decide the interest is a passion and a potential career option! No matter the outcome, your child wins because he or she learns. Your child should not feel like failure because a potential interest did not turn into a career. Instead, he should view each endeavor as a learning process and should continue his education through exploration.

Remember students do not have to pick the perfect career path in high school. Many career paths can lead to job fulfillment. People are dynamic individuals and have multiple interests. Thus, helping your son or daughter develop passions in high school is important.

## WORD OF CAUTION

Any time your child is involved in activities outside the home, you need to make sure to check out the adults in charge. Parents should never blindly assume the instructors are inherently well intentioned. You do not need to do a full background check on every teacher or scout leader, but make sure you do your homework. Ask questions about the instructor's background and teach your students how to react in inappropriate or dangerous situations. As a parent, it is your responsibility to protect your children; being informed is the best way to do so.

## HELPING YOUR STUDENT LEARN WHAT MOTIVATES THEM

Parents are often amazed how two siblings—who have lived in the same house, experienced the same things, and are similar in age—are vastly different in how they think and act. The disparity among students comes from multiple factors, such as personality traits, gender, and personal motivators. While this chapter is in no means intended to be a comprehensive psychoanalysis of your student's psyche, hopefully it will get him or her thinking. An understanding of personal motivation styles could potentially benefit every aspect of your child's life.

Talk with your daughter about the things that inspire her to accomplish her goals. Help her figure out ways her motivating factors can help her plan for success. Students who understand their motivating factors early in life can begin to tailor their goals so that they will have motivation to achieve them. Students with clear motivations are more likely to succeed in reaching the goals they set for themselves.

## PARENTS' HOMEWORK

Have your son or daughter take a motivation test (to understand what drives them), personality test (to find out what makes them tick), and career test (to discover possible job interests). Do not allow these results to pigeonhole your child into a certain box. These tests are merely indicators to help you understand and guide your child better. While these types of tests don't have all the answers, they can get you and your child on the right path early, which can save both time and money in the future.

Here are some books to help you get started.

*Ultimate Aptitude Tests: Assess Your Potential with Aptitude, Motivational and Personality Tests* by Jim Barrett
*Get Motivated!: Overcome Any Obstacle, Achieve Any Goal, and Accelerate Your Success with Motivational DNA* by Tamara Lowe
*Essential Enneagram: The Definitive Personality Test and Self-Discovery Guide, Revised & Updated* by David Daniels and Virginia Price
*The Everything Career Tests Book: 10 Tests to Determine the Right Occupation for You* by A. Bronwyn Llewellyn

You may also want to check out these websites:

www.keirsey.com

www.learnmyself.com

www.richardstep.com/self-motivation-quiz-test

www.strengthsquest.com/home.aspx

www.myersbriggs.org

www.outofservice.com/bigfive

# CHAPTER THREE: OWN YOUR BELIEFS

**B**ELIEFS COME in all different sizes and categories. From religion to politics, your beliefs exist as those things that you believe to be true and right in the world. The quest for truth is personal in nature. Holding onto someone else's faith (even your parents') will not be enough to sustain you when times get tough. We are all required to make decisions about truth. Someday you will have to ask, "What do I believe?" At that moment, it won't matter what your parents, friends, and other family members believe; it only matters what you decide. You do not have to make final judgments today, but start asking questions so when the time comes, you will be ready.

## DEVELOPING YOUR OWN BELIEFS

As you get older, you tend to get more curious about why your parents do what they do. You might start questioning your family's religious beliefs, or wondering why your parents raised you in a certain way. It is important to start asking tough questions. Asking questions now helps you get answers before other people start asking you the same questions later. In the future, you will have to make the decision to either follow what your parents have taught you or choose a different path. This is not a decision to take lightly. Without the right foundation, you will be unprepared to make it.

Do not just trust your family's traditions because they are familiar and safe. One day this reasoning will not be enough to sustain your beliefs. Similarly, do not rebel against what you have grown up believing because you want to do something different. Instead, make your beliefs your own. Consider what you have been taught, and decide for yourself whether you believe it to be true.

Start an open dialogue with your parents about their beliefs and why they believe them. Ask them serious questions and evaluate their answers. If they don't know the answers to some of your questions, then make it a family project to find out the answers. Search out people who do know and ask them. At first, your parents might be intimidated by your questions. They might be afraid that you are looking for ways to rebel or that you don't trust them. It is up to you to assure them that you are simply searching for the truth. Approach your parents with respect. Do not antagonize or belittle them. Make sure they know you are trying to make wise choices for yourself.

Never stop learning or asking questions. The more you know, the better you will be able to decide to accept or reject beliefs.

## YOUR JOURNEY

The journey to your own belief system can be challenging. You must be careful when you start. You must make sure that you are emotionally and mentally prepared. Are you ready to listen and ask questions? Be honest about your willingness to be open to what others have to say. If you start your journey believing that your initial beliefs are 100 percent right, you are less likely to honestly evaluate differing opinions or evidence. Finding answers may not be easy. Sometimes it will take deep soul searching to discover what you are truly looking for.

On this journey, you may have to drop a long-held belief because you find evidence to its contrary. This may strain your relationship with your family or friends. Nonetheless, sticking to your convictions is more important than making everyone else happy.

Maybe you will disagree with some of the finer points of a popular worldview. Not everybody who shares a similar belief will always believe the exact same things. There are different nuances to every belief system. The different denominations of major religions illustrate how groups can share common beliefs yet disagree about different aspects. Just because you do not agree with one element of a belief system does not necessarily mean the entire belief system is wrong for you.

The final destination of this journey is the discovery of what is true. Truth accurately reflects the way the world functions. There are entire libraries dedicated to defining truth, so go look for what is available. Utilize only good resources (people, reputable books, and so on) that you can trust to help guide you. Not every book or person is looking out for your best interests. Be careful whom you listen to because logical fallacies are abundant in the world and are easy to fall for. Some people can make things sound true that are far from the truth.

Once you have established your beliefs, own them completely. You should study to know your beliefs intimately, especially before you attempt to debate them. Although this journey can be difficult, it is exciting to know what you believe and why you believe it.

Lastly, choosing not to believe in anything is still a type of belief.

## CULTIVATING A DESIRE FOR VIRTUES

Your belief system defines your character. Your character is the essence of who you really are (especially when no one is around). A strong character, one that is full of virtue, allows you to make the right decisions, even when those decisions are tough.

As you grow up, you must focus on your character development. Worthwhile character qualities determine how you respond to hard situations. It takes both humility and discipline to become virtuous. You should think of virtue as a muscle in your body. When you use a muscle, it gets stronger and can then deal with more weight. In the same way, a strong character can deal with weightier moral choices. Properly handling small issues daily is a great way to prepare yourself to take on big issues.

For example, if the cashier hands back too much change on your purchase, the right (although not fun) action is to return the extra money. Practicing doing the right thing in easy circumstances prepares you for much harder situations.

Let your goal be to live by the "Golden Rule"—doing unto others as you would have them do unto you. Be motivated by always wanting the best for others. Guard your words and never say anything about someone else that you would not say in front of his or her face. Once said or written in public spaces (including on the Internet), hurtful words cannot be taken back.

When it comes to your character, you get out what you put in. Those who do not want to take the time to learn virtue do not deserve the rewards of it. It is important to remember that virtue is also a reward in and of itself. Virtue helps balance and control individuals, bringing peace of mind and strength. Success as an individual starts and ends with a strong character.

 **THINK ABOUT IT**

No one can make you desire a strong character. It is something you must want for yourself. Meditate on the following ten virtues. Think about how possessing these qualities could benefit your life, future career goals, and relationships with others. Try to imagine difficult situations that would require a strong character and imagine the virtuous response. Then imagine yourself performing that action. **Do not hastily read this list and go on to the next topic. In fact, if you get nothing else from this entire book but a strong desire to improve your character, your time will be well spent**. Take time to dwell on each virtue and its meaning. Ask yourself what your life would be like if you had more temperance, moderation, patience, etc.

## TEN COMMON VIRTUES AND THEIR MEANINGS

1. Temperance: the ability to maintain self-control
2. Moderation: the ability to find balance between two extremes
3. Patience: the willingness to forgo an immediate pleasure for a future reward
4. Discipline: the ability to do something unpleasant for the sake of doing what is right
5. Honesty: the ability to tell the truth, regardless of the consequences
6. Sincerity: the ability to mean what you say
7. Justice: the quality of being impartial and fair
8. Mercy: the ability to show compassion and forgiveness to those who wrong you
9. Frugality: the quality of using resources wisely
10. Chastity: the quality of having purity in conduct and intention, both with yourself and in your relationships with others

## QUESTIONS TO GET YOU STARTED

1. What exactly does my family believe about the world and its existence?

   _____

   _____

   _____

2. How do I feel about these beliefs?

   _____

   _____

   _____

3. What are the debates concerning my family's beliefs?

   _____

   _____

   _____

4. Where do I stand on those debates?

   _____

   _____

   _____

5. List some knowledgeable people whom I can talk to or whose works I can read?

   _____

   _____

   _____

6. Do the answers to those questions make sense in how the world works?

   _____

   _____

   _____

7. Are there contradictions in my belief system that need to be reconciled?

   _____

   _____

   _____

8. Can they be reconciled?

   _____

   _____

   _____

9. How will this new knowledge influence the way I think, act, and speak?

   _____

   _____

   _____

## WHAT ARE YOU GOING TO DO ABOUT IT?

Now ask yourself the following questions.

1. By cultivating the virtue of temperance I will be able to

   _____

   _____.

2. By cultivating the virtue of moderation I will be able to

   _____

   _____.

3. By cultivating the virtue of patience I will be able to

   _____

   _____.

4. By cultivating the virtue of discipline I will be able to

   _____

   _____.

5. By cultivating the virtue of honesty I will be able to

   _____

   _____.

6. By cultivating the virtue of sincerity I will be able to

   _____

   _____.

7. By cultivating the virtue of justice I will be able to

   _____

   _____.

8. By cultivating the virtue of mercy I will be able to

   _____

   _____.

9. By cultivating the virtue of frugality I will be able to

   _____

   _____.

10. By cultivating the virtue of chastity I will be able to

    _____

    _____.

11. How can I cultivate the virtue of temperance?

_____

_____.

12. How can I cultivate the virtue of moderation?

_____

_____.

13. How can I cultivate the virtue of patience?

_____

_____.

14. How can I cultivate the virtue of discipline?

_____

_____.

15. How can I cultivate the virtue of honesty?

_____

_____.

16. How can I cultivate the virtue of sincerity?

_____

_____.

17. How can I cultivate the virtue of justice?

_____

_____.

18. How can I cultivate the virtue of mercy?

_____

_____.

19. How can I cultivate the virtue of frugality?

_____

_____.

20. How can I cultivate the virtue of chastity?

_____

_____.

# GUIDE FOR PARENTS
# HELPING YOUR CHILD DEVELOP HIS OR HER BELIEFS

Regardless of how you raised your son, there will come a time when he will start looking into the family beliefs and asking if he really believes in them. This can be a scary time for both you and him. Parents sometimes feel their children's questions are an act of rebellion, and kids often feel alienated by their parents' responses. While neither are what the others intend to communicate, both can have a powerfully negative effect on the situation.

The first thing you need to understand is that not every child will go through this stage at the same age. Some children are naturally more curious while others happily go along with the status quo. If your daughter starts asking questions at the age of ten but your son does not until he is eighteen, it's OK.

Regardless of what age your child starts asking tough questions, you need to encourage him or her to search for the truth. No matter how strongly you might believe in something, your faith does not automatically carry over to your children. They must believe it for themselves. Ultimately, once your daughter leaves your house, either for college or for the real world, she will be forced to examine her beliefs. The best thing you can do for her is start an open dialogue about your beliefs early and encourage her to ask tough questions. Let her struggle and search out the truth with your guidance and encouragement. Listen honestly to her and try to understand her questions and concerns.

Do not regard your silent child as someone who does not care or as one who is solid in his or her beliefs. Your son may be too shy or uncomfortable talking about his beliefs with you. If he hasn't expressed curiosity before entering the last few years of high school, carefully broach this topic with him to check in on his personal journey. It is OK if your daughter is eighteen and isn't ready to struggle with the tough questions; everyone matures at different ages. If this is the case with your teenager, then bring up these topics every so often to help him or her start thinking about it. Some children need extra coaxing when dealing with personal topics.

## HELPING YOUR STUDENT BUILD STRONG CHARACTER

A strong moral character is essential to success after high school. No matter what they do after they graduate, the desire to live virtuously will serve them well. College admissions counselors, future employers, and military recruiters often look for students who exhibit a strong sense of virtue, which is useful in every aspect of their lives. As you guide your students into adulthood, do not neglect the most important aspect of adulthood—the desire to live a virtuous life.

To teach your child a strong moral character, you should live as an example. While no parent will ever be perfect, your daughter will know whether you truly believe what you are telling her if you live it yourself. During the teen years, children begin to notice any disparity between their parents' words and actions. "Do as I say, not as I do," is frustrating advice for a teenager. If you want your son to learn compassion, show him how to be compassionate. If you think your daughter is struggling with discipline, show her you understand by tackling a new task that requires a lot of discipline.

Teenagers are looking for the reasons behind your advice, and they want to know the purpose of the rules and instruction you give them. Simply telling your daughter to do the right thing probably won't work, but showing her how to exhibit virtue most likely will. Although she probably doesn't verbalize it, she looks to you for guidance and examples. Help her desire a strong moral character by showing her what one looks like.

## PARENTS' HOMEWORK

Set a time to have a family discussion concerning your family's beliefs and traditions, one that allows your student to respond to what you say and to ask questions concerning his or her own personal struggles or doubts. Be intentional to create a safe environment, one that allows for any question and is free from a defensive spirit by all parties involved.

Encourage your child to face difficult questions, ones that you might even struggle with, and seek out appropriate resources that can help guide the way. Help your son understand why you believe what you believe, which will in turn allow him to understand his own beliefs. It is far better to encourage this quest for truth under your tutelage than for him to pursue it when he is out in the world alone. While this meeting will be a good starting point for him, it will by no means answer all questions. The quest for truth is a lifelong endeavor that will continue to develop in your child throughout the years.

For bonus points: Give your child moral scenarios and ask him or her to reflect and respond. This will help teach the ability to think things through. For example, try posing this dilemma: "You go to a high school party with some friends. Although you did not know it before you came, there is alcohol there. Even though you choose not to drink, the friends you came with did. What should you do?"

# CHAPTER FOUR:
# BUILDING A HEALTHY YOU

Adolescence is a time of many changes. During this stage in life, you undergo rapid physical growth, which requires a special attention to your dietary needs. Unfortunately, you may have been ignoring key nutrients. This neglect can produce a variety of undesirable side effects including weight gain, acne, and hindered growth.

In addition to establishing and maintaining a balanced diet of fruits, vegetables, proteins, and carbohydrates, you need to focus on two main nutrients: iron and calcium.

Iron helps build lean muscles and promotes healthy oxygen flow in the blood. Throughout puberty, both genders have specific physical needs for iron. Males' rapid development of lean muscles requires an increase of iron in the diet. Females require an increase of iron to compensate for the loss of blood during menstruation. It is important to ensure you are including iron-rich foods in your diet. Great sources of iron are lean cuts of beef, liver, and iron-fortified cereals such as Wheaties or Total. Broccoli, spinach, soybeans, watermelon, and raisins are also high in iron.

Calcium is another important nutrient for teenagers. Because your skeletal mass is growing during this time, an increase of calcium in the diet will help promote healthy bone development. Unfortunately, many students overlook this crucial mineral. A lack of calcium can cause serious problems later on in your life. Female students are especially at risk for adolescent osteoporosis. One easy way to ensure an ample amount of calcium in the diet is by replacing other beverages with milk during meal times. Students also need to include two to three daily servings of low-fat dairy foods. Such products include milk and cheeses, low-fat cottage cheese, and yogurt. If you are lactose-intolerant or vegan, some options are to drink calcium-fortified orange juice, take calcium supplements, or find calcium-fortified soy products.

If you are an athlete, you need to make sure you are eating foods rich in carbohydrates and proteins. Carbohydrates fuel energy levels, and proteins help build and maintain muscles. Eating the right amount of good carbohydrates will strengthen your endurance. Great sources of carbohydrates are whole grains, beans, fruits, vegetables, and milk. To encourage muscle growth and repair, incorporate a serving of protein with each meal. Great sources of protein include chicken, turkey, fish, eggs, nuts, peanut butter, and dairy products.

Lastly, drinking enough water is the foundation of any healthy diet. Many students opt for any other beverage than water, thus denying their bodies one of the very keys to survival. While humans can live several weeks without eating, they can only survive a matter of days without water. Even though you may consume some amounts of water in other drinks and food, nothing can replace the benefits of pure water. Ideally you should drink six to eight 8-ounce glasses a day. However, this can be hard to do, so try and get at least four glasses of water daily. If you are having trouble getting used to plain water, you can add fruit like lemons, limes, cucumbers, or strawberries to help you enjoy the taste.

## WISER FOOD CHOICES

Along with knowing what nutrients are needed, you need to be aware of what types of food to avoid. Be very cautious of unnecessary sodium, sugar, and saturated fat, such as are included in soft drinks, fried foods, hamburgers, pizza, and high-calorie snacks such as cookies, candy bars, and chips. These foods contribute to a variety of health concerns including unwanted weight gain and a higher risk of heart disease. Substitute for these choices better options that have higher nutrient content and fewer calories.

Here are some ideas to help you replace bad food choices with good ones:

- Soda: a cup of juice or flavored water
- Potato chips: a bag of popcorn or baked versions of your favorite chips
- Candy bars: dark chocolate with more cocoa than sugar (60 percent cocoa or higher)
- Deep dish pizza: thin crust pizza with vegetables (avoid pepperoni)
- Hamburgers: turkey burgers on whole wheat buns with lots of vegetables
- Spaghetti dinner: whole grain pasta with vegetables (limit the bread sticks)
- Caesar salad: Garden salad with balsamic vinaigrette dressing

The possibilities are endless if you are creative. It is easier than ever to eat healthily these days with so many restaurants, grocery stores, and fast food chains offering healthy alternatives.

Junk food is acceptable in moderation. If you have issues with eating bad foods, cut down little by little over a period of weeks. It is easy to fail if you try too much too fast. If you get tempted to eat poorly when you go out, try keeping a bag of carrots or another highly nutritious snack with you. The goal is finding a proper balance between nutritious food and the occasional splurge.

Remember these are general guidelines to help you start thinking about your eating habits, and you should continue to research this topic. At your next checkup, talk with your doctor about creating a nutrition plan that's right for you.

There are many reasons to start a healthy diet now rather than later. Decide what it will take to motivate you to eat more healthily, lose weight, improve your health, etc.; and then make the commitment to do it.

## CONSISTENT EATING SCHEDULE IS KEY

Establishing a consistent eating schedule will help you maintain proper nutrition. Regularly eating breakfast, for example, will help ensure your body has the nutrients it needs to function in the morning. Too often students skip this important meal and suffer throughout the day due to this neglect. Research shows students who eat breakfast every day have greater concentration and more energy. Eating breakfast will also increase your metabolism, helping you burn more calories throughout the day.

Keep in mind: You will get the most benefit by eating a healthy balanced breakfast versus a sugary or high-fat meal. Eating a sugary meal will result in a midmorning blood-sugar crash, which can leave you less energized. Include good sources of protein in your breakfast such as eggs, meat, dairy, nuts, and peanut butter to keep you feeling full longer and to provide important nutrients for improved brain function. However, it is better to eat something, even if it's a poor choice, than not eat anything.

Try to spread out your meals throughout the day. Many dietitians recommend eating five or six small meals rather than three large ones. This stabilizes your metabolism and regulates your energy levels. One idea is to keep healthy snacks like granola or trail-mix in your locker, purse, or backpack. This way you can have something healthy to munch on during your breaks.

## THE PROBLEM WITH FAT

There are two very distinct problems facing people in regards to fat. The first is over-eating. This is probably more correctly stated as over-eating the wrong foods. It is rare to find a person who eats too many fruits and vegetables. Over-eating the wrong types of food leads to an excess gain of body fat. This can lead to serious health conditions and a negative self-image. The other extreme is the person who does not eat enough for the fear of getting fat. Both extremes are serious issues that must be dealt with professionally.

If you have excess body fat you should meet with your trusted physician to create a plan to help you establish a healthy body weight. Extremes are bad, and you should not try any starvation diets, health fads, or quick fixes. Make a plan and stick with it. Diet and exercise is the only formula that works 100% of the time. Not only will you be proud of your ability to stick with your plan and exhibit discipline, but also you will be satisfied with looking and feeling better. Your ultimate goal is not to lose the weight, but to establish a healthy lifestyle.

Being underweight is just as serious as being overweight. The normal human body needs a certain amount of fat. This fat helps to insulate parts of the body to keep them warm and protected from injury. Your body also needs fat as a store of energy reserves. These reserves become very important if you come down with an illness, receive even relatively minor injuries, or need to perform some physical activity. The healthy amount of fat you need is largely determined by your age, gender, and activity levels.

It is very dangerous to be overly concerned with losing weight. It is easy to believe that losing weight is a good thing, but choosing not to eat is very detrimental to your body. Do not neglect monitoring your eating habits and pay special attention to any significant changes in your attitude toward food. Learning how to view food in a healthy manner can save you a lot of pain and suffering further down the road. Carefully read the list and check any or all that may apply. If you or one of your friends suffers from any of the signs listed, seek help immediately.

Common signs of unhealthy food habits[1]
1. Sudden and severe weight loss
2. Obsessing about food and/or appearance
3. Counting exactly how many calories are in everything, or eating only specific foods because of their calorie count
4. Withdrawal from social environments
5. Lying about weight or food intake
6. Eating food in a ritualistic fashion
7. Large quantity of health problems
8. Abusing diet pills and/or laxatives
9. Vomiting after eating
10. Excessive exercising

---

1 According to www.mirror-mirror.com

11. Drinking several soft drinks a day
12. Eating fried or fast food every day
13. Snacking only on sugary or high-calorie snacks
14. Lying about how much candy or soda consumed
15. Eating junk food late at night

 **THINK ABOUT IT**

Now that you have learned the importance of establishing a healthy diet, take some time to think through these questions. Once you have answered them honestly, think about ways you can improve.

1. What do I consider junk food?

_____

_____

_____

2. How often do I eat that junk food? (Daily/Weekly)

_____

_____

_____

3. Do I routinely eat breakfast?
   ☐ YES      ☐ NO

4. What is my typical breakfast?

_____

_____

_____

5. What is my typical lunch?

_____

_____

_____

6. What is my typical dinner?

_____

_____

_____

7. How many glasses of water do I drink a day?

_____

_____

_____

8. What is one dietary improvement I can make today?

_____

_____

_____

## TACKLING CHANGE

Despite the fact that change is inevitable, many people are resistant to change and try desperately to avoid it. Many students look upon the impending change from middle school to high school or from high school to college with dread. Change is fraught with uncertainty. Most people fear the unknown, and by its very nature, change is an unknown.

Change gets a bad rap. In fact, for the most part change is actually one of the best parts of life.

But, you say to yourself, life isn't so bad now. Why change what works? Imagine you stayed the same age, living in the same place, with the same people, doing the same thing every day for eternity. Do you really want to be sitting in third-period algebra for the rest of your life? That doesn't sound very fun. Now imagine all the different things you did and experienced over the last couple of years. Think about all the people you have met and all the friendships you have made. Think about all the things you have learned. All of that involved some aspect of change. Imagine if life had stopped changing before you got to where you are now. Imagine being stuck as a baby, toddler, or even middle school student. Change can be just as good as it is scary. It is a neutral unstoppable force, so you need to learn how to handle it.

You go through hundreds of changes every day without ever taking notice. Were you in a panic when you woke up this morning and it was a new day? Today is different from yesterday, and different from tomorrow, but I bet you did not even think about it. You know how to cope with the change in days because you have some sort of guidelines that address the change. Even though the change in days seems very mundane, you can face monumental changes with the same type of assurance.

Here are some tips to help you lessen the anxiety that surrounds most forms of change.

1. Recognize that change is inevitable and often a good thing.
2. Approach change with a positive attitude.
3. Look for positives in the way things are changing.
4. Don't romanticize the past; things were never as good as you remember.
5. Create new habits to make the change familiar.
6. Establish and rely on your support system of family and friends.
7. Make and strive for goals in this new stage of life.
8. Always tackle challenges head on.
9. Bring your best self to the table and make sure to take care of your physical, emotional, and spiritual needs.
10. Be resourceful and look for ways to utilize what you have to make your situation the best it can be.

## DEPRESSION AND RECOVERING FROM SETBACKS

Setbacks are never fun and can hamper your ability to achieve your goals. After you have experienced a relatively minor setback, give yourself some time to be sad about whatever it is you have lost. It is important to grieve and acknowledge that you are disappointed with how things turned out. Once you have given yourself a couple of days to be disappointed, it is time to move on. Accept the outcome and make the best of it; there may be ways to mitigate the negative outcomes. There are many avenues to potential goals and dreams; often setbacks force you to find creative ways to obtain your goals.

If, however, you have recently faced a serious circumstance (the death of a friend, a major illness, a loss of a dream), it is much harder to recover. If you have faced a long series of crises, it can be even harder to recover. You might begin to lose confidence in yourself and lose hope in your future. You may feel lost and abandoned by those around you. You may also feel like no one understands your circumstances and that you have to face things on your own. This hopelessness and isolation can often lead to depression or worse. Nobody enjoys disappointment.

Disappointment, however, passes with time and is a natural response to a setback. On the other hand, if hopelessness lingers, it is not a natural response. If situations make you feel hopeless, desperate, and/or panicked, it is time to go talk to someone. These are often signs of depression, and true depression doesn't just go away. Depression colors your perspective and runs much deeper than the setbacks you have just faced.

People self-diagnose themselves all the time as depressed. If they feel bad or are having a hard day, they may say they are depressed. That is not depression. Depression is a serious situation that is not synonymous with being upset. Everybody gets upset, but not everybody becomes depressed. Depression can take on many faces, so it is important to recognize potential signs of depression and to get help right away. Only after you have dealt with your depression can you hope to recover from your setback.

If you are experiencing any of the feelings listed below it is time to go get help. Talk to a trusted adult and ask him or her to help you find a professional counselor. It might seem embarrassing to have to go to counseling, but it should not be. A counselor's job is to help people just like you get through tough times. You don't have to face difficult situations on your own; talk with the people who make it their profession to help. There is no shame in turning to someone who is knowledgeable and trained to tackle serious problems. Even the United States military recognizes the seriousness of depression and has taken steps to help protect and heal its soldiers, sailors, airmen, and Marines from this ailment.

The most important step is to make a commitment not to give up on life. Giving up on life does not solely mean suicide; it means abandoning your goals and ambitions. This is not a good way to beat depression. Take a cue from Winston Churchill and never surrender!

## RECOGNIZE THE SIGNS OF DEPRESSION

How do you know if you are depressed? Carefully read the following list and check any or all that may apply. If you or any of your friends exhibit some or most of these symptoms, it is time to talk with a trusted adult.

1. Sad or intense negative mood for an extended amount of time
2. Decreased self-image
3. Loss of motivation and interest in things you enjoy
4. Excessive guilt or self-blame
5. Constant feeling of fatigue
6. Abnormal sleeping habits (either too much or too little)
7. Increased emotional sensitivity
8. Difficulty concentrating or focusing
9. Lack of social interest
10. Excessive worrying
11. Abnormal eating habits (too much or too little)
12. Constant feeling of hopelessness
13. Dramatic shifts in moods (from extremely happy to extremely sad)
14. Constant need to cry or lash out at others
15. Reckless behavior

Remember, depression can be a serious situation, but it is not a hopeless one. People get help every day and recover from this malady. If you feel like you or someone you know is going through depression, talk to a trusted adult about it. The sooner you seek help, the sooner you will start to feel better.

## SUICIDE

According to the Centers for Disease Control and Prevention, suicide is the third leading cause of death for fifteen- to twenty-four-year-olds. Roughly 14 percent of students in high school seriously consider suicide. This means one out of every seven high-schoolers contemplates suicide as a means for escaping his or her problems. This issue could affect you, your family, or your community.

If you have either attempted or considered suicide as an option, realize that you do not have to face this problem alone. The fact that you hold this book in your hand is evidence that someone cares about you and your future. No problem is insurmountable; your current pain is only a drop in the bucket compared to the joy you have awaiting you in the future. Remember no situation is completely unique, and someone else has dealt with the exact same problems and made it through. Before you do anything irrecoverable, stop and talk to someone about the thoughts in your head. School counselors, a trusted adult, or a spiritual guide can all lend a listening ear. With the help of your support network, you can make it to your brighter future.

# ▌GUIDE FOR PARENTS
# HELPING YOUR CHILD ESTABLISH A HEALTHY BODY

Your child needs special guidance to establish healthy eating habits. Besides feeding your daughter all the right foods, you also need to teach her how to make good choices without your guidance. Don't let this discussion slack! Many students don't learn it, which is why so many college freshman gain an average of fifteen extra pounds. Help her avoid this mistake by giving proper instruction beforehand.

Your son does not need to become a health fanatic, but he does need to understand the benefits of healthy eating as well as how to make wise food choices. Understanding how to properly fuel his body now will save him a lot of time and energy and excess fat in the future. The best way to start teaching him how to live a healthy lifestyle is by ensuring these habits are displayed at home. As the parent, you are your student's best role model.

## HELPING YOUR STUDENTS ESTABLISH A HEALTHY MIND

The transition from childhood to adulthood can be scary for your child. While some teenagers cannot wait to grow up and start living their own lives, the reality of facing the future can be intimidating. Uncertainty is rarely fun; many youths panic when they confront the pressure of future decisions. Helping your son or daughter recognize and understand the fear of change will be invaluable. Students who learn how to cope with small changes in life are better equipped to handle the much bigger changes as well. After all, life will only continue to move faster as more and more things begin to change.

During this time, good communication can often be challenging, but it is vital to ensuring the health of your child. Teens are not always willing to talk to their parents about their fears and feelings. Sometimes they don't know how. If your daughter seems aloof and unwilling to talk to you, do not rashly make conclusions about why she is keeping silent. Look at the situation as a whole; notice changes in behavior, situations, and attitude to help you decide what approach is best to take with her.

Your son might become distant or confrontational when asked to have a serious conversation. Try not to be hurt by unnecessary outbursts or evasiveness. These often result from his feeling overwhelmed or insecure about himself, his future, and his place. Developing teenagers do not always think through their actions or words. While age is no excuse for disrespectful behavior, sometimes remembering that he is still an adolescent can give you enough patience to respond properly to him.

Do not give up, nor let your frustrations muddy communications. Your teenager needs you. That may mean sometimes your daughter needs some space to figure things out, or it may mean that your son needs you to take action to keep him from doing something harmful or stupid. Other times it may mean seeking outside help. No matter what situation you find yourself in with your child, take an honest evaluation and seek what is best for him or her.

There is no shame in turning to others for help; many parents speak with counselors about how to have a better relationship with their children. Some parents falsely believe they have failed at parenting if their child goes to counseling. This is a mistake. Teenagers handle life differently and sometimes can greatly benefit from getting professional advice about what is going on in their lives. Topics discussed in therapy can be as mundane as trying to fit in at school or as serious as contemplating suicide. It may be embarrassing for parents to admit they do not know how to handle certain situations with their kids. However, there is no shame in getting help. Good parenting is getting help for your kids when they need it, even if it means seeking help outside of the home.

Awareness of your child's health is vital during adolescence. If you notice any signs of unhealthful behavior, you need act immediately. Erratic intense emotional states or dramatic weight gain or loss may be signs that your son or daughter needs outside help. Don't wait for a dramatic event to incite action, but rather try to remedy problems before they develop into major life issues.

## PARENTS' HOMEWORK

A healthy diet is the foundation of a healthy lifestyle. Teaching your children how to recognize good, OK, and poor food choices is one of the best things you can teach them. Take some time out of your day to examine your pantry, refrigerator, and cabinets. Identify the three different types of food choices and instruct your child how often he or she should partake of them (good: throughout the day, OK: once a day, poor: once or twice a week). Try to highlight the value of moderation versus excess.

Good food choices: Apples, carrots, almonds, raisins, low-fat cottage cheese, turkey slices, eggs

OK food choices: Peanut butter, avocados, granola, low-fat popcorn, whole wheat bread, low sugar cereal

Poor food choices: Fast food, cookies, chips, candy, breakfast pastries, white bread, potatoes

# CHAPTER FIVE: YOUR FINANCIAL INDEPENDENCE

URING HIGH school, many students do not worry about managing a budget, saving for the future, or learning how to invest. Simply put, financial security may not seem relevant to you. However, understanding finances is important now! Don't make the mistake of waiting until college to start tackling your financial situation. You may already be making serious financial mistakes, and these problems will only compound as you get older and more responsibilities demand both your time and money.

According to www.creditcard.com, the average undergraduate student will amass more than two thousand dollars in credit card debt while in college, on top of student loans. That credit card debt alone (assuming you don't put any more debt on your card and it does not accrue interest, which rarely happens) will cost you more than six hundred dollars annually for three years after you graduate. You might be thinking, "So what? If I get a good job, I can afford the extra six hundred dollars a year in debt." Remember that two thousand dollars of debt is an average, which means some students amass substantially more and on multiple cards. In fact, half of American college students had four or more credit cards in 2008.[2]

---

2    According to www.creditcard.com.

Before you start thinking about what you can buy with those four credit cards, think about the bills that you will have to pay after school: rent, utilities, groceries, insurance, car payments, and/or car maintenance, etc. If you get married while in school or soon after, you will have even more financial responsibilities. Debt is much easier to accrue than pay off. You may occasionally use your credit line to make ends meet or to splurge on a nice item. So many things in life clamor for your money, paying down your credit cards becomes a low priority. Without proper planning, your financial situation can get out of hand quickly.

To add insult to injury, companies looking to hire new associates may investigate to see if your credit history indicates that you will be an asset. Companies are generally risk averse; they do not like taking risks unless they have to. If you have a history of mismanaging money, future employers may see you as irresponsible. Additionally, some government jobs will not hire you if you have credit issues. Do you want to work for the CIA? Not if your credit history indicates that you will be at risk for bribes or other improprieties. Recently a panel of agents and officers from the country's national security agencies all remarked that poor credit history is a serious issue because it can lead to problems with operational security. Thus, if the government thinks financial security is important enough to consider it a national security issue, then you should consider it a serious issue too. Take your credit and financial situation seriously.

## MAKE A BUDGET

You probably don't make a ton of money right now, nor do you have a lot of bills to pay. Regardless, learning how to make a budget now will be a very rewarding habit for the future. To make a budget, you need to add up all the money you make and subtract the amount of money that you need to pay.

Ask your parents to help you figure out how to make a budget. There are also great resources online (like mint.com) that can help you get started. Calculate every source of income that you have; include your allowance, part-time job paychecks, and other sources of revenue. That will be your total income. Then subtract all of the things you will have to pay for the next month. You may not have any bills right now, but in the future this will include your rent, utilities, cell phone, etc. Make sure your account for all the areas you need to spend money, including your "savings bill." It is also a good idea to put some spending money in the budget to reward yourself for your discipline.

Once you have subtracted your bills from your income, you can allocate the rest of your money to wherever you like! Decide how much money you will save, spend, and give away. Calculating exactly how much money you have to spend and where you will spend it is a great way to keep from overextending your resources.

## KEEP TRACK OF YOUR DOLLARS

While making a budget is rather simple, sticking to a budget is a lot harder. Have you ever noticed how quickly your money can evaporate right before your eyes? A few dollars here, a few dollars there, and before you know it, your money is gone. All of the little purchases over time can really add up.

Get in the habit of keeping a log of every purchase you make, both big and small. It might be tedious at first, but you will be glad you did in the end. A money log can help you evaluate your purchases and keep yourself on track. It can be easy to overspend on items you don't really need—like unnecessarily eating at a restaurant when you can pack a lunch instead. A few weeks of wasting money and you will quickly run out, which will likely make you miss opportunities for things you really want.

## THE IMPORTANCE OF A CHECKING ACCOUNT

Learning how to balance your checking account and monitor your savings goes hand in hand with keeping a budget. If you do not have a checking account, go get one! Do not put it off until after graduation. Do not wait until you are on your own. It is much easier to learn how to protect yourself from some serious financial mistakes under the guidance of adults you trust.

If you are younger than eighteen years old, you will most likely have to open a joint checking account with one or both of your parents. While this might seem like an insult to your independence, remember you only need to have your parents on your account until you turn eighteen. Once you turn eighteen, you can file for a sole account.

Although at times inconvenient, there are actually tremendous benefits to having a joint account with your parents. Your parents will be able to cash checks for you and freely transfer money into your account without any extra steps to get your approval. On the flipside, having your parents on your account will also allow them the freedom to withdraw money if they feel like they need to and monitor your spending activity online.

For most cases, having a joint account with your parents should be perfect. However, if you feel that there is good reason to avoid having your parents on your account, then talk to your bank to see if you can have another trusted adult as a co-signer.

You should shop around before picking your checking account as some banks offer specials for students. Check into student banking accounts that are free from fees.

## THE RIGHT SAVINGS ACCOUNT

When picking a savings account, it is important to decide if you want one that is connected to your checking account or one at a separate institution. Either type of savings account has benefits and drawbacks. You will have to decide which type of account is best for you.

Joint accounts allow you free access between your savings and your checking account. They can often offer you overdraft protection coverage in case you take too much money out of checking. Likewise, you can easily transfer money back and forth between the two accounts. This allows quick access to all the cash you have on hand. Unfortunately, it also allows you the opportunity to spend the money easily in both of your accounts.

Having your savings account at a separate institution from your checking allows you greater protection from spending your savings. In many ways, having two accounts at different banks or credit unions operates on the principle of out of sight, out of mind. However, this great amount of security from your spending habits comes at a price. It is a lot harder to get cash into your checking account if you need it immediately.

If you are someone who has a hard time saving, it might be a good idea to have separate accounts. If saving comes easily to you, then it might be a good idea to get joint accounts so you can have the extra degree of flexibility. Some people like to have both a joint savings account with their checking and a separate savings account at another financial institution. They keep enough money in their joint saving account in case of an emergency and put the rest of the money in their other account.

Look around, talk to banks, and decide which option, or combination of options work for you.

## LEARN HOW TO SAVE

Like any form of discipline, learning how to save money can be a challenging task. As with most things that require hard work, discipline in finances pays great dividends in the future. Having money in the bank allows you financial freedom. When there is a crisis and you need fast cash, savings can come in handy. Savings can also allow you to participate in things you otherwise would not have the ability to do, like a cruise to the Bahamas!

Another great thing about saving is that money grows. The longer you save, the less amount of actual money you need to accrue enormous wealth. Let's say you have a goal of being a millionaire by the time you retire. The earlier you start putting money into the bank, the less money you will need to invest to reach that goal because interest rates work to your advantage. The longer the money sits in your bank account, the more interest compounds. Therefore, a key to future financial freedom is starting early.

Decide today what percentage of your allowance or paycheck you are going to dedicate to savings and put that amount in the bank every month. Treat saving like every other bill that you have or will have to pay. Saving is the most important bill because it actually pays you back! Even if you put only a dollar in the bank every month, you will have one more dollar in your savings that can start working for you.

## THE FABULOUS RULE OF 72

In finance, the Rule of 72 is a way of devising the amount of time it takes for compound interest to double your savings or investment. This is only an estimation, but it can quickly show you the power of compound interest. To begin, divide the number 72 by the annual interest rate to obtain the amount of time it will take for your investment to double. For example, the rule of 72 states that one dollar invested at 10 percent would take 7.2 years (72/10 = 7.2) to turn into two dollars.

Let's just say, at the age of eighteen, you start saving (or investing) one thousand dollars every year (which is approximately eighty-four dollars a month) and continue until you are seventy. Accordingly, with this approximation, at the age of seventy, you will have the following amounts if your interest rates are 8, 12, or 18 percent, assuming your monthly contributions remain consistent and the interest is compounded monthly.

8%- $783,632.69
12%- $4,168,138.86
18%- $60,667,808.11

Not too shabby! Although these are just approximations, it does show the effectiveness of compound interest and continued savings. Interest rates available for student accounts are dependent upon the economic climate, and young students are not likely to get a savings account with interest rates as high as those above. However, the main point remains: Saving at a young age leads to large growth over time.

## LEARN ABOUT INVESTMENT OPPORTUNITIES

Investments are a lot like savings except they have a higher risk. Investments may pay dividends and can sometimes be sold at a hefty profit. The riskier the investment, the higher the potential payoff can be, or the better chance of losing everything!

Investments involve putting money into a certain product, industry, or company. There are many reasons to invest. If you think a certain company is great and going to be very profitable, you should consider investing in it.

Investing in a company means you become part owner, and therefore you get a share of its profits—or losses. Or you can invest in a certain type of industry. If you think energy is the future, then you can put money into a mutual fund that will distribute your money into several companies from the energy sector.

Before you ever decide to invest, seek professional guidance. You don't necessarily have to hire an investment firm, but you need to get wise counsel. It is just as easy to lose money in investments as it is to gain it. Don't make any hasty decisions.

Be an ethical investor. You should only put money into companies or ideas you believe in. If you think a certain product or company has immoral or unethical practices, don't invest in it, even if you think it will make a lot of money. Companies that practice immoral, unethical, or illegal activities are at high risk for problems. Enron is a great example of the dangers of investing in unethical companies. Many investors lost their shirts when Enron collapsed. Keep a long-term perspective in mind and do not settle for get-rich-quick schemes.

You may not be in a position right now to get involved in investments; however, now is the time to start learning about them. Do some investigating and learn about the difference between stocks, bonds, certificate deposits, and mutual funds. While these are probably unfamiliar terms right now, they can be great tools for your financial planning. Even if you have no money for investments right now, you can still make a hypothetical portfolio on paper and track potential investments. See how much your stocks grow or shrink in a matter of months. It's a good learning process with zero risk!

## THE TRUTH ABOUT CREDIT CARDS

Deciding whether you should get a credit card right now is a very important decision that you need to make with your parents. Do some research and talk to some financial experts. Gather as much information as possible to make the best possible decision. **You should not, however, get a credit card if you have no way of paying it off, or use it to purchase things you cannot afford!**

Never keep a balance on your credit card. Similar to your savings accounts, interest on credit cards accrues over time. Compound interest is your best friend in savings and your worst enemy in credit cards. Right now the savings interest rate is around 1% or less with credit card interest rates generally greater than 10%! The more money you put on your card, the harder it will be to pay off.

Only use your credit card to pay for things that you can pay off right away. This will help you establish a credit score that will help you get a home loan or car lease in the future. The credit score is the primary value of a credit card. It is not a resource for getting frivolous purchases now that you cannot afford.

## THE BEST INVESTMENT YOU WILL EVER MAKE

Do not make this small section of this book your sole authority on wise financial choices. One of the best purchases you can make is a resource on financial planning. There are tons of books written for all different levels and backgrounds to help with your financial situation. Your local library should have at least a few to choose from. Learn about different types of savings and investment plans. Set money goals for yourself and strive to achieve them. Knowing how to handle money is one area in life that you will need no matter what you decide to do or where you decide to go.

 **THINK ABOUT IT**

Challenge yourself to keep track of your purchases for one month to see where the bulk of your money goes. You may be surprised at how easy it is to spend on unnecessary items (such as candy bars, fast-food lunches, or one-time-use items). Create a money log (either in a notebook or on the computer), and write down every purchase, no matter how small. Be sure to include the exact price (tax included), a description of the item, and the date of the purchase. Be faithful and diligent in your bookkeeping. Once the month is over, total up all the purchases, evaluate the items, and think about what other things you could have bought if you had eliminated certain things. After you have completed the exercise, answer the following questions.

1.  How much money did I spend this month?

    _____

    _____

2.  What were some of the main things I spent my money on?

    _____

    _____

3.  Were these items worth purchasing? Was the enjoyment worth the price I paid?

    _____

    _____

4.  If not, what else could I have purchased (either at that time or in the future)?

    _____

    _____

5.  What lessons about money did I learn from this exercise?

    _____

    _____

# GUIDE FOR PARENTS HELPING YOUR CHILD LEARN ABOUT MONEY

It's never too early to teach your student how to save. If you give your daughter an allowance, make sure she puts some away in savings. Sit down with her, discuss why saving is important, and decide what percentage she will save.

Also, talk to her about the importance of making a budget. As she gets older, you might want to think about giving her responsibility for purchasing things like school clothes or family Christmas presents. Give her a certain amount and let her spend it however she wants. If your son decides he really wants a new pair of jeans that cost the same as his entire clothes budget, let him make the purchase. If he asks for more money, tell him no; he had a choice, and he chose one expensive pair of jeans over all the other clothes he could have purchased with his budget.

Your child needs to learn that spending has its limits. If you offer to give your son money every time he wants something, he will have a harder time managing his limited resources once he leaves your home. When a teen becomes accustomed to a certain lifestyle, he or she will try to maintain the same quality of life, even if that means using credit cards to do it. Curb this mentality now by requiring your child to live on a restricted budget. Your daughter will not be happy about it, but she will be better off in the long run.

## PARENTS' HOMEWORK

Discuss the importance of financial planning and budgeting. When discussing how to allot the given revenue, a good rule of thumb is the 10-10-10-70 rule. Your child should give 10 percent of their income to a church or charity (this teaches them to be generous to others), give 10 percent to savings (which allows them to establish a financial cushion), give 10 percent to a long-term investment (for right now this money will likely also go into their savings until they have enough to put into a mutual fund or the stock market), and lastly use 70 percent for their living expense (bills, gas, and other expenditures). Teaching children to live on only 70 percent of their total income will keep them from living beyond their means.

 10% Giving

 10% Savings

 10% Long-term Investment

 70% Life Needs

 Also, talk to your kids about income tax. Guide them through the appropriate forms and stress the importance of filing on time. Make sure they understand how their wages will be reduced, and have them add income tax as an extra bill in their monthly budget.

## GOOD BOOKS TO HELP YOU

*Financial Peace Revisited* by Dave Ramsey

*The Ultimate Financial Plan: Balancing Your Money and Life* by Jim Stovall and Tim Maurer

The Money Tree program, which empowers youth with financial literacy (for a substantial discount, go to www.themoneytreeusa.com and use code: HSPG)

# CHAPTER SIX: BUILDING A STRONG SUPPORT SYSTEM

JOHN DONNE, a famous English poet, once wrote that "no man is an Island, entire of itself; every man is a piece of the Continent." Those words, written in 1623, still have a profound meaning today. Donne spoke of people in relationship to one another—that they are connected as parts to a whole. This is true for you. While at times you may feel alone, you are not.

Other people will always influence you. This will never change. However, you get to decide what types of people have an influence and how much. It's your job to surround yourself with individuals who will support and encourage you to achieve your goals. A strong support team will help you succeed.

First, you need to make sure the people in your support team have your best interests at heart. It is common for other people to confuse *their* goals for *your* goals. Make sure that your trusted allies are interested in you for you, not for themselves. It doesn't matter if your support system is made up of mostly family members, teachers, or friends, as long as it is made up of people who believe in you and are willing to invest themselves in helping you.

Second, you need to make sure you are someone who is willing to work hard to help others achieve their goals. A good support system is a two-way street. You need to find people whom you can encourage as much as they can encourage you. (Although it may seem like adults will not need your help to achieve their goals, sometimes a positive attitude is a great encouragement to them!)

Don't just settle for your current group of friends. Make sure your support team has members who offer different perspectives than those of your peer group alone. Pick family members, teachers, mentors, etc., to help you get the best team possible. You don't have to consult every team member every time you have an issue, yet having a diverse group ensures a good variety of expertise to help you.

Here are some things to keep in mind when you are constructing your team.

## BE A PERSON PEOPLE WANT TO BE WITH

Before you can begin searching for a good support team, you need to make sure that you yourself are a good team member. It is so much easier to love someone who is lovable. People will want to help you if you prove yourself someone worthy of helping.

Think about the type of people that you like to be around. Are they happy or sad? Are they willing to help you out after you have helped them? You will get so much more out of your relationships if you are willing to give back to them. If you expect your teacher to write a letter of recommendation for you, then be the type of student he or she is excited about recommending.

When people help you out, show them you appreciate it. Nobody likes to be used, and no one likes to help someone who is ungrateful or lazy. Try to follow wise counsel and be thankful for it! Be mindful of your support team with thank you notes and birthday cards.

## LOOK FOR PEOPLE WHO GENUINELY CARE ABOUT YOU

Who is always there for you no matter what, even when you act mean or bratty? Take a moment and think about the people you know. Whose actions always show they care about you? It may be a parent, a friend, a youth pastor, or a teacher. If you think hard enough, you might be surprised at how many people you can come up with! These people are the ones you want to keep around. They are the people who know you for exactly who you are and still love you. You can't ask for better family or friends than that.

Don't take these people for granted! Just because someone forgives your misbehavior doesn't give you an excuse to behave poorly. People will get fed up with being mistreated. Truthfully, people like this are hard to find; you should do everything in your power to treat them with the highest respect and honor.

## PARENTS, TEACHERS, AND MENTORS

Your support system should begin with your parents or guardians. Good parents always seek the best interests of their children. Thus, you should respect their decisions and judgments, even if you feel that they don't understand you or your circumstances. While no parent is perfect, good parents try to safeguard your wellbeing. If you ever feel like your parents' guidance or decisions are wrong, keep a line of communication open and be courteous. (Rash actions or decisions rarely lead to positive long-term results.) As a rule, take your parents' advice seriously. They want your best future, and they can offer you an adult's perspective on your situation.

Right now, your main job is school. Who better to guide you than your teachers? After all, teaching is their occupation. Work with them, not against them, and you will be amazed at the results. Don't be afraid to look to them when you are struggling with your studies, when you have issues at school, or when you have serious questions about the world. Incorporating teachers into your support system will make the journey through high school, and even college, so much easier.

For advice that goes beyond the expertise of your parents, guardians, or teachers, you should seek a mentor. Mentors can be a huge blessing by helping you navigate personal, spiritual, professional, or academic endeavors. Try to look for a mentor when you have to meet a goal or challenge that has no clear guidelines. Find someone who has done it before, and ask him or her to help you.

Mentors come in all shapes and sizes; you can have more than one mentor. If you have lofty career goals, find someone in that field who is willing to talk to you and give you advice. If you have a particular interest, find someone who shares it. If nothing else, find someone who is wise and whose life you would like to emulate. A good mentor is a trailblazer who has already achieved a goal (personal, academic, athletic, vocational, spiritual, etc.) and can point you down the right path to success.

Look for mentors who have time and willingness to help you. If a mentor cannot invest in you, the relationship will do you no good. When you ask someone to be a mentor, let him or her know that it is OK to say no if that person is too busy or does not feel up to the job. It is better for someone to say no and for you to find another resource than to have someone say yes who cannot commit to helping you.

If a mentor says yes, it is up to you to make the relationship work as smoothly as possible. You have to be willing to work around your mentor's schedule. Never forget that a mentor is helping you. He or she does not owe you time; you have not earned it. Make sure you treat your mentor's sacrifice with appreciation.

## DEVELOPING NEW FRIENDSHIPS

Strong social connections influence a person's happiness. Everyone needs close long-term relationships. Good friends will offer you a place to belong, a source of support, and an avenue for self-growth. People learn to be good friends by having good friends.

During adolescence, developing worthwhile relationships can positively affect the rest of your life. Likewise, aligning yourself with destructive companionships can negatively affect the rest of your life. Therefore, it is imperative you learn not only how to develop but also how to evaluate those friendships.

Whether you go to a completely new high school, start a co-op program, or rejoin your middle school classmates in high school, there will be times in your life when you'll have to make new friends. Although it might not seem like it, being forced to develop new relationships is a good thing. Making friends is a lifelong skill, and it's better to learn it now than later on in adulthood. Meeting new people and learning about their lives is a very rewarding and enriching experience.

Not to deny the importance of having a few close friends, continuously expanding your social circle should always be a goal. However, it is impossible to meet new people if there is nobody new around. To make new friends, you should go where the people are. Group activities or student organizations are great places to start.

Try joining a club connected to your interests. You will likely find people with similar interests to you; new friendships quickly spring up between people who share something. Get out of your comfort zone and say yes to different activities. This might mean joining a new group of classmates at the lunch table, taking an outside class, playing a pickup game of basketball, or going to a school-hosted party.

Make sure you are open to meeting people. If you don't want to make new friends, chances are you won't. Have a good attitude about meeting people and think positively about your new situations. Feeling good will put you in a positive mood and make you more appealing to new friends. While this does not mean you need to always be a ray of sunshine, it does mean you will have a hard time getting to know others if you are constantly moping around. Even if you don't feel great, put on a smile. If you start to act happy, most of the time you will start to feel happy.

Leave the electronics at home! It's pointless to go to group activities if you spend the whole time messing with your phone or listening to your MP3 player. Electronics can wait until you are somewhere else. If you go somewhere to make friends, then focus your attention on getting to know the others around you.

If you are feeling self-conscious, remember everyone else feels the same way you do. Remember you have just as much to offer new friends as they do you. If you get snubbed by someone, don't let it get you down. Realize if someone doesn't want to get to know you, then he or she wouldn't be a good friend anyway.

Once you have found someone you want to get to know better, show that person you are interested in getting to know him or her by asking questions and sincerely listening. This shows a person that you care about his or her personal journey, and it gives you more information to evaluate that person as a prospective friend. For example, ask your new companion what his or her favorite book is and why. This will give you great insight into this person's interests, which will help you decide if you two could be good friends or just acquaintances.

When talking with somebody new, it is always nice to find something you like about that person and tell him or her. If you find out something that really interests you or impresses you, let that person know. As long as your compliment is genuine and meaningful, that person will enjoy the nice thing you said.

After you have met a few people, talked with them, and developed an interest in getting to know them better, you can make plans to hang out. The foundation of a friendship is quality time. Try to find something you both can enjoy and make a plan to do it.

## QUESTIONS TO GET YOU STARTED

1. What do you want to do after high school, and why?
2. What's your favorite type of music, and why?
3. If you could go to any time period, which one would you go to and why?
4. What do you do in your free time?
5. If you were given a million dollars (and couldn't give any to charity), what would you spend it on?

## EVALUATING FRIENDSHIPS

It is not always easy to know whether your friendships are healthy. You may not have spent enough time with some friends to know if they have the potential of being great friends, or you may not know what a great friend looks like and you have settled for some less desirable options. No matter the reason, the type of relationships you find yourself in will greatly influence the type of person you will become. Take time to think about your closest friends, your acquaintances, and people you might like to get to know better. Think about your interactions with them, how they make you feel, and whether they are good for you. Does the person you are hanging out with bring out the best or worst in you?

When evaluating your friendships, look at the whole picture. Remember that no friendship will ever be perfect. Conflict arises in even the healthiest relationships. Also, people learn and grow throughout their lives; someone who might have once been a bad friend might turn out to be a great friend in the end.

Friendships do not have to be all or nothing either. Not everyone needs to be your best friend, and therefore you do not have to hold everyone to the exact same standard of friendship. If there is someone you really enjoy hanging around with but you do not necessarily trust, it's OK to hang out with that person but not confide in him or her.

When picking your friends, remember that they are going to have just as much influence over you as you will over them. Make sure your friendships are helping you become a better person and not a worse one.

Below are some characteristics of healthy and unhealthy friendships to help you evaluate your relationships.

## CHARACTERISTICS OF HEALTHY RELATIONSHIPS

1. Friends put an equal amount of effort into the friendship. Both parties share the responsibilities of making plans and communicating.
2. Each party encourages the other and does not try to tear the other individual down.
3. Friends never try to make the other party feel bad for doing something good.
4. One never encourages the other party to do something harmful or puts pressure on him or her to do something he or she knows is wrong.
5. Friends recognize each other's faults and have patience with one another.
6. Friends celebrate each other's successes.
7. What is shared in confidence stays in confidence unless it is in the other person's best interest to get someone older involved.
8. The friendship encourages both parties to be better people.
9. Each friend is willing to give an honest and gentle critique of the other person if necessary.
10. Friends show respect for the other person's ideas and interests.

## CHARACTERISTICS OF UNHEALTHY RELATIONSHIPS

1. One person does all of the planning and communicating.
2. At least one "friend" makes the other person feel bad about himself or herself.
3. One tries to get the other person to do something harmful.
4. Friends hold the other party to an impossible standard of perfection.
5. One party feels the need to always compete with the other person.
6. At least one party assumes the worst about the other person.
7. At least one party talks about the other person behind his or her back.
8. Friends feel the need to criticize the other individual unnecessarily.
9. Friends show disrespect for the other person's ideas or interests.
10. Friends are manipulative or make the other person feel guilty.

**A CAVEAT FOR DATING RELATIONSHIPS**

If you are dating (and it's OK if you aren't!), there are some things you should consider when evaluating romantic relationships. Firstly, romance should demonstrate all the aspects of a healthy friendship and none of the attributes of an unhealthy friendship (listed above).

Dating relationships can be very special as they can teach you how to serve your romantic partner. True love is looking out for the other person's best interests. This means doing what is right for the other person and looking out for that person's future while guarding his or her reputation. Be considerate and respectful in these relationships, so that your time with your boyfriend/girlfriend will be a blessing to the other person and not a curse.

Keep in mind: Every action has a future consequence. Since most teenagers are not ready for the responsibilities of a totally committed relationship, it is best to avoid situations of temptation. Try going out with a bunch a friends instead of one-on-one scenarios. If you choose to date in high school, never take advantage of your partner or allow your partner to take advantage of you. Romantic partners should never manipulate, intimidate, or coerce.

## DEALING WITH PEER PRESSURE

Peer pressure is part of the high school experience no matter where you go. It is normal for students to want to belong with their friends. Although normally treated in a negative context, peer pressure can sometimes be a good thing. Just as negative influences can pressure you to engage in harmful activities, positive influences can pressure you to do beneficial things. The goal of this section is to make sure that your decisions lead you to positive outcomes.

Do not do something just because everyone else is doing it. Think for yourself. Do not let the thoughts or actions of others heavily sway your decision-making process. Always ask yourself about the consequences of following the crowd, and don't gloss over potential risks just because they are unlikely. "Nobody ever gets caught," is logic that falls to pieces when a police officer arrives on the scene.

Also, don't let the fear of what others will say keep you from doing what is right. Even though you might be smart enough to avoid harmful actions, sometimes doing the right thing can be extremely challenging. This might mean speaking up against certain behaviors. Do not be afraid to stand up for the boy who is getting made fun of, or tell your best friend that she shouldn't sneak out her house.

## DITCH THE DOWNERS

Just as rotten food can cause adjacent good food to rot, bad influences will have a negative effect on you. If you have a friend who is always getting you into trouble or an outside adult who tells you that you will never succeed, these people don't need to be in your support group. You should remove them from your life or limit the amount of time you spend with them.

People's actions tell you a lot about their motivations toward you. If someone claims to be your friend but his actions prove otherwise, then you need to reevaluate that friendship. You need to do what is best for you and your future, even if it means saying goodbye to your best friend. It's a tough lesson, but for every bad influence there is another good influence you can find to takes its place.

## BULLYING

Unfortunately, bullying is a common problem. There is no cure-all solution for handling bullies, but you must refuse to be a victim if faced with a bullying situation. Do not keep it to yourself; immediately tell a parent or trusted adult.

Bullying is no longer limited to the confines of the physical world, but has now found a place in the cyber-world as well. Cyber-bullying can happen through emails, social networks, and blogs. This type of bullying can be more devastating than traditional bullying because a person's Internet identity follows him everywhere. A negative comment in cyberspace sticks with a student and follows him even to places where the bully has no context, like a personal home computer.

If you are a victim of cyber-bullying, try to remember that it does not matter what bullies say about you; your real friends know the truth. No matter what, your family will always love and support you. You do not have to defend yourself to people who believe what the cyber bullies say. Don't give them the satisfaction by even valuing their opinions. If this becomes too much at a school, then ask your parents about homeschooling. There is life after high school, and most of these people you will never see again.

## RESOURCE FOR DEALING WITH BULLYING

Barbara Coloroso Bullying Handout
www.kidsareworthit.com

## THINK ABOUT IT

1. Using the above criteria, am I a good friend? Yes/No
2. If not, how can I improve as a friend?

   _____

   _____

   _____

3. Which friend(s) is a good influence and wants only what is in my best interests?

   _____

   _____

   _____

4. Which friend(s) is a bad influence and creates an unhealthy relationship?

   _____

   _____

   _____

5. How do I know this to be true? (What are some examples?)

   _____

   _____

   _____

6. What do I want from a friendship?

   _____

   _____

   _____

7. What are important values that I want those friends to have?

   _____

   _____

   _____

# GUIDE FOR PARENTS HELPING YOUR CHILD BUILD A GREAT SUPPORT SYSTEM

Those who are most successful in life are successful not because of themselves but because of people who took the time to help them become successful. As your child continues to develop into a productive member of society, she will need a strong group of people who will help her achieve her goals and future aspirations. Students who surround themselves with positive role models, mentors, and friends have a huge advantage over people who try to go at life alone.

As their parent, you are your child's most important role model and instructor. Your son will look to your guidance throughout his developing years. While you hold the head coaching position in his life, having several assistant coaches along the way will greatly benefit him. Having several role models outside of family members allows students to learn different things and helps develop other aspects of their character. No one person does everything perfectly, and allowing your child to learn from numerous positive influences will enhance his or her development.

## HELPING YOUR STUDENT PICK GOOD FRIENDS

Teenagers need friends their own age to share common experiences. The sense of companionship that accompanies a group of good friends helps your child have both happy and productive teen years—if the friends are chosen well.

While you cannot always pick your daughter's friends—although you might want to—you can always help her evaluate her friendships. Watch how she acts around certain friends and see if those friends have a positive or a negative effect. Then, in private, discuss those friends with her.

Openly telling your son that his friends are bad influences might not always work. Instead, try to help him figure it out on his own. Encourage him to look honestly at all friendships and to decide if those friendships are good. If, however, he is involved with people who are dangerous, you should step in—especially if he does not want to end the friendship or is afraid of ending the friendship.

## HELPING YOUR STUDENT DEAL WITH PEER PRESSURE

It can be difficult to know if students are struggling with peer pressure. Peer pressure—good or bad—often happens when you are not around. Picking good friends and hoping that your child experiences the good type of peer pressure, however, is not enough. Parents need to instruct their children how to properly handle peer pressure.

Students need to learn to think for themselves. Help your daughter recognize when her peers are influencing her behavior so she can effectively determine how to respond. Teach her to pause and reevaluate the situation any time she feels like she is being pressured. This should help her overcome potentially harmful peer pressure, and help her develop critical thinking skills that will follow her after high school.

A helpful tool for overcoming peer pressure is giving your child the ability to call you to "not get permission" to do something. If your son is in a situation in which he doesn't feel comfortable, he can call you as a way to escape. You get to be the bad guy and act as protector during times when he might need extra help standing up for himself.

## PARENTS' HOMEWORK

Surrounding your students with positive and like-minded people can make your job as a parent easier. Now is a good time to identify and examine the people who are influencing your teen. Sit down with your student and write lists that categorize his or her support systems. Talk with your student about good and bad influences and try to help create a support system that will provide benefit not only during the high school years, but also in the future.

Here is a short list to help you get started.

Best/closest friend(s)_____

Good friends_____

Friend(s) of the opposite sex _____

Spiritual mentor_____

Financial mentor_____

Vocational mentor_____

# PART III:

# Foundation for Academic Success

# CHAPTER SEVEN: ACADEMIC DEVELOPMENT

## WHY IS EDUCATION IMPORTANT?

**Education:** the act or process of imparting or acquiring general knowledge, developing the powers of reasoning and judgment, and generally of preparing oneself or others intellectually for [a] mature life.[3]

When was the last time someone described education to you as a means to prepare yourself for a mature life? How often is education viewed solely as a means to get a job? Or a necessary evil all students must overcome?

Imagine for a moment that you live in a developing country, where only the elite of the nation have access to higher education, the middle class have access to grade schools, and the lower class have no access to any sort of formal schooling. Those born into wealth would be able to stay wealthy, those in the middle class would stay in the middle class, and those in poverty would stay in poverty. This scenario is due to the lack of education. Education opens doors to new skills, which in turn open doors to better jobs, which in turn open doors to better opportunities, which ultimately open doors to a higher quality of living.

---

3   As described by www.dictionary.com

Throughout the ages, people have fought for the right to be educated. Having the ability to read this book is the direct result of someone else's struggle for your right to literacy. You are reaping the benefits of the hard work of those who fought to learn. Therefore, it is very important for you to understand that education is a privilege and not a right.

Why does this matter? After all, doesn't going to school every day seem more like a curse than a blessing? What purpose does learning all those mathematical equations serve, and why do you have to read the works of a bunch of old dead people? These questions are merely reflections of a bigger question: Why is education important?

To answer this, let's go back to the definition of education. The dictionary defines education as the act or process of imparting or acquiring general knowledge, of developing the powers of reasoning and judgment, and generally of preparing oneself or others intellectually for a mature life.

Great, but what does that mean? The purpose of education is to form the frameworks in your mind to help you understand the world in which you live. Education is a vehicle for viewing and understanding life. Education is also a means of learning and developing new skills. Thus, education in its most basic and practical sense gives you the tools needed to live everyday life better. Now that sounds much more important than education being a necessary evil, and more meaningful than just an avenue to get a good job.

While it is fine to say that education makes your life better, it is also important to see how education is doing that. Below are some concrete examples of how education serves to improve your life. Although it is not exhaustive, this list includes some very important benefits you will receive from your education.

## BENEFITS OF EDUCATION

1. **Education teaches you to learn:** Going to school teaches you to gather, study, and apply information. Teachers train you in the process of learning.

2. **Education teaches time and task management:** Homework has several benefits: Not only do you have a chance to learn material with

hands-on projects, but it also teaches you how to manage projects and deadlines and complete assignments efficiently and effectively. These skills will benefit you tremendously later in your career.

3.  **Education teaches from the experience of others:** When you study the life works of great thinkers, you are learning from their hard work and experience. Education opens the door to studying a variety of topics with information from the people who really knew their stuff.

4.  **Education opens the door to new interests:** There are many exciting and interesting things in the world. By dedicating time to explore various topics, you have a greater chance of finding things that you really enjoy.

5.  **Education provides information to make wise decisions:** It is hard to make good decisions without critical thinking skills and useful information, which education provides.

6.  **Education frees you from assumptions:** It is easy to assume things about the world, but it's another thing to know them. Education is the process of obtaining knowledge so you can know if your assumptions are correct.

7.  **Education teaches values and work ethic:** Learning something new can be hard work. It takes time, effort, and dedication to master new skills, and thus the very process of learning is beneficial.

8.  **Education matures the mind:** As you age, your mind continues to mature and develop. Continuing education helps strengthen your brain's development. Learning is a mental workout for your most important organ.

9.  **Education teaches you to be resourceful**: Answers to difficult questions aren't always readily available. The more practice you have looking for answers, however, the better you get at finding those answers. Education teaches you to think beyond your readily available resources and search for information in some of the most unlikely places.

10. **Education opens doors to the rest of the world:** You live in a global world. Travel from nation to nation is the easiest it has ever been, and the communication pathways are wide open. Now more than ever it is important to study different cultures, customs, and

languages, and to become familiar with what is going on beyond your own borders. Through the Internet, curriculum, books, and other resources, you have the opportunities to discover so many things beyond the world around you.

## EDUCATION IS FOR LEARNING… NOT JUST MEMORIZING

Did you know there is a huge difference between memorizing information and actually learning it? Memorizing information works fine for facts, formulas, and historical dates, but learning is necessary for understanding ideas and concepts. The educational process is formed by a combination of the two. There will be times when you need to memorize information, but more often than not, you need to learn the information to understand how it affects your world.

Students often make the mistake of thinking it is enough to read the information repeatedly and then regurgitate it back on a test. This process does not constitute learning. It simply makes a student an information parrot, blindly repeating things that were taught without understanding, which leads to promptly forgetting all of the information once the class is over. Memorizing can be a great way to get good grades, but it is a terrible way to learn.

While at first the difference between memorizing and learning is subtle, the truth is they are fundamentally opposite. Consider this story of Bill and Sally.

Bill is smart, and he knows how to get an A in his history class by cramming the night before each test. Bill spends all night reading and rereading the information repeatedly until he knows the answers cold. He goes into the test, recognizes the information he has studied, and puts down the correct answers. He knows that George Washington crossed the Delaware River on December 25, 1776, and in doing so changed the tide of the American Revolution. Why does he know this? Because he memorized it from his textbook.

Will Bill remember this information after his history class? Most likely Bill will forget it once he has finished his test. Why? Because knowing when and where George Washington did something has little importance to Bill's life. He might retain some of the information because he read over it so much, but most likely Bill will only retain disconnected details and ideas. This type of studying is a waste of Bill's time.

Now consider Sally. Sally is in the same class as Bill, and she too wants to get an A on the history test. She reads the same information Bill does, listens to the same class lectures, and is studying for the same test. She too knows that George Washington crossed the Delaware River in December and in doing so helped changed the course of history. However, Sally approaches her studies a little bit differently. Instead of reading and rereading the right answers—the way Bill did—Sally stops and asks questions. She asks why Washington's boat trip had a dramatic effect on the war. She finds out it was a surprise attack and the victory inspired the Revolutionary troops.

Sally looks for connections from what was happening in America during 1776 to what was going on in the rest of the world at that time. She makes connections between the American Revolution and the French Revolution a decade later. Sally is not satisfied with just the correct answer but wants to know why it is the correct answer. She wants to learn the material and not just memorize it. Chances are Sally will come across things that are much more important than just dates and actions—things that she can apply to both her other studies and her personal life.

On the surface both of these students look exactly the same. Sally, however, didn't waste her time because she got something useful out of the course. She now has viable information she can add to how she views and interprets the world around her. Sally has a better appreciation for one of America's great heroes, and maybe for America itself. Sally might even have learned something she can apply to other classes to help her understand that material better. She has matured her mind. Unfortunately for Bill, he all but wasted a semester. He might remember a few key facts from the class, but he has no idea how those facts fit into the bigger picture. Although he might graduate with an admirable GPA, the knowledge he takes away from high school will be very limited and most likely useless.

Students who memorize information are not necessarily lazier students. On the contrary, memorizing concepts in many ways is a lot harder than actually learning the subject material. Most students who memorize just aren't taught the difference between memorizing facts and learning information. Nonetheless, recognizing the difference will greatly improve any student's education.

Below are some keys to help you better recognize learning versus memorizing. When approaching your studies, you should try to follow these five steps.

## KEYS TO LEARNING THE MATERIAL

1. **Read for understanding:** You won't get much out of reading by simply skimming materials. Be an active reader and think through a text as you read it.

2. **Look for the author's main points:** People don't write books to make you read them. Authors want to teach you something they have learned. When reading your textbooks, no matter what the subject, look for the main themes behind each chapter and the overarching thesis of the entire book.

3. **Look for the author's evidence for those points:** Your textbooks will have main themes and ideas, and then evidence to back up those ideas. Once you have identified the main points of your text look for examples that back up those ideas. If you understand both the author's conclusion and how he reached that conclusion, you are well on your way to understanding the material.

4. **Ask yourself relevant questions:** The best way to know if you have learned something is to ask yourself questions about it. If you can clearly answer your own questions, you know the material. If you can't, look over the material and ask your teacher or friends for help. Here are some example questions.
   - What was the author teaching me in this chapter?
   - What evidence did the author use to back up his or her point?
   - How did the author reach his or her conclusion?
   - Was it good evidence?
   - What did this historical document mean to the people the author first presented it to?
   - What does the information mean for people today?
   - Did the information add to or change the way people viewed the world?

- What is a practical example of this information being used in my life?
- How can I use this information to better understand other concepts in this book?
- How does this information apply to other subjects I am studying?

5. **Teach the information to someone else:** Once you have a grasp on the material, find someone else to teach it to. You can help a friend who is struggling or explain the concepts to your parents. Learning how to effectively communicate the information from your textbook to someone else will help solidify concepts in your mind. Being able to translate the book's concepts into your own words proves you know the material.

 **THINK ABOUT IT**

Students who wish to make the most out of their academic years must first understand why school is important. Before you go any further in this book, stop and think about how getting an education can benefit you personally. Think about the previous list, and come up with some of your own ideas.

_____

_____

_____

_____

_____

_____

_____

_____

When it comes to learning something new, make sure to focus on the hows and whys. (How is this important? Why did X happen?) Once you can answer the relevant questions, you can be confident you understand the material.

Before you go any farther in this book, stop and think about whether you are in the habit of learning material or simply memorizing it. After thinking about it, answer the following questions.

1.  Do I tend to learn or memorize my class materials?

    _____

    _____

    _____

2.  In which subjects do I tend to simply memorize information?

    _____

    _____

    _____

    _____

    _____

3.  What can I do better to help me learn the materials?

    _____

    _____

    _____

4.  How can learning the material benefit me personally?

    _____

    _____

    _____

5.  Who can I get to help me be accountable for learning and not memorizing the materials?

    _____

    _____

    _____

## GUIDE FOR PARENTS HELPING YOUR CHILD NAVIGATE ACADEMICS

It can be tempting for parents of high school students to take a hands-off approach to their students' academic studies. Many parents begin to let their students ask for their help instead of offering it outright. As your son gets older, he needs less help on his homework and he becomes more responsible for his academic performance. It is important that he learn how to take responsibility for his own performance. Students who never learn to take initiative to do their own work will have a hard time becoming successful in college or the workplace.

Nonetheless, you still play a vital role in your child's academic career. You must make sure that your daughter learns how to be successful in academics, so she can be equipped for the challenges that lie beyond the high school years. It's important to make sure she understands the importance of gaining an education, meeting deadlines, performing her best, and keeping an organized schedule. These are fundamental skills not only for high school, but for her future.

## PARENTS' HOMEWORK

One way to become actively involved in your son's academics is to ask him questions about his studies. Parents should ask questions about what their child is learning and challenge him about how he is questioning the materials. Any student can be a passive learner—simply digesting the information given by his or her teachers—but you should encourage your student to be an active learner and delve into the material. Persuading him to get involved by asking questions is a great way to encourage him to learn the material and not just regurgitate it.

Start a discussion over any or all subjects taught in school each day. Find out what your daughter learned and how it can be applied to her personally. Challenge her to go beyond what was taught in class and to question stated conclusions.

Example questions to get you started:
1. What was the most interesting thing you learned today in each class?
2. Why was it interesting?
3. What conclusions did the teacher or the book have?
4. Do you agree with those conclusions?
5. Why or why not?
6. What evidence do you have to back up your opinion?
7. Is it good evidence? Why or why not?
8. Can you think of any practical applications to your lessons?
9. Can you think of a way to connect the information learned in this class with another class?
10. What was the most boring aspect of your studies, and why?
11. Is there anything you are struggling with or confused about?
12. Are there other resources that can help you understand this subject (movies, documentaries, books, Internet)?

# CHAPTER EIGHT: EFFECTIVE STUDYING

STUDYING CAN be one of the most frustrating aspects of high school if you do not do it properly. You can waste a lot of time unnecessarily if you do not have a plan for how you are going to attack it. Although there is no magic formula that will work for everybody, this general method can help you establish your own study plan.

High school introduces you to a lot of new topics and ideas. Although no person is able to be an expert in every field, you can greatly increase the amount of information you understand and retain by establishing and practicing effective study habits. This process can be difficult at first, but all the hard work up front will pay off in the end. You will not only get those great grades, but you will also be able to use the information outside of the classroom.

No matter what classes you take during your high school years, you must become a master of self-directed study. Doing things on your own, without the need for anyone to tell you what to do, must become a habit. When things get tough, practice critical thinking by breaking apart information and reevaluating it. Get help when you need, but it is critical for you to start becoming independent in your learning.

## YOUR STUDY ENVIRONMENT MAKES A DIFFERENCE

Not everyone runs on the same biological cycle, and therefore each person has his or her own peak productivity periods. Find time to study when you are at your best, whether that is the morning, afternoon, or evening.

A peaceful place is necessary for effective studying. Having an environment that is conducive to productivity will help you stay focused and enable you to get the job done faster. Before you study, make sure your space is prepared in a way that works for and not against you.

Making your workspace a success could be as simple as keeping everything in its proper place. You don't have to be the most organized person in the world, but you do need to set up your space in a way in which you know where everything you need is located. This can save you from a lot of frustration and distraction during the studying process. If more storage space is needed, think about adding a bookshelf or cleaning out some drawers. Having a clean workspace makes a huge difference, and your mom and dad won't complain either.

People like to work in areas where they feel comfortable. Sit in a comfortable chair. You will spend several hours every day working on homework; you might as well make the study room a place you like. If your bedroom is your main study area, then decorate it in a way that is calming and happy.

Here are few tips to enhance comfort in a workspace.
- Make the temperature something you like.
- Make it smell good.
- Add some plants and a little color.
- Put on a little bit of background music (ideally classical).
- Keep a glass of water nearby.

Dress in comfortable clothing for optimal study time. Come home and put on something loose-fitting and temperature-appropriate. Just be careful not to change into something that will make your bed more appealing than the homework that needs to be done.

Proper lighting also contributes to comfort when you study. Working in a poorly lit room can have profound effects on your studying ability. If the room is dark, you may find yourself feeling sleepy or distracted. Also low light causes your eyes to strain, which might result in a headache. Before you sit down to solve the world's greatest problems or read your history book, you should open the blinds or turn on the overhead light. This will help you feel more awake and able to conquer your homework assignments.

No matter how comfortable your study environment, your study time will be ineffective unless you try to limit distractions. If you can, keep the door shut to your study room. Shutting the door not only blocks out sounds from the rest of the house, but it also is a visual representation that you are busy. This should help minimize the number of interruptions from family members. If small siblings like to walk in and out of the room, get your parents involved. Parents will be more than willing to help minimize the things that keep you from doing your homework. Make a sign that says "do not disturb while studying" and hang it on the doorknob.

If you don't have any space at home to study, you should try going to a library to get some work done. Libraries have computers and study rooms, which are open to the public. Don't let a noisy house keep you from getting good grades.

Another distraction you must be mindful of is your cell phone. If you are fortunate enough to have your own cell phone, show your parents that you are responsible by either turning it completely off during your study time or leaving it in another room with your parents. You will be surprised how much work you can get done without the temptation of texting or talking.

Also, have a light snack so that you give your brain enough fuel to function and a growling stomach won't distract you.

## THE EVILS OF TEXTING

OK, so texting really isn't evil, but it can be a habit that is detrimental to your success in school. If you are texting while in class or when you are trying to study, then you are not paying attention to what you are supposed to be learning. Texting in class is not only rude to your teachers, but it is also a distraction to your peers. Save yourself some trouble, and break the habit of texting during class and while you are trying to study. Not to mention, the habits of texting will not help you when it comes to actually writing. Good essays require punctuation, proper sentence structure, and correct spelling.

## READING TO LEARN

Reading is the foundation for learning new materials, and like most things in life, effective reading is a process and takes a plan to fully obtain and utilize its benefits.

**Step One: Be prepared to learn.**
- Come to each reading session with a positive attitude. If you don't want to learn something new, then no matter how long you sit there you won't learn anything.
- Block out time in your schedule solely for going over materials in order to avoid any distractions.

**Step Two: Get a feel for the information.**
- Pick a subject and study only one thing at a time.
- Survey each chapter by skimming the index, headings, graphics, pre- and post-questions, and introductory paragraph to establish a framework in your mind.
- Look over any charts and pay attention to any bullets.

**Step Three: Read the text for understanding.**

- Once you have surveyed the information, go through the chapter slowly; make sure to read the material thoroughly.
- Take notes on key ideas and the evidence that backs up those ideas. Also, make sure to mark any ideas and concepts that are unclear.
- Make flash cards for any unknown words and learn their definitions.

**Step Four: Put your book away.**

- Once you have carefully read the chapter, put the book aside and let the material sink into your brain.
- Get up, stretch your legs, and grab a snack or a glass of water to clear your head.

**Step Five: Come back and ask yourself key questions.**

- Return from your short break to the material and ask yourself the key questions for understanding.
- Look over the concepts that were confusing; do you understand them any better? If not, write out questions for your teacher, tutor or other people who might be able to explain the information better.
- Read over the material again if necessary.

**Step Six: Invent your own examples.**

- Once you grasp the information, come up with personal examples of how the information is useful in your daily life.
- Now think of examples of how the information is applicable to the lives of others.

**Step Seven: Extend your knowledge.**

- Go beyond the textbook and look for alternative sources of the information. Find at least one article on your topic other than your textbook. Read what others have to say about the information.
- Make up questions that you would ask an expert on that topic. This will help you manipulate the information in your head. If you are curious, go out and find someone who can answer your questions.

**Step Eight: Reflect on what you learned.**
- Review the material and the format in which it is presented. What questions, criticism, or praise would you give the author?
- Reflect on the practical applications of the information.

**Step Nine: Review previous material.**
- As you continue to learn new information, review previous material to help grasp new concepts. Most ideas build upon one another.
- Review your key themes, supporting evidence, and questions to help prepare you for tests on the material.

**Step Ten: Reward yourself for a job well done.**
- Once you have tackled one subject, reward yourself with another short break. Your mind can handle only approximately 45 minutes of good study time without a break. Therefore, give your mind a rest and do something else for 10 minutes.

In essence, don't just read information; explore it. Join discussion groups, make up projects, and find audio/video materials that help you discover a new way of considering the information. There are many different techniques to help you understand your materials; why not try them all?

It is important to establish effective reading habits early on in high school when the material is less challenging and you have more time to experiment. Do not make the mistake of coasting through easy high school classes without making good habits because this will make any future advanced courses harder.

## ENCOUNTERING UNKNOWN WORDS

Many textbooks or reading assignments contain unfamiliar vocabulary words. To enhance your reading, don't skip these words but rather have a dictionary nearby and look them up as you come across them. Then, write them down along with their definitions in a notebook designated specifically for new

words. Reviewing these words periodically will help elevate your quality of communication, raise your test scores, enhance your speech, and improve your writing ability.

Here are some tips for remembering vocabulary words:
1. Write the word on a flash card
2. Include: definition, book title and the complete sentence context
3. Assign a mnemonic for easy remembrance
4. Repeat out loud
5. Write a paragraph/story using the word(s)
6. Review often
7. Meditate on it
8. Use it in a sentence several times a day
9. Use it in games
10. Teach it to someone

*To easily and painlessly learn SAT-level vocabulary words in a fun, wholesome story, visit www.vocabcafé.com. Each book contains 300 specifically chosen words placed in the context of a narrative story with the definition and pronunciation at the bottom of the page for easy reference and instant reinforcement.*

## GOOD NOTE-TAKING IS ESSENTIAL

As you read your textbooks, it's important to also look over your class notes. There may be key points that your teacher referenced that were not in the text. Your notes will also provide some explanations to advanced ideas referenced in the chapters.

During class, it can be hard to know what you should write down. A good rule of thumb is to pay extra attention to anything your teacher says more than once, writes on the board, or intentionally emphasizes with either gestures or vocal inflections. If your teacher thinks it is important, you should think it is important.

As your teacher lectures, be sure to write down any questions you have in the margin of your paper. This way you can come back to those questions after the class period. If your teacher did not clear up a question during the lecture, make time to ask about it after class. Be sure to make headings for different topics as the lecture progresses. When it comes time to review for a test, these headings will be a great help.

Write legibly! If you can't read what you wrote in class, you can't study from it. For those with notoriously bad penmanship, before the day is over, go over your class notes and make sure they make sense. If you need to sit down and organize them, make sure to do it immediately, before they get out of hand. Take a little bit of time to refresh yourself on what you learned that day to solidify it in your mind.

## KEEP YOUR NOTES ORGANIZED

Make sure you keep all the information for each class organized. If you take notes or do homework on the computer, make separate computer folders for each class. Make sure you have everything together, so when it comes time to read or study for a test, you will have everything you need in one place.

If you need help with note-taking, try the Cornell Note-Taking System. The following website offers a simple PDF to help you organize your notes:
http://lsc.sas.cornell.edu/Sidebars/Study_Skills_Resources/cornellsystem.pdf

When all your notes are organized, they are easy to find and look over. Before you go to class, pull out your notes for that class and review what you are discussing and what you have learned. Look over any questions you have written down and see if you've found any of the answers yet.

## HOMEWORK ASSIGNMENTS & PROJECTS

If you are keeping up with your reading schedule, additional homework assignments should be easy. Generally, homework assignments correspond directly to the reading assignment, so you should be able to complete them with the information you have just covered. A typical assignment will assist you in understanding the materials by providing questions, examples, and practice from the text.

Sometimes you will be assigned a group project, which can be fun and rewarding. Nonetheless, they can also be challenging because your grade is reliant on everyone in the group. If you are assigned a group project, make sure the group is in agreement over the project criteria, timeline, and deadlines. If you are not the group leader, or if there isn't one, make sure that someone who is reliable is in charge. Be sure that everyone knows his or her responsibilities and that the workload is divided equally. Group projects run smoothest if everyone participates and feels included.

## WHEN YOU DON'T UNDERSTAND THE MATERIAL

Sometimes no matter what you do, things just don't make sense. It might be that you don't grasp a concept or you can't seem to solve a problem. Whatever the reason, times like these can make you feel lost or stupid. There are very few things that are more frustrating than trying your best and it simply is not enough.

Do not despair! You are not unintelligent just because some things don't make sense. People's brains are built differently, and something that might be natural for your best friend may be completely foreign to you. That's OK. There are ways to get around challenging topics and to retrain your brain to let difficult concepts and problems make sense. Nobody has the ability to be a master of all fields of study, but all students do have the ability to understand important concepts from every subject.

You need to recognize that there will be topics that are hard to grasp. That isn't an excuse to quit. You should always try your best to understand as much as possible, and once you have reached your personal best, let the rest go. Sometimes that means accepting a less-than-stellar grade. That is OK. All anyone can ask of you is that you try your best.

Sometimes in order to understand a subject you need to approach it in a different manner than you would another subject. Interpreting Shakespearean literature requires different skills than solving a math equation. Be open to tackling new concepts in ways that may seem foreign to how you naturally think. Here are some tips to help you wrestle with challenging topics or confusing problems.

1. **Rethink the problem:** Look at your situation from a different angle. Try to find new perspectives you haven't thought about. Ask others how they have or would have tackled the situation. For example, if you are having trouble with a math problem, ask your more mathematically inclined parent how he or she would solve it. Follow the suggested steps and see if it helps you better understand the concept.

2. **Use visualization:** Sometimes it is easier to think about things through stories, pictures, or diagrams. Draw up your problem, and see if there is something you are missing. Sometimes getting something down on paper is enough to spark inspiration. For example, if you are having trouble writing your English essay, scribble out an outline and possible thematic concepts.

3. **Make connections:** Draw up a concept map of things you are learning, and see how they fit together. Try to find relationships between different ideas, where they came from, and the problems or solutions they provide. See how smaller ideas contribute to bigger ideas. For example, if you are having trouble memorizing dates for your history test, write out a timeline of events. Seeing the whole picture can help you remember when things happened and how they influenced history as a whole.

4. **Inverse your problem:** Try working backwards to solve a problem. Choose a solution and find the steps to get there. Reversing the problem may provide an avenue to a solution that you haven't thought of before. For example, if you are having trouble understanding the grammar of your Latin lesson, translate the Latin phrases into English. Seeing a backwards translation can help you put the pieces together.

5. **Think in analogies:** See if you can create an analogy by comparing the difficult concept to something you can easily understand. If you are having trouble understanding the way red blood cells function, associate these cells with things that are familiar (e.g., red blood cells are like taxis because they transport oxygen from one place to another). If you can't think of anything on your own, ask your teacher to explain the information with an analogy.

## A FINAL THOUGHT ON STUDYING

If you find that one method of studying is not helping you learn, then ditch it and try something new. It might be that you are a hands-on learner and need a method of studying that requires projects and at-home examples. If you have a hard time reading and remembering the subject matter, try finding an audiobook or podcast on the subject matter. It doesn't matter which way you learn, as long as you take advantage of your own study style.

At the end of the week, try to go over your work. You don't have to spend your whole weekend studying; just take some time to review what you learned that week in each class. You can skim over the chapters you have read and think about what each one discussed, or review the flash cards you made.

Don't wait until the end of the semester to reward yourself for a job well done. Although good grades are a great reward, make up your own reward system. At the end of each week congratulate yourself for completing your work with things that motivate you. This should help you consistently maintain a regular homework schedule.

# GUIDE FOR PARENTS
# HELPING YOUR CHILD DEVELOP EFFECTIVE
# STUDY HABITS

Discipline is the foundation of any good study routine. Students must learn how to put aside the things they want to do, in order to do the things they need to do. Learning how to study is a process that does not necessarily come naturally.

Emphasize the importance of taking good notes in class. Not only is this especially important for accurately knowing the reading and homework assignments, but it will also help your child understand the more advanced concepts in the textbook.

Try to help your daughter develop practical ways to tackle her subjects. Help her create a reward system for consistent and effective work. Make sure to allow her space to take the initiative, but also ensure that her work gets done.

Students who know how to study will be able to get the most out of their classes and be better prepared for projects and tests. Teaching these skills now will enhance all future academic endeavors.

## PARENTS' HOMEWORK

Many students struggle with finding a quiet place to study that is free from distractions. You can aid your son tremendously by helping him find a time and place that he can do his homework unimpeded. Talk with him about the type of atmosphere he needs, and brainstorm some ideas that can help him improve his study space.

Establish and enforce rules for your child's study times. For example, if the living room is your daughter's afterschool workplace, be sure that other siblings respect that area and keep out. That may mean family habits will need to change or adjust (i.e., the TV must remain off until after dinner) to accommodate your studious high school student.

It's especially important that wherever she chooses to study, the lure of video games, cell phones, and the Internet is removed. Electronics can be too tempting for a student to avoid without parental intervention. Many students can "sneak" these distractions while still haphazardly completing their study assignments. Reward students with these things after they have done their work properly. If your son needs a computer to do research, monitor his time carefully. Internet research can quickly become goofing off.

If students need extra tutoring, check out an informational website like www.khanacademy.org. This is a free site, created by a not-for-profit organization, that features instruction in many basic subjects, such as math, physics, chemistry and advanced topics that may go beyond a parent's abilities. The video lessons and interactive practice sessions may help your child understand the material better.

## SPECIAL NOTE FOR READING ASSIGNMENTS

During high school, your child will be asked to read a lot of books, some of which you may not feel comfortable about. Parents also often have the ability to negotiate the high school reading list. If you do not agree with a book that is assigned to your son or daughter due to its controversial subject, religious affiliation, or content matter, ask for an alternative. Most schools offer alternative reading lists for any parent who asks.

*A list of great works of literature can be found in Appendix C.*

# CHAPTER NINE:
# TESTS AND PAPERS

## HOW TO STUDY FOR TESTS

Tests are one of the main sources of academic anxiety. Fortunately, studying for a test is merely an extension of general studying habits. The great thing about good study habits throughout a semester is that you don't have to cram when it is time for the exam. You merely have to review the material a few more times to make sure you are able to put the information down on paper.

Lucky for you, you are rarely tested over more than a couple of subjects on any given day. This means when it comes time for your tests, you can adjust your study methods to focus the majority of your time on those topics being tested while getting the bare minimum done on the other school subjects. Although it may not seem like it, teachers understand students are taking more than just one class and try not to overwhelm their students with overlapping exams.

# WHAT WILL BE TESTED?

By understanding what you will be tested on, you can save time by focusing solely on those chapters or materials. Teachers won't always say what exactly will be on the test, but they will often give you a guideline of what to expect. Ask your teacher for a study guide if you are unclear of what is expected of you.

Find out the format of the test. Knowing if the test will be multiple choice, short-answer, true or false, essay, or some combination will help you tailor how you study. Below is a brief overview of these different formats.

## ESSAY

Essay questions can be some of the easiest questions on a test if you know how to articulate your thoughts in a clear, consistent, and concise manner. No matter the length of the essay, you will want to write an introduction and conclusion. You will also need to support your thesis throughout your answer.

If you have an essay test, practice writing a timed essay (thirty minutes or less). You can ask your teacher for an example prompt (a prompt is a starting point from which your essay derives, like a question) or make up your own about the subject. Practice getting your thoughts on paper in twenty minutes, then use the last ten minutes to polish up your writing. It is important to leave time at the end to reread your work; otherwise you could turn in incomplete thoughts or an essay that doesn't make sense.

## TRUE OR FALSE

True or false questions are both easy and difficult at the same time. You will always have a fifty-fifty chance of getting the correct answer; however, the questions are often trickier than multiple choice ones. When it comes to true or false, there are some things you need to keep in mind.

First, every part of the sentence must be true for you to mark it as true. If even a tiny part of the sentence is false, then the whole sentence is false.

Also pay close attention any time there is a negative (no, not, cannot) in the sentence or a qualifier (sometimes, often, mostly) that changes the overall meaning of the sentence.

Avoid answering true to questions that do not allow for exceptions. If the sentence has an absolute word in it (no, never, none, always, every, only), then that sentence is implying that the concept is 100 percent true for every occasion. Absolutes are very rare in reality. Most of the time if a sentence includes an absolute word, the answer on the test is false.

**MULTIPLE CHOICE**

For multiple-choice questions, the key is to read the questions and answers critically, mark off any answers that cannot be true, and always double check that you circled the right letter or number. If you do not know the answer to a multiple-choice question immediately, do not spend too much time on it. Put a star by it, skip it, and come back to that question after you have had time to finish the rest of the test. Your mind will continue to work on this problem even after you have consciously moved past it.

One way to study for multiple-choice questions is to create matching games for your information to help you familiarize yourself with what information goes where. For example, if you have to match up names with dates, then write out both the lists of names and dates. Then cut them out and see if you can match them back up correctly. If you do this, be sure to have a master list, so you know when you got the answers right.

**SHORT ANSWER**

Short answer questions are great because you are given room to explain your thoughts on a given topic, but can be tricky if you don't already know something about the subject of the question. When you prepare for your test, focus on keywords, events, vocabulary, and overall concepts. Don't just practice recognizing the information, like you would for a multiple choice test, but practice writing out thoughts or explaining the information to others.

## HOW TO REVIEW

First look for the key concepts of each section and know why those concepts are important. This will give you a good overview of the material. If something happens—an event, discovery, a person, or an idea that changes the focus of your readings—then chances are it is an important shift. Throughout history, every subject has undergone some sort of change. Most books address monumental events in a subject's history and note it in the text. Make sure you understand what was happening before the shift, what exactly happened, and why and how it changed your subject. Teachers love to test on these types of things.

If your teacher has given you any outside materials, projects, or assignments, make sure you review that information before the test as well. This review can help you think about the material in different ways, and sometimes information from these items will show up on your actual test. Also, review any old tests, which you have corrected, to help you study for any comprehensive exams.

During your study time, if you discover any unanswered questions, write them down and make sure to find the answers before the day of the test. Usually understanding these types of questions is essential to getting a good test grade. Don't be afraid to ask your teachers to make an explanation more clear; that is why they are there. This could be a great time to find an analogy that will work for you.

Flash cards are great ways to quiz yourself, and they can be taken anywhere. Write down key concepts, dates, people, events, formulas, and so on. You can even write down your key questions and put the answers on the back. Make a game out of your flash cards and get other friends in your class to play along.

Study groups can be helpful if they are actually used to study. Don't waste your time goofing off during a study group, but use the time to gain insights from your fellow classmates. Sometimes this can be a great opportunity to explain important concepts to your peers. Teaching the information will only help solidify the information in your mind and bring a real-world context to the subject.

In the end, if you have been reviewing your notes throughout the semester, doing your homework, and keeping up with your assignments, then you have already done most of your test preparation. Studying for a test should only be an in-depth review and nothing else. Don't spend all of your time studying. Remember it is possible to study too much.

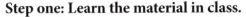

**Step one: Learn the material in class.**
- Follow the general study method to learn the material throughout the semester.
- Make sure to take good notes.

**Step two: Make a test prep plan.**
- Estimate how much time it will take for you to review the material.
- Draw up a test prep schedule and stick to it.

**Step three: Review your materials.**
- Review notes, supplementary materials, and homework assignments.
- Look over all of your questions and make sure to have the correct answers.

**Step four: Give yourself a break.**
- Don't try to cram all the material in at once; take short breaks in between studying.
- Let your mind work on the material even if you aren't physically looking at it.

**Step five: Test yourself.**
- Quiz yourself on the information.
- Write up mock test questions if it will help.

**Step six: Get others involved.**
- Take advantage of study groups to gain new insight.
- Teach the information to someone else.

**Step seven: Leave it alone.**
- Once you are sure you know the information, put it away and don't worry about it.
- Make sure you sleep on it; your mind assimilates new information as you sleep.

## DEALING WITH TEST ANXIETY

Test anxiety can be a real problem and can lead to poor performance on exams. This type of anxiety can also have a dramatic effect on a student's self-esteem and overall confidence. While test anxiety may seem untreatable, it is usually a learned habit. Some students may be prone to this type of anxiety, but it doesn't mean they are forced to live with it forever. Knowing some facts about anxiety itself and ways to beat it will greatly reduce its power over your life.

It must be noted: A little bit of nerves can be a good thing because it helps motivate you to perform well on your exams. The term *test anxiety* is used for extreme cases of anxiety that go beyond motivation and interfere with your ability to perform well on a test or to be productive outside of academics.

## SYMPTOMS OF TEST ANXIETY

Knowing whether you personally suffer from test anxiety is the first step. You could suffer from test anxiety and not know it or not know how to classify it. Here is a general, partial list of symptoms to help you determine whether anxiety is playing a role in your academic performance. This list is meant only as a guideline to recognizing common symptoms of test anxiety, but is by no means an official diagnosis.

There are two manifestations of test anxiety: mental effects and physical effects. Students who suffer from anxiety may have some or all of these symptoms. If you can relate to two or more of the symptoms, you may suffer from test anxiety.

Mental Effects
- Mental Blanks
- Racing Thoughts
- Difficulty Concentrating
- Consuming Negative Thoughts
- Knowing Answers Only After the Test

Physical Effects
- Increased Heart Rate
- Cramps/Nausea
- Intense Sweating
- Headache
- Dry Mouth
- Heavy Breathing
- Tense Muscles

If you believe you suffer from test anxiety, it is important to speak with a professional about your concerns. While learning how to help yourself is important, it can be harmful to try to solve all your problems on your own.

## FIGHTING TEST ANXIETY

There are many reasons a student might be suffering from test anxiety. Below are some common factors that produce anxiety and how you should properly tackle each one. The biggest key to reducing test anxiety is recognizing why tests make you anxious. You must be honest with yourself and look at how you really think about tests. Once you understand why you are anxious, you can work on changing how you think about tests. Here are some common reasons for test anxiety.

**I am afraid of the test itself.**
*Tests are nothing more than opportunities for students to show what they know.*
    Does the subject freak you out? Are you terrified because you have heard some scary rumors about the test? People often fear the unknown and avoid learning because they are afraid of it. Before you let yourself get worked up over a test, familiarize yourself with the material. If you are dreading next week's chemistry test because you aren't sure what will be on it, go to your teacher and ask. He or she will point you in the right direction.

**I do not know the material well enough to be tested on it.**
*As long as you have paid attention in class and used a study plan, you should be prepared for the test.*

A lot of people accept defeat before they even begin. Don't sell yourself short. Go through your class notes and identify your weaknesses and strengths. If there are concepts you are unfamiliar with, then spend more time focusing on those. Make a study schedule and stick with it. If you allow yourself time to study, then you can go to the test with confidence.

**Every time I think about the test, I am consumed with negative thoughts.**
*You have the ability to control your thoughts; you can determine how you think about the test.*

Do you feel that, no matter how much you study, you are going to do poorly on every test? Do you believe just because you have done poorly in the past means you will do poorly in the future? Thinking negative thoughts about yourself and the upcoming test will only ensure that your fears come true. It is time to start thinking positively.

This does not mean positive thinking alone will make you do well. It means an attitude change can have a positive effect on your test outcome. Identify your negative thoughts, evaluate them, and change them. Go study, and then tune out the negative thoughts. You can control what is going on in your head, so think some positive thoughts.

**The very thought of taking a test makes me tense.**
*You can control how your body reacts to tests; you have the power to calm yourself down.*

Do you get a headache whenever you try to study? Do your shoulders get tense and does your back begin to ache? These are physical reactions to stress. Along with working on controlling your mind, you can learn to control your stress levels. You have the power to calm yourself through relaxation, prayer, and meditation. Learn relaxation techniques, and every time you start to feel stressed, practice calming your thoughts and body.

**I try to focus, but there are so many distractions when I take a test.**
*You have the ability to train your mind to stay focused, so you can do well on the test.*

It is time to learn how to tune out distractions. If you spend your time worrying about the other students in the room, or the fact you can hear people walking up and down the hall, you are focusing on the wrong things. When you are taking a test, the only thing you should worry about is your test.

The best way to tune out distractions during a test is to practice doing it while you are studying for the test. Turn on small distractions while you are studying and practice ignoring them. It may seem impossible at first, but over time you will get better.

If this proves to be too difficult for you, ask you teacher about using earplugs during the test. Many schools allow students to block out distractions with the assistance of earplugs.

### When I take a test, I find myself thinking about everything else other than the test.

*Not thinking about the test means you are avoiding the test.*

Do you find yourself thinking more about how much you would like to be done with the test than about completing the test? If so, you will have trouble doing well on the exam. Practice staying focused on the task at hand. Prepare your mind before you sit down to focus only on the questions you are being asked. Recall the information you have studied, why it is important, and how it fits in with the question. Keeping your mind on each question will help you stay focused on the test and not what you are having for lunch next period.

You also should consider why you are paying attention to other things and not the test. Avoiding the test can be a sign of a much deeper test anxiety problem. Consider if you are avoiding the test because you are afraid of it or believe you cannot do well on it.

Also, keep in mind that working on an empty stomach or lack of sleep can be detrimental to staying focused. If you find that your growling belly is distracting you and your classmates, consider keeping healthy snacks in your bags that you can eat during breaks. Taking a test on a full stomach can dramatically help.

### I don't know how to study for this test.

*Different tests require different study habits; acknowledge the differences and make a plan.*

It is important to note that different subjects and formats require different studying habits. Essay tests are different from multiple choice tests. Knowing the differences between the types of tests will help you plan how to study.

It is also important to know different subjects take different amounts of time to master. If you are great in math but not so great in history, then you will need to spend extra time studying for your next history exam.

### I am struggling in this subject.

*If you are struggling, ask for help.*

It's hard to ask for help when you don't understand something or if it seems like you are the only person who doesn't get it. However, if you let yourself struggle and don't seek help, you are only hurting yourself. Because many classes build on the information you have already been taught, the longer you wait to get help, the more difficult it becomes to understand the information.

If you are having trouble, you need to find a tutor. Students learn in different ways, and a tutor might explain something in a new way. Chances are you *can* grasp the material; you just need it explained in another way.

### I just don't feel well enough to study.

*It takes time and energy to do well on test. Make sure your mind as well as your body are prepared.*

A great way to boost your energy or blow off some extra anxiety is to exercise. Not only will this improve your overall health, but it can also greatly reduce the effects of test anxiety. Get in the habit of a regular exercise program. You will love the results, and it will combat stress. It's a win-win situation.

### I am smart, but I always make dumb mistakes.

*Dumb mistakes on a test are the easiest mistakes to remedy.*

Do you know the material but find yourself making careless mistakes when you take your test? This is probably because you are rushing through the exam and not taking the time to read the directions of *every* question carefully. Don't make assumptions about the test. Read a question thoroughly, answer the question, and move on to do the same for the following questions. Once you are finished taking a test, double-check your work. Don't get a bad grade because you forgot to go over your answers.

**I find myself too tired to focus on my test.**
*Students often do poorly on tests because they do not get enough sleep.*

If you don't get the amount of sleep you need, your mind and body won't work as well as you need them to work. You will have trouble staying focused, and you will wear your body down, making it more prone to illness. It is not only important to get a good night's rest the night before an exam, but also to get in the habit of getting enough rest every day. Studies show that students need on average nine hours of sleep each night. Do yourself a favor and cut off the things that are keeping you up (TV, music, the Internet, and cell phones).

**I don't want people to think I am stupid.**
*You are not competing with anyone else. All you need to do is your best.*

Are you thinking about your classmates and how they are doing? Are you embarrassed if you are the last one to finish? Are you afraid of what your parents might say if you don't do well? It is time to stop thinking about other people. The only person that matters during a test is you. You are competing solely with yourself at that moment and no one else. Worrying about other people only takes away from your ability to concentrate.

**I can't focus because I feel weak or my stomach is upset.**
*Students do better if they make the time to have breakfast.*

Eat breakfast before you go to school. Breakfast helps fuel the mind and body and prepares you to tackle the rest of the day. If you are in the habit of skipping breakfast, then it is time to break that habit. If you aren't feeling your best when you go into a test, you probably won't perform your best. So take time to eat.

**I spend all my time trying to figure out the questions I don't know.**
*Your mind is incredible and can work on problems even when you don't think about them.*

If you go blank on a question, the best thing to do is to skip the question and go on. Your mind is an amazing organ and actually works on problems subconsciously, so if you skip a question it doesn't mean your mind has forgotten about the problem. Let your mind work for you and come back to answer that question.

Make sure you mark the question, so you know you have skipped it. Come back either when you have finished the rest of the questions or something else on the test has sparked your memory.

**Once I learn about a test, it is all I can think about.**
*Your brain can get tired out too.*

If you have done all you need to prepare for a test, then stop thinking about the test and focus on something else. Obsessing about any aspect of the test will raise your anxiety levels. It may help you to wake up early on a test day and, instead of studying, spend some time dressing up to look your best. Not only will the extra time focusing on your appearance keep your mind off the test, but also you will feel more confident going into the test.

*Once you understand the reasons for test anxiety, you can fight it more effectively. Appendix D is dedicated to several relaxation techniques that can help you fight the physical and mental effects of anxiety. Students who suffer from test anxiety should practice these techniques daily to help relieve some or all of their symptoms. If, however, these general tips do not help, you should seek professional assistance. You can talk to your guidance counselor, family doctor, or other trusted counselor for help. If you don't know any counselors you can find one at a local church, school, or do a quick Internet search for counselors in your area. Don't be anxious about using the web to find a counselor; many websites rate counselors in the area and you can read about what other people say about their experiences.*

 **THINK ABOUT IT**

If you are still unsure whether you suffer from test anxiety, take time to answer the following five questions. If you agree with two or more of these statements, there is a good chance you suffer from test anxiety. Test anxiety can be a serious problem. If you may be suffering from it, talk to someone who can help.

1. I always expect to perform poorly on a test even when I have seriously studied for it. YES/NO
2. The very idea of taking a test makes me want to freak out. YES/NO
3. I think I am a failure if I perform poorly on a test. YES/ NO

## WRITING A HIGH SCHOOL PAPER

For some people, taking a test is the most terrifying aspect of high school; for others, it is writing papers. Just like learning how to study properly, good writing skills are something that can be learned. While your teachers should instruct you on how to write different types of papers (research, essays, analytical, timed, etc.), some methods can be used for any and all papers you will need to write in high school and beyond.

**Step One: Create a Concept Map.**
- Your thesis is the subject of your essay; it is what you want to talk about and develop. Define your thesis, and draw up a concept map to connect what you want to say. A concept map is a diagram that shows how different ideas relate to one another. Write out the different thoughts that you want to incorporate into your paper, then circle them and see where they connect. If you are still confused about a concept map, ask your teacher to help you start one or do an online search to help you get started.

**Step Two: Start Your Research.**
- Whether you are writing an actual research paper, or simply critiquing a piece of literature, you need evidence to support your

thesis. Use the library, Internet, or books you have read in the past to find your supporting arguments.

### Step Three: Write an Outline.

- The easiest way to write a coherent paper is to have a clear outline. Take a few minutes to write an outline, and it can save you hours of rewrites.

### Step Four: Write and Rewrite.

- Most papers need to be written, then rewritten a couple times. The first thing you produce will not be your best work. Final drafts are the result of rewriting your work multiple times.
- Have someone other than yourself look over your final edits. Be sure to hand him or her a printed copy to review. It is easier to catch mistakes on paper than it is on a computer. Once you have your editor's notes, polish your paper with strong vocabulary and final tweaks.

### Step Five: When Necessary, Properly Cite Sources.

- Ask your teachers or professors whether they prefer endnotes, parenthetical citations, or footnotes.
- Different teachers prefer different styles, so make sure you know what type of bibliography they want you to use. One resource that can help you is www.biblme.org.

### Step Six: Turn in a Stellar Paper.

- Review the previous five steps to make sure you have everything covered. Print out your cover paper and staple it to your final draft.
- Hand in your paper with confidence.

The purpose of writing papers is to showcase your knowledge on a topic. Polish your paper-writing process so that you can produce quality work every time. Two good books that can help you learn to write better are *The Elements of Style* by Strunk and White and *On Writing Well* by William Zinsser.

## PLAGIARISM

Plagiarism is a major academic offense. While it might be tempting to steal an idea here or there for your papers, copying other people's work and claiming it as your own is never OK. You may get away with plagiarism in high school, but you certainly will not get away with cheating in college. In fact, many high school and college classes will require you to turn in your papers electronically to ensure that you didn't cheat. Cheating may seem like the easy way now, but it can result in serious academic consequences.

# GUIDE FOR PARENTS HELPING YOUR CHILD STUDY FOR TESTS

When it comes time for tests, encourage your son to make a test prep schedule that establishes how and when he is going to study for his tests. Remind him that too much studying can be a waste of time if he does not learn how to take breaks and let the material sink into his brain.

You can also help your daughter study by participating in the process. Once she has spent sufficient time reviewing materials, help her out by giving her a mock quiz, or turn studying into a game. Finding new ways to study information is a great way to make it stick.

## PARENTS' HOMEWORK

There are lots of strategies to taking tests, especially standardized ones. Research test prep curricula that can help your son or daughter think through questions critically and effectively. If you have not done so already, check into the *College Prep Genius* program. Although mainly an SAT and PSAT/NMSQT study guide, it contains testing strategies that can apply to all testing scenarios.

# CHAPTER TEN: GETTING ORGANIZED

ORGANIZATION IS essential to high school success. The amount of required homework increases significantly from middle school to high school. That's not to mention the increased opportunities for afterschool activities. From football to the drama club, high school is a wonderful place for students to try new things. Even if you do not go to a traditional high school, there is still a wealth of activities in the community you can, and should, get involved in. However, more classes plus more opportunities for extracurricular activities can create a hectic schedule, and if you are not careful, it can be the cause for slipping grades. Don't let this happen. Although there may be a lot of stuff on your plate during this time, if you are diligently organized, you can keep yourself from being overwhelmed.

Drive your schedule—instead of having your schedule drive you—by keeping everything organized. Although everyone is different and some things won't work for everyone, below are some practical tips to help you organize your academic life. Feel free to adjust some or all of these tips to better suit your personal needs. By learning how to organize a schedule now, you will save yourself a lot of stress throughout high school, college, and your career.

## HAVE NOTEBOOKS THAT CORRESPOND WITH YOUR CLASS SCHEDULE

Keep together all the information that goes together. It's very easy for a student to lose information if one page of history notes is in the science notebook, or if a couple of the math notes are in the language notebook. Keep *everything* from one subject together and separate from all other subjects.

If you have the same classes every Monday, Wednesday, and Friday, then purchase a three-ring binder that is big enough to hold all the MWF schedule information. Each class should have its own section in the binder. Do the same for the Tuesday/Thursday schedule. (The days may vary depending on how your high school periods are broken down.) It is also a good idea to have a binder with pockets for any additional handouts from each period. Once you are home, you can find a hole-punch and put the handouts into the correct section of the notebook.

## BUY A DAY PLANNER

Having a day planner is an important step in keeping all your obligations straight. It will allow you to write down all of your club meetings, volunteer commitments, and hangout sessions while ensuring you never overbook yourself. Knowing that everything has been properly scheduled allows you to better enjoy your free time. You don't have to worry if you are missing something or if you were supposed to be somewhere else.

You could also use your phone, handheld computer, or any other electronic device with a calendar application. However, be aware that many electronic devices have a dismiss option for any reminder alarm. Don't use the dismiss button like a snooze button on an alarm clock. This is an easy way to forget an obligation. Use electronic schedules and reminders as back-ups in case your physical planner is lost or misplaced.

A hardcopy schedule is the best option for most people. It is much easier to plan your week when everything is easily seen. There is also something special about the feeling you get when you write something down in ink. It makes the commitment seem more real, and if a commitment is more real, you are less likely to forget it.

However, just buying a day planner doesn't make you organized. You must commit to using it. Get in the habit of writing all appointments down in the day planner. It does you no good to have a planner if you frequently forget to write things down and then miss them.

You also must get in the habit of reviewing your planner's content. Make it a daily task to review what is coming up in your week, so that you can appropriately plan your schedule. This way, if your best friend invites you to the movies, you can make sure it doesn't conflict with your other obligations.

## DON'T USE THE DAY PLANNER ONLY FOR EXTRACURRICULAR ACTIVITIES

Writing down social activities is a great way to keep from being overbooked. The day planner is also an excellent tool for keeping all your schoolwork in order. You don't have to write down every class period, but it is a great idea to write down what homework is due on which particular class period. You should also break down larger assignments and write down when you are going to work on them throughout the week.

Keeping a record of all class assignments in one place will ensure that you do not miss something. Students often get into trouble when they write down their assignments in different places. If the assignments are in a day planner, they will always be readily available to you. Even if you accidently leave the class notebook at school, you still have a record of what is due.

Here is an example of how to organize schoolwork and homework assignments.

During the first week of a new semester, you may receive a class syllabus or class outline. This outline should give you an overview of the course (subject matter), a homework schedule (timeline of assignments due), and an estimate of when each test is scheduled. This outline can be your best friend if you let it. Teachers do their students a tremendous favor by breaking down the courses and letting the students know exactly what is expected of them during the semester. If you don't get a syllabus, ask your teacher if he or she will create one for you.

Once you receive the syllabus or course outline, write down what homework is due on each day in your day planner. When writing down future assignments in the day planner, always use a pencil! Because a syllabus is a tentative schedule, it is subject to change so it is best to keep the planner as neat as possible.

Don't let all of the information in the course outline be overwhelming. Realize an outline shows you all the things the teacher hopes to accomplish throughout the course. No one expects you to know all the information before you take the class. If that were true, the class would be unnecessary. You will accomplish each task over the *entire* semester. There is no reason to panic.

## BREAK IT DOWN INTO MANAGEABLE CHUNKS

There is no rule that says you have to complete an entire assignment in one day. If you have a lot of reading due for a class and a couple days to complete it, then divide the pages over the days and read a little at a time. This way you won't get bored with a subject and don't feel overwhelmed by one class.

This is also a great way to handle long or complex assignments. If you have to write a fifteen-page paper for your history class, break up the paper into smaller assignments. Do the research one day, the bibliography another day, write half the next, and write the other half later. As long as you give yourself enough time to complete the project, you can tackle the assignment in any way you want.

Giving yourself breaks from long assignments helps prevent burn-out on a particular subject or class. Giving yourself diverse assignments can help you enjoy your study time better. It is more fun to study a variety of different things than spend all day on just one thing. Look at the examples in this chapter of how to schedule your time.

Once you break the assignments down, schedule the segments into days or times when you can complete them. You might find it helpful to sit down one day a week and chart the week's to-do list. Decide how much time you have each day to complete your homework and schedule the amount needed to get it all done.

If you have a couple of really busy days when there's no time for homework, perhaps because of sports practices or club activities, you can schedule your homework around those days. If Monday nights are always full, make them light homework days. Even if you have a major project due on a Tuesday, if you schedule most of it earlier the week before, you can still get all your homework done before your Monday night practice.

Once you have the to-do list from the day planner on a separate piece of paper, you can put your assignments in order of importance. The first few are the things that *must* be done that day, the next *should* be done that day, and the last ones can be delegated, omitted, or put on the next day's list.

By creating a proper schedule, you don't have to worry about projects or assignments catching you by surprise. This means fewer late nights and more time to do well on the project—which in turn means better grades.

## THINK ABOUT IT

Let's say you have American history every Monday, Wednesday, and Friday at 10:00 am. The syllabus says you have a reading quiz every Monday and a test every fourth Friday. In your day planner, go to every Monday and in the 10:00 am spot write, "Reading Quiz Amer. Hist pg [the pages it covers]." Then on every fourth Friday in the 10:00 am spot write, "Amer. Hist Test ch [the chapters it covers]."

Do this for every class. Not only do you have a record of what is due, but also when it is due. It takes a little bit of time to discipline yourself to write it down, but this small action can save you tons of headaches in the future.

A great way to keep subjects separate is by color-coding the different classes (e.g., Spanish—blue, physics—black, math—orange).

| September | | | | | | |
|---|---|---|---|---|---|---|
| **M** | **T** | **W** | **T** | **F** | **S** | **S** |
| 2<br>Labor Day-No school! | 3 9:00<br>Spanish Chapter 3 homework questions<br>1:00 Physics Chapter 5 homework questions<br>2:00 Math Chapter 4 homework questions<br>3:30 Band Practice | 4<br>10:00 History read Chapter 5<br>11:00 Eng. Lit quiz Chapter 12<br>3:30 Band Practice<br>6:30 Youth Group | 5 9:00<br>Spanish Chapter 4 homework questions<br>1:00 Physics Chapter 6 homework questions<br>2:00 Math Chapter 5 homework questions<br>3:30 Band Practice | 6<br>10:00 History test over Chapters 1-5<br>11:00 Eng. Lit quiz Chapter 13<br>5:30 Football game AWAY | 7<br>9-12:00 Volunteer Hilltop Hospital<br>Research Literature Paper | 8 |
| 9<br>10:00 History read Chapter 6<br>11:00 Eng. Lit quiz Chapter 14<br>3:30 Band Practice | 10 9:00<br>Spanish Chapter 5 homework questions<br>1:00 Physics Chapter 7 homework questions<br>2:00 Math Chapter 6 homework questions<br>3:30 Band Practice | 11<br>10:00 History read Chapter 7<br>11:00 Eng. Lit quiz Chapter 15<br>3:30 Band Practice<br>6:30 Youth Group | 12 9:00<br>Spanish Chapter 6 homework questions<br>1:00 Physics Chapter 8 homework questions<br>2:00 Math Chapter 7 homework questions<br>3:30 Band Practice | 13<br>10:00 History read Chapter 8<br>11:00 Eng. Lit quiz Chapter 16<br>5:30 Football game HOME | 14<br>9-12:00 Volunteer Hilltop Hospital<br>Write rough draft literature paper | 15 |

**September**

| M | T | W | T | F | S | S |
|---|---|---|---|---|---|---|
| 16 10:00 History read Chapter 9 11:00 Eng. Lit Test over Chapters 12-16 3:30 Band Practice | 17 9:00 Spanish test over 1-6 1:00 Physics Chapter 9 homework questions 2:00 Math Chapter 8 homework questions 3:30 Band Practice | 18 10:00 History read Chapter 10 11:00 Eng. Lit quiz Chapter 17 3:30 Band Practice 6:30 Youth Group | 19 9:00 Spanish Chapter 7 homework questions 1:00 Physics test 5-9 2:00 Math Chapter 9 homework questions 3:30 Band Practice | 20 10:00 History test over 6-10 11:00 Eng. Lit quiz Chapter 18. Turn in Literature Paper 3:30 Band Practice 5:30 Football game AWAY | 21 9-12:00 Volunteer Hilltop Hospital | 22 |
| 23 10:00 History read Chapter 11 11:00 Eng. Lit quiz Chapter 19 3:30 Band Practice | 24 9:00 Spanish Chapter 8 homework questions 1:00 Physics Chapter 10 homework questions 2:00 Math Chapter 10 homework questions 3:30 Band Practice | 25 10:00 History read Chapter 12 11:00 Eng. Lit quiz Chapter 20 3:30 Band Practice 6:30 Youth Group | 26 9:00 Spanish Chapter 9 homework questions 1:00 Physics Chapter 11 homework questions 2:00 Math test over Chapters 1-10 3:30 Band Practice | 27 10:00 History read Chapter 13 11:00 Eng. Lit test over Chapters 17-20 3:30 Band Practice 5:30 Football game HOME | 28 9-12:00 Volunteer Hilltop Hospital | 29 |
| 30 10:00 History read Chapter 14 11:00 Eng. Lit quiz Chapter 21 3:30 Band Practice | 31 | | | | | |

Now that you know how to organize your schedule, it is time to purchase your own day planner. Even if it is already the middle of the semester, writing down the rest of your assignments will be a great help. If you have lost your class outline, you can always ask your teacher for a new one. Day planners aren't very expensive, so don't wait another day to start reaping the benefits of using one.

## ALWAYS MAKE SURE TO HAVE WHAT IS NEEDED FOR EVERY CLASS

It is a big disappointment to keep up with all the assignments, do the work at home, and then leave it sitting on your desk in your bedroom. This is a silly mistake, and over time, late or missed assignments can really hurt your overall GPA.

Showing up to class prepared shows a teacher that you take your responsibilities seriously. Not to mention, if you are in the habit of forgetting work, your teacher is less likely to give leniency when it might really be needed. Even if you aren't what someone would call a dedicated student, making sure you are prepared for class will make you feel like a dedicated student. By acting dedicated, you will in turn become a dedicated student.

An easy way to make sure to always come to class prepared is to place your finished assignments in the right class notebook. As soon as something is completed, put it in the folder where it belongs. This way if the notebook gets to class, so will the homework assignment. Now you only need to make sure all your notebooks come to school. Get in the habit of going over what is needed for the next day the night before. It doesn't take long to check and pack your backpack. If you prepare the night before, you will be less rushed in the morning and have time to do the things you enjoy more—perhaps catch an extra five minutes of sleep!

Homeschooled students also need to get in the habit of preparing things for class. Even if you take every class at home, getting in the habit of being organized and having your assignments ready will help prepare you for the time when you will not be working at home. Students can get themselves in a lot of trouble after high school if they are not in the habit of arriving prepared.

## DRESS FOR SUCCESS

No matter what dress code you might have to follow at school, any student can adopt the habits of dressing for success. If you get out of bed, skip a shower, and throw something on that may or may not be dirty, then you are not starting the day off on your best foot. Appearances—although they aren't the most important thing in life—play a large role in a person's self-esteem. If you feel gross, which often comes from not taking the time to get properly dressed, then you will probably act like you feel gross. Alternatively, if you look confident, you'll start to feel confident. Students don't have to spend an inordinate amount of time on their appearances, but you should get up and start the day off fresh. Make sure you wear neat and clean clothes. Every morning is a new chance for you to reach your goals and enjoy your life. Why not start the day in the best possibly way?

## TACKLING TIME MANAGEMENT

The better you get at organization, the better you will become at time management; the two ideas go hand in hand. The execution of time management, however, is a little more difficult for students. Many teens and even adults never learn how to effectively manage their time and suffer the consequences. Learn how to do this now and save yourself frustration later on in life.

### THE GOAL IS TO GET THINGS DONE, NOT TO STAY BUSY

Let's say you have all afternoon to write a paper. Even if the paper should only take about an hour or so to write, chances are the paper will take all afternoon. Yes, you will accomplish the goal of getting the paper done; however, think about all the other ways you could have spent the afternoon. Dragging out a task isn't the most effective use of time.

Instead of letting a task take all day, estimate how long a task should take, and then strive to meet that time requirement. It might take a while for you to accurately estimate the time needed, but you can always keep track of how long it did take and adjust the next estimation when necessary. The more practice, the better you will get at estimating.

The faster you get your homework done, the more time you have to play video games, hang out with friends and family, or study a subject you enjoy more. You can decide if something will take you all day or if you will tackle it head on and complete it.

## PRIORITIZE YOUR OBLIGATIONS

Not every task is created equal, and therefore some tasks are more important than others. Some assignments have earlier deadlines, and harder projects need more time. It is essential to complete these important tasks first. When thinking about how to prioritize a workload you should ask these simple questions:

- When is this assignment due?
- How long do I expect it to take?
- Are there many steps I need to do to complete this project?
- Is this a group assignment or an individual project?
- What is required of me to get a good grade on this project?
- How much weight does this project have on my total class grade?

Be careful not to prioritize assignments strictly by the ones that seem like more fun. Just because you like one assignment better than another doesn't mean that assignment is more important.

Also, because group projects rely on other people and not just the individual student, you need to start these projects early. Not all students care about their grades, and their laziness can affect the grades of others. Be proactive in group projects to ensure your grades don't suffer because of someone else's laziness or mistakes.

## BALANCE THE OBLIGATIONS

Another important strategy is to maintain a balanced schedule. Very rarely in life are people required to spend all their energy on one particular thing. That is a recipe for burnout at a very early age. Practice taking breaks from certain tasks and doing something else with the free time. You might just find that you enjoy the tasks more. Recent studies by cognitive psychologists have said learning to balance work and play promotes overall mental health and can help students live a happier existence.

This doesn't mean you should spend one hour on homework then one hour practicing basketball. Balance doesn't mean you split your time down the middle between the things you have to do and the things you want to do; it means you make time in your life for both.

## BEAT PROCRASTINATION

Procrastination is a serious obstacle to time management. No matter what type of student you are, there will be times when you will feel the pull to procrastinate on a project, homework assignment, or test preparation. While a little procrastination is reasonable, allowing procrastination to rule your work ethic can be detrimental to your grades.

If you have something you really don't want to do, don't put it off. You should complete it as soon as possible, so you can have the weight of that obligation off your shoulders. *If you complete your hardest task first (if your priority list allows), everything else you have to do will seem easy.*

Often procrastination comes from fear. If a project feels overwhelming, you are less likely to want to start on it. Don't forget you can tackle it step by step. Don't be afraid of failure. The only real failure is the failure to try. Even if something turns out in the worst possible way, you can at least say you gave it a shot. If you never try, then you are already doomed to failure. However, if you try, there is always a chance of success. Most likely, the task is not as hard as you imagined and success is just around the corner.

Realize your work doesn't have to be perfect. There is a huge difference between doing your personal best and being perfect. Everyone expects you to do your best; no one expects your best to be perfect. As long you try for your personal best, then you can be proud of your accomplishments. It's okay to have weaknesses and strengths; everybody does.

One way to help you evaluate your work is by creating a grading rubric. A rubric is a scoring chart that distinguishes different levels of work. See if there are any national standards or levels of achievement to help you evaluate your efforts. For example, if you are preparing for the SAT, see what scores qualify you for acceptance at the top universities, then at state schools, and then for your local community college. This will give you a rubric of achievement for the SAT. If you have an athletic goal, try to work with a coach to establish a rubric. If you have academic goals, a teacher may be able to help you find a rubric to rate your accomplishments.

Once your difficult task is completed, you should reward yourself for doing it. Giving yourself rewards for completing goals will make unwanted tasks more pleasant. Your rewards don't have to be big, just something to celebrate a job well done—maybe even something as small as watching your favorite TV show because all your work is done.

Remember, rewards must be proportional to the goals completed. Running half a mile doesn't mean you get to eat half a chocolate cake.

## DISCOVER THE TIME WASTERS

It is very important to understand how and where your time is spent. If every time you sit down to write a paper you find yourself checking email, Facebook, or twitter, then you aren't really spending that time writing a paper. Keep track of habits like these and learn how to eliminate time wasters and increase your overall productivity. This way you can keep your mind focused on the tasks needing to be done.

If something is a big distraction, then get rid of it completely. Check email before starting, and then close the application. If you think the Internet will be a distraction, then turn it off before you get started. If people like to call or text you, then put your phone on silent.

Avoiding unwanted distractions (like little siblings) doesn't require much discipline; however, it is much harder to remove the wanted distractions, like phone calls and the Internet. You must treat all distractions equally, whether you like them or not. If a phone call is missed, you can return it later, and chances are the Internet isn't going anywhere any time soon.

## DON'T WASTE THE WAITING TIME

Think about all the time you spend waiting for stuff, perhaps at a doctor's office or at home waiting for a computer program to load. Don't waste the time sitting and thinking about how nothing is getting done. Find something else to do in the meantime. There are so many little tasks that you can accomplish while you are waiting to accomplish something bigger. This way you will have more free time later on.

For example, if you are going on a vacation and you will be waiting at the airport for two hours, then bring something that you need to work on. It could be homework, it could be the letter to Grandma you have been meaning to write, or it could be deleting old emails.

You don't have to do this just when you are out and about either. If you are waiting for your computer to run its updates and you need it to write a paper, then think about what you want to write about or jot down notes to help you write it faster.

## LEARN HOW TO DELEGATE

No one can do it all, and the sooner you learn this truth, the better off you will be. Splitting up tasks gets the job done faster. On group projects, make sure everyone has a task. If you are planning an event for a volunteer organization, assign smaller duties to the people who are supposed to help out.

You can also use the skill of delegation in other areas of your life. Good leaders know when it is best to delegate.

Remember: You should only delegate group assignments and not individual ones. Claiming someone else's work as your own is plagiarizing and can get you into serious trouble.

## LEARN TO SAY NO

There are tons of demands on your time, and there is no way you can finish everything. When you are offered a job that you don't have time to complete, feel free to say no. Although saying no may disappoint someone, it is far worse to agree to something and then back out at the last minute or do a poor job. You are actually doing the person who asked you a favor by being honest and saying that you can't or don't want to do something. This way that person can find someone else who is a better fit for the job.

It's easier to say no if you think about the consequences of saying yes. For example, if you add a Wednesday night babysitting gig for the rest of the summer, then you can't hang out with your friends on Wednesday night. "No" can actually save you from missing other opportunities.

## KEEP IT IN PERSPECTIVE

If you make a mistake, forget an assignment, overbook yourself, or just do a poor job on something, it is only as big a deal as you make it. Failures may seem huge now, but the consequences can be mitigated by owning up to the mistakes and working hard not to repeat them. This works for every area of your life. If you miss a meeting, call the leader and apologize. If you do poorly on a test, work harder for the next one.

However, don't make excuses. No one likes it when someone tries to excuse away mistakes. People are more likely to forgive if you accept that you messed up and take care of the consequences.

Also don't get into a habit of expecting people to forgive you just because you apologize. Saying sorry goes a long way in pacifying the offended parties, but only for a time. When a mistake is made, it is your responsibility both to apologize and then to do everything to avoid making the same mistake a second time.

# GUIDE FOR PARENTS HELPING YOUR CHILD CREATE A SCHEDULE

Organization is an important skill for any student to possess. One of the best ways to help your son become organized is to teach him the importance of meeting deadlines and keeping a schedule. Students who understand how to keep track of all their obligations and know what is expected of them will be able to keep themselves organized.

Help your daughter beat procrastination by teaching her to prioritize the most unfavorable tasks. It is also a good idea to encourage her to break complex tasks into smaller, more manageable chunks. This will teach her to start working on big projects early so she doesn't have to be consumed by them in the end. Students can break down any project into simple parts and tackle it systematically.

One way to encourage students to do well is to make sure your child understands that you expect her to do her best, but not to be perfect. Help her realize that if she tries her best, she can be proud of her accomplishments. Students often fail to try because they are afraid of disappointing their parents, teachers, or classmates.

## PARENTS' HOMEWORK

In this chapter, students learned the importance of having a day planner to organize their schedules. This tool is only valuable if it is used. While your son might have the best of intentions of using a day planner, he might need help implementing it in his daily life. Periodically, review his day planner and to-do lists to make sure he is staying on track. Be sure to continue to encourage him to keep up with his work.

# CHAPTER ELEVEN: HIGH SCHOOL MECHANICS

THIS CHAPTER will focus on the basics of high school mechanics to help you navigate the next four years. Regardless if you are in public, private, charter, or home school, you will need to have a firm grasp on these fundamentals. You will learn about grades, transcripts, and essential courses you need in order to graduate from high school.

## GRADES COUNT FROM DAY ONE

Many students are under the false impression that grades are not important during their first year of high school. Mistakenly, they think grades don't matter in senior year either. For the most part this is not true. Grades will count throughout the entirety of high school. There is no excuse to slack off at any time during your high school experience. Grades are the only thing that counts when calculating your grade point average (GPA) and class rank. Don't sabotage your GPA at the beginning or end of high school by not taking your classes seriously. Because your GPA is cumulative, if you start high school with poor grades it is very hard to bring your GPA up.

Although most of this section will talk about the importance of grades, it is equally important to mention that grades reflect only one aspect of academic achievement. Rather than spending your time obsessing about grade point average, it is better to view your high school experience as a chance to learn. While many people look to grades as a way to evaluate your academic success, the best way to measure your education is to look at how much you have learned. Straight As without any understanding or practical knowledge of your class work is all but useless in the real world. When focusing on doing well in your studies, always strive to obtain the highest possible grades, but do so because you spent the time learning the material.

## HOW GRADING WORKS

Grades are an evaluation of your academic performance. Teachers will read and assess the quality of your work and grade you according to their grading scales. Like many things in high school, there is no one set grading scale that every high school uses. While most high schools are consistent in using one particular grading scale, if you take classes outside of your high school, you are likely to encounter a different type of grading scale. Before each class begins, it is important to understand what type of grading scale your teacher will be using to evaluate your grades. This way you can self-evaluate how well you are doing in the class throughout the semester.

Also, check to see if the majority of your grades will be made up of tests, papers, or homework assignments, and know what percentage each assignment is worth in your total class grade. This will help you gauge how much time and energy you need to focus on particular projects. If your homework is worth only 10 percent of your grade and your tests are worth 90 percent, then do a good job on your homework to be sure you understand the basics and put extra effort into reviewing and practicing what you've learned so you do really well on your tests. This does not mean you can blow off your homework assignments; it just means that you need to pay extra attention to your tests.

Also realize, some teachers include attendance and participation in the overall grades. Stay alert, ask questions, and show your teacher you are actively involved in the subject. Showing your interest in a subject will go a long way in helping your teacher accurately evaluate your class performance.

Here's an example of several grading scales:

Sample: Typical Grading Scale

90-100= A

80-89= B

70-79= C

60-69= D

0-59 = F

Sample: Plus and Minus Grading Scale

97-100= A+

94-96 = A

90-93 = A-

87-89 = B+

84-86 = B

80-83 = B-

77-79 = C+

74-76 = C

70-73 = C-

65-69 = D

0-64 = F

Sample: Alternative Grading Scale

93-100= A

85-92= B

77-84= C

70-76= D

0-69= F

Regardless of the type of grading scale your teachers choose to employ, it is always important that you strive to produce your best work during your high school years.

## WHAT IS A GRADE POINT AVERAGE?

Your grade point average (GPA) is essentially your academic record of accomplishment. GPAs measure a student's academic achievement throughout high school. Traditionally GPAs are on a 4.0 scale—though some use a 5.0 scale—and the points awarded each letter are as follows: A = 4 points, B = 3 points, C = 2 points, D = 1 point, and F = 0 points. Some high schools give additional points for honors and AP courses, and others vary the point system by using a plus and minus scale.

GPAs are calculated by adding the total points for each letter grade and then dividing that number by the number of classes taken. For example: If you get an A in biology (4 points), a B in history (3 points), and a C in math (2 points), you would calculate your GPA by adding all the points together (4+3+2=9) and then dividing by the number of classes (biology + history + math = 3 classes): 9/3= 3. For that semester you would have a 3.0 GPA.

Your total GPA is a running average of every semester taken in high school. If you got a 3.0 your first semester, but then 4.0 second semester you would add up the total points for both semesters and divide it by the total number of semesters.

3.0 + 4.0/2= 3.5 GPA for both semesters

## WHAT'S THE BIG DEAL ABOUT GPAs?

Colleges and even future employers look at a student's GPA to see what type of effort that student put into each class. Students who take their classes seriously and strive to excel usually have higher GPAs than those who don't. Of course, the types of courses taken can influence a student's total GPA. If one student takes all easy courses and gets straight As and another takes all AP and honor courses and gets straight Bs, the first student might have a higher GPA, unless the school weights harder classes differently.

## WEIGHTED VERSUS UNWEIGHTED GPA

An unweighted GPA uses the simplest point system, described above, to turn your letter grade into a GPA. A weighted GPA reflects the rigor of your high school course load. In an unweighted scale, similar letter grades count for the same points (e.g., All As = 4 points). In a weighted scale, AP or honors courses may count for more (e.g., As in an AP class = 5 points).

Colleges view the two scales differently, and it is important to talk to specific admissions counselors to address any questions you might have about how your college choices view unweighted and weighted GPAs.

## CLASS SELECTION AND GPA

Is it better for you take an easier class to get an easy A or take a harder class and risk lowering your GPA? Simply put, there is no clear answer for that question. When considering what level course to take, it is important to consider three things: your high school grading scale, your future colleges, and your personal goals. You should decide on the classes that are best for you and your plans.

For the first item, remember that grading scales vary from school to school, and what might typically be an A at some schools could be considered a B at another. This is why colleges often refer to the SAT or ACT as the determining factor for entrance since it puts all students on an equal playing field.

Your prospective colleges are a factor that should help you decide. Some colleges look only at the unweighted GPA, which means an A is an A and a B is a B, regardless of class rigor. In this case, a college does not consider the B you got in AP calculus any different from the B you got in general history. Other colleges understand the increased work involved in AP and honors courses and value those grades differently than other courses.

The decision to take harder courses ultimately depends on your personal goals. If you love to learn and enjoy tackling challenging material, then you should probably take the hardest classes available. If you have specific career goals, you should take higher-level courses offered in your field of study.

## CLASS RANK

Your class rank is a measurement of your performance compared to all the other students in your class. If you have a class size of 100 and your GPA is better than 75 other students, then your class rank will be 25.

Class rank is also commonly expressed as a percentile. To calculate your class rank as a percentile, you simply take the number of students in your class minus the number of people who are ahead of you in your class rank. Next you divide that number by the total number of students in your class. Then multiply that number by 100. This is important as some states guarantee acceptance into state schools for students who are in the 90th percentile of their class.

For example, pretend you are number 25 in your class. You would calculate your class rank as follows.

**Step one:** Take the total number of students minus the students are ahead of you. **(100-25=75)**

**Step two:** Divide that number by the total amount of students. **(75/100= .75)**

**Step three:** Multiple that number by 100. **(.75*100= 75)**

**At the rank of 25, you are in the 75th percentile of your class.**

Some schools choose not to rank their students. If your school chooses not to use the ranking system, it is important to note that fact on your college application. If your school does not rank or you are homeschooled, then most colleges will use your GPA and standardized test scores to evaluate your high school performance.

## ESSENTIAL COURSES STUDENTS NEED

While no school's curriculum will be exactly the same, every state determines how many classes each student needs to complete to graduate from high school. There may be a minimum of courses in English, history, mathematics, science, fine arts, physical education, and health. Along with these core curricula, you will also have the option of taking several electives to finish out your high school career.

There are also non-required courses you should take to help you prepare for the rigors of college. We recommend taking logic, Latin, economics, speech and/or debate, and a college test prep course.

Logic is a skill that is universally applicable to every subject. Knowing how to formulate, critique, and explain arguments will help you evaluate material that is presented to you both in high school and in college. Logic will help you write and think better, as well as help you assess what you are learning.

Latin is another course you should consider taking. Although Latin is a dead language—meaning nobody speaks it anymore—it is one of the easiest foreign languages to learn. It is also the foundation of many of our modern languages, so Latin also helps you learn other foreign languages. It is the mother of Romance languages—French, Spanish, Italian, among others—and has practical applications for English. Many of the vocabulary words found in the SAT and ACT tests are words derived from Latin. Understanding the grammar and structure of Latin can help you master other grammatical structures.

Economics is another important class offered by many high schools. If it is not required, then you should make it a personal requirement. Economics is the science of analyzing the production, distribution, and consumption of goods and services. In other words, it is the science of how business works. Along with being an interesting subject, economics has practical applications for your life. By understanding the importance of ideas like incentives, opportunity costs, and supply and demand, you will gain great insight into the mechanics of the real world. Economic concepts are applicable to any future career and not just important for future economists.

Speech and debate can also enhance your high school experience. This can teach the principles of public speaking and logical argumentation, which can come in handy throughout your life. Young professionals who can confidently speak on their feet are more likely to climb the corporate ladder of success quickly. Likewise, the art of articulating complex arguments will aid you in diverse endeavors that range from defending your beliefs to solving multifaceted theoretical problems. Practice what you learn by volunteering to speak at local groups, churches, and public-speaking forums.

Lastly, you should take an SAT and/or ACT prep class *early* in your high school years. Ideally, students should take a class in the ninth grade, so they can spend a good amount of time preparing for these tests. The longer you have to study, the more time you have to improve. Many schools schedule SAT and ACT prep classes during the school year. Make sure that you check with your school and see what classes are being offered. Remember that not every prep class is created equal. You want to take a class that teaches to the logic of the test and shows you how to conquer the recurring patterns. If your school does not offer any SAT or ACT prep classes, you can see what classes are offered in your area or purchase a program that you can do at your home. Chapter 15 offers more information on college entrance exams.

## HIGH SCHOOL TRANSCRIPT

Your high school transcript is essentially your academic résumé. Transcripts are a record of every class you took and the grade you received. Your transcript is maintained by your counselors at a public, private, or charter school or by your parent if you are homeschooled.

A transcript is one of the most important pieces of information when applying to colleges and seeking scholarship opportunities. Transcripts help colleges evaluate your academic course load and performance. When applying to colleges and universities, you will need to send an interim transcript when you first apply and a final transcript once you graduate (both from your school in a sealed envelope). The only difference is that final transcripts have your finalized grades from all four years of high school, and your interim transcript does not. You have to send in a preliminary transcript first because, more likely than not, you will be applying for college before you actually finish high school. Additional information other than your grades that may be on your transcript are absences, plus or minus grades, rank or percentile, weighted GPA, and citizenship record.

For many colleges the transcript you send in must be in an envelope that is sealed by the high school and includes the school seal or stamp or has the administrator's signature. Colleges and universities call these transcripts "official" because they are clearly marked from the schools.

Those students who have an administration staff recording their transcripts should take it upon themselves to periodically check their transcripts for accuracy. Mistakes can happen, and sometimes it can be too late to fix those mistakes after graduation. You do not have to constantly bother your guidance counselor or school administrative staff about your transcript; just get in the habit of looking over your transcript at the end of each year, and at the end of each semester during your senior year.

## REQUESTING YOUR HIGH SCHOOL TRANSCRIPT

The process of requesting a transcript can vary from school to school. It is important to speak with your high school guidance counselor about any forms you need to fill out and what documentation is required to receive your transcript. Today many administration resources are on-line. Requesting a transcript may be as easy as simply logging onto your school's website and filling out the forms on your computer.

It is also a good idea to request a couple of extra transcripts to keep for your files. You never know when you might need an additional transcript. It is much easier to have a transcript on hand than to have to go through the process of requesting another one.

## HOMESCHOOL TRANSCRIPTS

For home-educated students, the adults in charge of your education will record and maintain your transcripts. Home educators must also be aware of the state's requirements for high school graduation and ensure their students take the necessary courses. It is also important to remember any high-school-level courses a student completed before ninth grade can be added to a student's high school transcript.

Creating your own transcript is rather an easy task as long as the parent or student has maintained a good record of the high school courses. Transcripts can be constructed in a Word document, Excel spreadsheet, or other similar programs. Home educators can use a basic transcript format or create a new one. There is no wrong way to create a homeschool transcript. As long as the transcript has some essential elements, the format doesn't matter. Another option is to create and organize a transcript by subject rather than by year. See Appendix A for transcript samples.

Make sure the person in charge of your transcript is taking the time to record all the details of your curriculum, academic performance, and extracurricular activities each semester. Doing this every semester will save time and frustration later on. Don't let your parents wait until your senior year of high school to work on your transcript. Trying to remember all the classes you took during high school can be tricky after the fact. Waiting until the end allows more room for mistakes and the possibility of forgetting some important information.

Remember that transcripts will be used to determine a student's qualifications for college admissions and scholarship awards. Therefore, it is important to be as detailed as possible when constructing a transcript. Be sure to keep a record of all extracurricular activities, awards, and academic achievements. If you want to mark something down for class rank, then you may consider showing percentile rank on the SAT (e.g., scored in the 95th percentile of all juniors who took the test).

It is also a good idea to keep a hard copy and a backup file in case something happens to your computer and you lose the original transcript file.

# GUIDE FOR PARENTS ESTABLISHING AN ACADEMIC FOUNDATION

Whether students go to public or private schools, or are in home schools, parents should want them to get the very best education. A strong academic foundation goes beyond the basics of reading, writing, and arithmetic. Students need to develop skills in critical thinking, foreign language, English grammar, and vocabulary. Younger children who learn logic, Latin or Greek, and strong fundamentals of grammar will have a much easier time in high school and college. These curricula will also help prepare them to take college entrance exams like the SAT and ACT. Building an academic foundation now will save time and frustration later.

Do not let your son neglect these fundamental skills in his middle school and early high school years. It is much easier for him to master basic concepts first, than to play catch-up later on in school.

Even if your daughter's school does not focus on these critical skills, make it a priority in her education. If her school has limited resources, then supplement her education with outside classes. Building a strong academic foundation is an essential key to high school and college academic success.

# SPECIAL GUIDE FOR HOMESCHOOLING PARENTS
## HOMESCHOOL ADMINISTRATION RESPONSIBILITIES

Parents who homeschool serve as teachers, principals, registrars, and guidance counselors. Homeschooling parents are also in charge of making curriculum decisions and ensuring that their students meet their state's high school graduation requirements (if applicable) as well as college entrance requirements. If you are a parent of a homeschooled student, you will wear many hats. These hats necessitate that you gather as much information as possible to help your high school student be successful. As you know, homeschooling throughout high school can be a very challenging, as well as a very rewarding experience.

*A detailed explanation of how to build transcripts and example transcripts can be found in Appendix A.*

## STATE REQUIREMENTS FOR HOMESCHOOL STUDENTS

Today's society considers homeschooling as an acceptable alternative to public or private school. Many colleges and universities accept homeschooled students with little or no hassle as long as the students have completed the required courses for high school graduation.

While homeschooled students are generally required to complete the same types of courses as public or private school students, the state in which you homeschool will determine any specific requirements, if any, for your homeschool curriculum. Some states will have stricter laws and requirements than other states. It is important for homeschooling parents to understand and follow the guidelines so that their students can graduate on time.

While it can be difficult to navigate the legal aspects of homeschooling, you do not have to go through this process alone. The Homeschool Legal Defense Association is a nonprofit organization created to help homeschooling parents protect their right to educate their children. The purpose of the Homeschool Legal Defense Association is to help you understand and protect your decision to educate your children. As a part of their services, the organization has dedicated a section of their website to specific requirements for each state. This website is a great place to start when learning what your state requires of you as a homeschooling parent. For more information on the laws concerning homeschooling in your state, visit www.hslda.org/hs/state/.

## GRADING YOUR HOMESCHOOL STUDENT

Grading your homeschool daughter can often be a difficult task. Yet grades are still very important for her. As mentioned earlier in this chapter, grades determine her GPA, and colleges use GPAs to help evaluate their applicants. Therefore, it is important for you as the parent to keep a detailed record of your student's assignments, grading scales, and grades.

Like many aspects of homeschooling, how assignments are graded is up to you, and it does not matter what type of grading scale you use with your children as long as it is consistent. When constructing a class for your child, sit down and decide the structure of the class and how grades will be given. You can grade your son on assignments, tests, participation, and so on. Once you have established the grading criteria, do not neglect keeping a log of his grades throughout the duration of the course. Keeping up with his grading will help you later when you give him an overall grade for the course. Organization and consistency are the two most important keys to accurately evaluating your student's work throughout high school.

## THE IMPORTANCE OF DEADLINES

All homeschooled students must learn how to meet a deadline. While some homeschooling parents choose to teach their students in a very traditional setting with daily homework assignments, scheduled tests, and projects, many homeschooling parents choose not to follow a strict academic schedule. These parents allow their students to complete projects on the students' timeline and take tests when the students feel ready to take the tests. Some parents structure their classes using a combination of these types of schedules.

It does not matter what type of class schedule you follow; however, it is important for your students to understand the importance of deadlines. Once your child leaves your house for college or career, he or she will face deadlines. Knowing and understanding the importance of deadlines is crucial for success in the real world. Bright homeschooled students often find themselves struggling in college or the workplace because they fail to turn in work or projects on time. Deadlines do not have to be the core of your curriculum; just make sure that your students understand that, while Mom and Dad might let some deadlines go, college professors and future bosses won't.

A great way to teach your students the importance of a deadline is by getting them involved in extracurricular activities like newspaper or yearbook classes that may be offered at their co-op. Newspapers and yearbooks are great avenues to teach the importance of deadlines because they are two organizations that rely heavily on deadlines. Finding an extracurricular activity that emphasizes deadlines will help your students appreciate and understand the vital importance of deadlines in the real world.

## UMBRELLA SCHOOLS

Umbrella schools are another option for homeschooling parents. These schools help homeschooling parents meet the government education requirements by overseeing the education of the students involved. Umbrella schools vary in their requirements, benefits, and costs. Some schools offer curriculum, outside classes, extracurricular activities, and even standardized tests. Many students who participate in umbrella schools can receive a graduation ceremony and official diploma from that school. Parents who are interested in enrolling their students in an umbrella school should do some research and talk with others who have participated. Depending on the needs of the parents and students, umbrella schools can be a viable option for reducing the amount of school administrative duties of homeschooling parents.

## PARENTS' HOMEWORK

Before your child enters high school, make sure you understand the mechanics of his education avenue. If he is in a public, private, or charter school, make time to meet with the academic advisor or guidance counselor. Be sure to ask about the school's grading scales, class ranking, and transcript requirements. Having this information early will help you chart his path for success. After meeting with the proper administrator, sit down with your son and share the information that you learned. Make him aware of what will be expected of him regarding grades and be sure to emphasize that grades count from the beginning until the end.

If your daughter is homeschooled, be sure to establish the type of grading system you will use, or will be experimenting with, before classes start. Once you have implemented this system, clearly explain your methods to her. Be sure to formulate a system for good record keeping and be diligent in your data entry. Record keeping can be easily tracked in a Word document or spreadsheet. It doesn't matter which format you use as long as you keep up with the data input. Be sure to include the subjects, grades, dates of completion, and any additional notes that are relevant.

# CHAPTER TWELVE: GOING BEYOND THE BASICS

IN HIGH school you will become responsible for deciding what courses you are going to take each semester and making sure you are signed up for those courses. A high school degree plan is your road map to high school success. It's a good idea to plan ahead because it will give you the freedom to change your plans in case something important comes up, like a new class that is only offered your senior year or a foreign exchange program that sends you to Europe for a semester. This chapter is dedicated to familiarizing you with a variety of options that can enhance your high school education experience.

Before you start your first semester of high school, meet with your middle school or high school guidance counselor. (If you are homeschooled your high school guidance counselor will be one or both of your parents and/or guardians.) Find out what courses are required for graduation and when they are offered, along with any prerequisites or age requirements for advanced classes. Once you have a list, you can plan your tentative high school degree plan. Your plan will guide you throughout your four years and keep you on track for graduation.

When making your high school schedule, you will be given some freedom in deciding which classes to take and when. Many students do not realize the wealth of resources available to them when building their high school course loads. You do not have to settle for the cookie-cutter plan established by your high school administrators. Even the basic required courses can be tweaked to fit your future goals. There are basic classes, honors and AP, dual credits, and outside classes. When thinking about your path through high school, be sure to include all the options available to you. Do not settle for the course load that everyone else is taking; be creative and make the most out of your high school curriculum.

When choosing what courses to take, there are a couple of things you need to keep in mind. First, the material you cover in high school lays the foundation for any future studies. Most colleges and universities require a certain number of general education classes. These classes often build upon the classes you take in high school. In college, you will most likely need to take at least one course each in history, mathematics, science, and English. It is much easier to learn the foundations of these subjects in high school than to play catch-up in a harder course.

Second, if you are interested in a particular field, you will want to get as much experience in related classes as possible. By getting experience with a subject now, you will have a better understanding of whether you actually want to pursue that subject in college. Not to mention, if you are planning on applying to a competitive program, your experience and grades in the subject will influence a college's admission decision.

## DISCUSSING CURRICULUM WITH SCHOOL ADMINISTRATORS

Your education is ultimately your responsibility. Although your guidance counselor is there to help you navigate high school, he or she often has too much on his or her plate to take the time to specifically make the best schedule for you. Thus, the burden falls on your shoulders.

Although your school administrators are very busy people, they will still have time to meet with you. Come prepared to the meeting in order to use their time wisely. Guidance counselors will appreciate your efforts because it shows initiative and saves them time.

## QUESTIONS FOR YOUR SCHOOL ADMINISTRATORS

1.   What are the school requirements for graduation?
2.   How much flexibility is there to choose my own classes?
3.   Are the syllabi available to look at before I register for my classes?
4.   What types of advanced classes are offered?
5.   What are the prerequisites or other requirements (age, class year, etc.) for an advanced class?
6.   Do I have to be involved in an honors program to take advanced classes? Or can I pick and choose what advanced classes I take?

## HOMESCHOOL CURRICULUM

The flexibility of homeschooling allows parents to choose an individual degree plan for each student. Curriculum can be purchased on-line, at bookstores, and through homeschool book fairs. Advanced courses, honors programs, AP classes, dual credit, and College Level Examination Program (CLEP) resources are available to students who are educated at home. There are also individuals who can assist in helping tailor your student's education and helping you to implement a plan that meets your family's needs.

## GOING BEYOND THE FOUNDATIONAL CURRICULUM

Limited by budgets, facilities, and resources, not every high school can supply every student with the resources to pursue all interests and academic aspirations. If you find that your school does not have all the classes you would like to take, you can always add supplemental classes to your high school experience. The potential for supplemental classes is limited only by your imagination, creativity, and financial resources. Your high school education is not limited to the walls of your high school or your homeschool. Education exists anywhere you learn something new.

You can take classes at community centers, local colleges, on-line, community organizations, friends' houses, local libraries, and so on. You can employ the help of tutors to assist you with subjects you are struggling with or wish to learn more about. A job can serve as practical hands-on class experience. All you need is an interest in a topic, material to study, and someone who will teach you.

Here are some examples of supplementary classes you can take in a variety of locales.

**Community College**
>   Astronomy
>   Advanced calculus
>   Medieval history
>   Theater history
>   Multimedia and animation
>   Computer programming

**Community Center**
>   Pottery
>   Painting
>   Martial arts
>   Gymnastics
>   Racquetball

**Private Lessons**
>   Vocal instruction
>   Musical instruments
>   Language instruction
>   Academic tutoring

**Internship Opportunities**
>   Business management
>   Veterinarian training
>   Photography
>   Talent management
>   Promotional marketing

## HONORS PROGRAMS

High schools can really boost your academic experience by providing new opportunities to learn. If you are interested in being involved in an honors program, talk with you guidance counselor or your school's honors program coordinator. Although homeschool students are not eligible for some honor society memberships, there are still plenty of honors programs available to them.

The most widely used and recognized honors program is the National Honor Society (NHS). NHS chapters can be found in all 50 states; over one million students are currently involved in the program. NHS membership is available only to students who are enrolled in either public or private schools that have NHS chapters. Students who wish to become NHS members must have a minimum cumulative grade point average of 85 percent (3.0 GPA) or the school's equivalent, and must meet the requirements of the specific school in service, leadership, and character. Benefits of being a member of the NHS include national recognition among U.S. colleges and universities, school-organized honors program functions, and NHS-exclusive scholarship opportunities. For specific information concerning the NHS, more information can be obtained at www.nhs.us.

Another prestigious high school honor society is the National Society of High School Scholars (NSHSS). Unlike the NHS, the NSHSS is open to public, private, charter, and homeschool students. Membership advantages include on-line forums, society events, monthly publications, and exclusive NSHSS scholarship opportunities. Students must be nominated for membership by their schools or be extended an invitation by the NSHSS program. Students can request an invitation by following the request-an-invitation procedure. For more information on the NSHSS and how to request an invitation, please visit www.nshss.org.

Programs created for the homeschool community include the Eta Sigma Alpha National Homeschool Honor Society and the National Math Honors Society for the Homeschool Community. According to the Homeschool Legal Defense Association, these programs are equally prestigious as the NHS and have rigorous membership standards. Along with meeting the specific requirements for membership, both organizations require students to submit an application for membership as well as standardized tests scores. Benefits of joining a homeschool honors program include recognition of academic excellence, enhancement of college applications, and participation in service opportunities. For specific application requirements and more information on the Eta Sigma Alpha National Homeschool Honor Society, please visit www.etasigmaalpha.com. For the National Math Honors Society, please visit www.mathhonorsociety.com.

## ADVANCED PLACEMENT COURSES

Advanced Placement (AP) classes are college-level courses taken in high school. While students take these classes during the school year, students must take the official AP exams, administered by the College Board, at the end of the year to qualify for college credit. AP scores demonstrate to the colleges that you have mastered the college-level coursework. This is one way to prove you are one of the best and the brightest.

You do not have to take every AP class offered, but with over thirty AP courses available, chances are you will be interested in at least a couple. AP offerings include English literature, U.S. history, European history, American government, psychology, economics, art history, music theory, French, Spanish, German, physics, chemistry, biology, computer programming, calculus, statistics, and so on. The exams require students to pay a fee, and all scores are sent in the mail.

These exams are scored on a scale of 1 to 5. Students who score between 3 and 5 may qualify for a college credit in that subject at most colleges and universities. Depending on the high school, AP students may not have to take the exams for high school credit. The exams are usually used for obtaining college credit.

Let's say you take an AP chemistry class during your senior year of high school. If you score a 4 on the AP test, most colleges will accept that score as proof of your competency in introductory chemistry. Therefore, you will get credit for basic chemistry in your college schedule. This can save tuition as well as help you concentrate on other classes.

AP courses also help prepare you for college writing assignments and harder coursework. Other benefits to receiving these college credits include the possibility of graduating earlier or easily adding on another major or minor.

Students can generally only take AP courses in their junior and senior years of high school, but there are exceptions. Some larger schools make Advanced Placement courses available for prepared younger students, particularly courses like human geography, environmental science, world history, and European history. Or a student with advanced foreign language skills (often a native speaker) may take an AP level course of the language earlier in his high school career. For more information on appropriate grade levels for AP courses, visit http://apcentral.collegeboard.com/apc/public/repository/Appropriate-Grade-Levels-for-AP-Courses.pdf.

Although there are many benefits of taking AP classes, they are also a huge time commitment. Most likely, you will need to devote between five and ten hours per week to each AP course. Therefore, if you already have a very busy schedule, you should be discriminating about which AP courses to take. Also, if you struggle in a particular class, you may not benefit from taking an advanced course in that subject. You know better than anyone else how much time and energy you are willing to put into your class work. If you want to take all AP courses, great! But don't waste your or your teacher's time by knowingly signing up for a class you aren't going to take seriously.

## ADVANCED PLACEMENT WITHOUT AP CLASSES

There is a distinction between AP courses that have been reviewed through the College Board course audit process and courses of study that can prepare a student to succeed on an AP exam. The transcript notation "American History with AP Exam" would refer to a course that was not audited by the College Board. Still, a high score on the AP exam would mean the same for any student regardless of whether the student took "AP U.S. History" with official course approval. An officially approved syllabus will have little value if the exam score is not 3 or better.

Homeschool students can also participate in "official" AP classes by taking instruction from a certified AP teacher or an official on-line AP class. Self-motivated students can study on their own by using a guide—found in bookstores—and following the class work schedule. No matter how you take an AP course, you will still have to take the AP exam offered in May to receive the AP college credit.

For more information on AP courses, or to sign up for an AP exam, visit www.collegeboard.com.

### CLEP

This is the College Level Examination Program. Students earn credit by taking qualified tests that correspond to a one-semester class. The tests are ninety minutes long. They can be taken at any age. CLEP tests can help someone finish their degree.

### DUAL CREDIT/EARLY ENROLLMENT

Dual credit/early enrollment credit can be obtained when a student is simultaneously enrolled in both high school (public, private, charter, or homeschool) and a local college or university. (Some schools may even offer distance-learning courses as dual credit.) By taking college classes during high school you can earn credit for both your high school graduation requirements and college credit.

To qualify for this college credit, you will need to fill out an application and fulfill the requirements for enrollment into your specific course-offering school. In many cases, students are required to take an entrance exam (e.g., SAT, ACT, or placement test) to prove their academic readiness for college.

Not every college has the same credit transfer policy. You must contact your prospective colleges to see how they feel about dual credits and discuss their specific transfer policies. These classes may not always result in college credit but could perhaps be used as honors courses on the transcript or for internal class placement and college prerequisite requirements. Be aware of how many possible credits you will be able to transfer into particular schools, too. Transfer credits can reduce the college workload; however, they can also affect your future enrollment status. **Students who accumulate a large number of college credits from dual enrollment, AP, or CLEP exams may not be considered incoming freshmen when they enter college, but instead transfers student. The difference in enrollment status can influence your application**

**consideration and scholarship opportunities**.

You must also consider how the dual credit will influence your experience at your future school. For example, if you are considering majoring in history, then it might not be a good idea to take your core history classes at the community college instead of at your university.

Look to these resources to find out how college credit transfers:

www.collegetransfer.net

www.transfer.org

Be sure to make good grades in dual credit courses because poor marks could possibly affect your graduation plans, honors society requirements, or even college GPA. While many colleges transfer only the credits, others will apply your grade in a dual-credit course to your college GPA. No matter what, this grade will directly affect your high school GPA.

Dual-credit/early enrollment opportunities are usually limited to high school juniors and seniors, but exceptions for younger students can be made. Documentation is usually required for younger students to prove their exceptional academic ability to undertake college-level class work, which can be provided by your high school, and/or your parents or governing homeschool association.

The cost for these courses varies, but many colleges have tuition-assistance programs. Some schools even allow students to participate at no charge.

Entering college with some credit has several benefits: Skipping classes that you are already know will not only save money but can also allow more time for classes that you want to take, possibly add on another degree, or graduate early.

## INTERNATIONAL BACCALAUREATE PROGRAM

Many high schools today are now members of the International Baccalaureate (IB) program. The IB program is a rigorous pre-university program that aims to prepare students for the challenges of continuing education as well as the unique challenges of living in a global world. Students who participate in IB programs are evaluated by IB standards and are required to take standardized assessments including written assignments and final examinations that are evaluated by their high school and IB evaluators. This ensures the high standards of the program remain consistent across all schools participating in the program. IB programs are traditionally taught over two years in high school and include curriculum covering foreign language, social studies, experimental science, and mathematics. Most students who graduate with an IB diploma are eligible for IB scholarships, which can result in a full ride to some universities.

Only students who are enrolled in IB schools can participate in the IB program, and homeschool parents cannot use the IB program at home. Individual schools set their own IB enrollment requirements; students must contact the school for further information. For more information on the IB program and to find out what schools in your area participate in the IB program, visit www.ibo.org.

## ACADEMIC AWARDS

Along with enrolling in advanced classes, keep a record of all of the honors and awards that you receive during high school, no matter how small. If you keep a record of your success, when you apply for colleges and scholarships you will have all your information readily available. While you can keep your awards, trophies, and certificates anywhere you like, you should keep a catalog of your awards on a spreadsheet in your college and career notebook. Make sure you divide the catalog by grades, subjects, explanations, and dates. You should save your catalog and print it off once a year.

Having a catalog of your awards and honors will come in handy not only during the college application progress, but also when you look for scholarships. There are tons of scholarships out there. Look for scholarships that match any of the honors or awards that you have obtained. You might be surprised by how many different scholarships you are eligible for.

A very impressive award that very few people apply for is the Congressional Award. Students are eligible to apply for this award between the ages of fourteen and twenty-three. They will need to set goals in four areas: volunteer, personal development, physical fitness, and expedition. There are three medals awarded. Once you have completed all of the qualifications and requirements, you will be invited to Washington, D.C., in June to receive the Gold Medal

Award. This is a super program for students who wish to get extra distinction outside of the classroom. For more information on the Congressional Award, go to www.congressionalaward.org.

## POSSIBLE AWARDS AND HONORS

1. Eagle Scout
2. Honors societies
3. National Merit scholar
4. Student of the *year*
5. *Who's Who Among High School Students* listing
6. Girl Scout Gold Award
7. Congressional Award
8. Leadership certificates
9. National Piano Guild
10. Writing contest awards
11. Community service awards
12. Mayor for the day
13. Fine arts recognition
14. Volunteer of the year

## VOLUNTEERING

Volunteering is a wonderful way to round out your high school experience. Giving time to help those in need is not only rewarding on a personal level, but it is also beneficial to your future. College admission departments and prospective employers look favorably on your volunteer résumé. Admissions staffers like knowing you are willing to become active in a community, so that your presence on campus will enrich the overall environment. Employers like knowing you have experience in a variety of jobs and can make commitments and fulfill obligations.

Helping others has positive psychological benefits. People who spend more time thinking about others and less time thinking about themselves are, on average, happier people. Being able to assist someone in need gives a person a sense of worth and greater purpose. On a purely psychological basis, volunteering for a cause you believe in can do you a world of good.

There is no telling what you will learn about yourself and others when you volunteer. You will get life experience and an overall broader worldview. Perhaps when you are at the soup kitchen, you learn to appreciate your own mother's cooking. Seeing people who lack modern conveniences can help you appreciate the things you have. Maybe on your weekly visits to the nursing home you befriend some really interesting people and hear life-enriching stories.

Volunteers also get the chance to do jobs they might otherwise not be able to do. Organizations don't usually hire inexperienced workers, but they may be willing to train workers in exchange for their unpaid time. Therefore, volunteering at different places will increase your work experience and job skills. Exploring different job fields, without the incentive of a paycheck, will give you good insight into whether you want to continue in that field. If you want to become an architect, then working with Habitat for Humanity is a great way to get real-world experience. If you want to work with animals, volunteering at the local animal shelter will give you hands-on experience with pets.

Lastly, volunteering is a sign of commitment. People like to see examples of strong work ethic and dedication to a certain effort. Thus, don't wait until it is too late to start thinking about volunteering; do it now. The longer you volunteer at a single place, the better it will look on your résumé. Don't volunteer at 100 places just to pad your application. Skipping from one volunteer place to the next demonstrates the opposite of commitment. Colleges want applicants who have fully committed to the goals and purpose of a certain organization or program by showing passion and dedication.

There are also scholarships available for students who continue volunteering through college. Also check into volunteer vacations or programs that allows families to volunteer together.

Here are some websites to get you started.
www.volunteermatch.org
www.cogito.org
www.handsonnetwork.org
www.idealist.org

www.DoSomething.org
www.allforgood.org
www.service.gov
www.jhu.edu/gifted/imagine/index.html

## GET STARTED AS A VOLUNTEER

1.  Make a list of your interests and possible volunteer opportunities that match.
2.  Call local organizations and associations that are related to your interests. Ask if they have volunteer opportunities, or see if they would like some help in the particular area in which you are interested.
3.  Surf the Internet for possible organizations or businesses you might have overlooked.
4.  Check with your guidance counselor or church bulletin board for possible service opportunities.
5.  Talk to your friends about their interests and volunteer opportunities.
6.  Read the local newspaper or visit nonprofit organizations in your area to see if they need help with any upcoming charity events.
7.  Ask area sports teams if they need help.
8.  Talk to people who work at places you are interested in, and see if they need help.
9.  If you can't find a group to match your particular interest, make your own. All you need to do is find a need and figure out how to fill it.
10. Schedule dates and times with the organizations and make sure to mark them on your calendar.

## AFTER YOU VOLUNTEER

1.  Keep a log of date, hours, job performed, supervisor, etc., for each organization that you volunteer with. This will start to build your volunteer résumé and is an important part of your college and career notebook. *Some places will allow driving time as volunteer work.*

2. Get a letter of recommendation from your supervisor stating what jobs you accomplished and how well you did. (Make sure it is on the organization's letterhead.)

3. Send handwritten thank you notes to your supervisors and anyone who helped you obtain the position or trained you on the job. It doesn't have to be a long letter; just thank them for their help and tell them you appreciated working for them.

4. Start looking for your next volunteer opportunity, or make plans to volunteer at the same organization when they need you again.

5. Feel good about how hard you worked.

## COMMUNITY SERVICE SCHOLARSHIPS

Students who take an interest in making a difference in their world can be rewarded with scholarship money. Some may not be specifically labeled as community service scholarships, so definitely mention any volunteer experience on your application or in your scholarship essay.

Here are some possible scholarship for volunteers:
Alliant Energy Community Service Scholarship
The Disneyland Resort Scholarship Program
Prudential Spirit of Community Awards
Samuel Huntington Public Service Award

Below is a list of forty possible volunteer ideas to get you started.

### Organizational Opportunities
1. Counseling centers
2. Animal hospitals
3. Nursing homes
4. Retirement communities
5. Animal shelters
6. Garden centers or nurseries
7. Libraries

8.  Aquariums
9.  Television studios
10. Homeless shelters
11. Food banks
12. Children's wish foundations
13. Parks and outdoor centers
14. Tutoring centers
15. Special Olympics
16. Habitat for Humanity
17. City government
18. Blood banks
19. Political campaigns
20. Telethons
21. Boys and Girls Clubs
22. Destination Imagination
23. Ronald McDonald House
24. United Way
25. Red Cross
26. Salvation Army
27. Meals on Wheels
28. Prison outreach
29. Big Brother/Big Sister
30. Guideposts Sweater Project
31. Hospitals
32. Senior citizen centers
33. Guiding Eyes for the Blind
34. Culinary Corps
35. Summit for Someone
36. Citizen Schools
37. Twilight Wish Foundation
38. Box Project
39. Public Lands Day
40. Crisis hotlines

**Individual Opportunities**

1. Start a recycling program in your area.
2. Help the elderly in your neighborhood.
3. Do lawn work for someone who can't.
4. Clean up a vacant lot.
5. Create a mural or public display to beautify an area.
6. Stuff backpacks with school supplies and deliver them to schools.
7. Collect used books and donate them to libraries, jails, or shelters.
8. Write appreciation letters to teachers and administrators.
9. Manage school book orders for teachers.
10. Befriend someone with special needs.
11. Visit those who are ill.
12. Adopt a grandparent.
13. Give through the mail.
14. Share the holiday spirit through giving.
15. Create a blog to bring awareness to an issue.
16. Mentor someone younger.

## SUMMER JOBS CAN WORK TOO

While volunteer programs are awesome, a part-time job during the summer is another wonderful idea. It helps build a solid work ethic and gives you the opportunities to learn new skills. Working jobs while in high school builds your résumé and looks good on both college and job applications. Don't just settle for an average job. Try to find jobs in your areas of interest; this way you have "real" world experience. If you can't get a paid job in a field you enjoy, think about trying an internship. Internships are a great way to learn about a business in exchange for your time and effort. Talk to people you know in the careers you are thinking about, and see if they have any opportunities for you. If you need to earn money, and can't find something in your desired field, there is no shame in having a "regular" job. Any job presents you with opportunities to learn.

## THINK ABOUT IT

Sure, you can settle for the classes handed to you, or you can actively pursue other options to fit your personal goals and motivations. In today's society, you have so many options to supplement the basic curriculum offered to you by your school.

Think about what you have to learn and what you want to learn in high school. Decide what goals you want to accomplish in the next four years and what subjects you really want to focus on. Honestly evaluate whether you can handle all, some, or none of the advanced classes. Research the policies of colleges you are considering toward advanced courses.

Once you have decided what path you want to take, talk with your school administrators about the options available to you. Write down which courses you hope to take and activities you wish to pursue in order to achieve your goals.

_____

_____

_____

_____

_____

_____

_____

_____

_____

_____

_____

_____

*Once you have all the information, you can begin to work on your own high school degree plan. A detailed explanation of how to create a high school degree plan and a sample degree plan can be found in the section on your college and career notebook.*

# GUIDE FOR PARENTS
# HELPING YOUR CHILD UNDERSTAND
# ADVANCED COURSES

Many schools offer different types of advanced classes for students to take during their time in high school. Three specific types of advanced classes include Advanced Placement (AP) classes, honors classes, and the International Baccalaureate program. Schools have various requirements for such programs, so it is important to speak with your child's guidance counselors to see what options are available. It is also possible that your child's high school offers more than one type of advanced class. Therefore, you and your student need to evaluate what options are best. Parents, it is important to research the options available to you and your student. Gather as much information as possible, and make an informed decision.

Never be afraid to ask the school's administrative staff any of your questions. While the teachers and administrative staff all want your student to succeed, they do not have the time to personally advise every student on which path is best. If you think something would be good for your child, like being enrolled in both the honors program and the AP courses, ask if it is possible. The worst thing that can happen is the school says no. Parents must take the lead role in determining their child's path for high school academic success. This is especially important for homeschooled students. Because homeschooled students do not attend an organized institution, their parents must seek out opportunities to allow their students to excel academically.

Many homeschool co-ops now offer AP classes, or homeschooled students can find AP classes through other channels. These teachers follow AP-level curriculum and teach their students how to prepare for the AP tests. If schools, co-ops, or outside classes do not offer AP courses, any student—public, private, charter, or home-schooled—can do an independent study. The same people who write the PSAT/NMSQT, SAT, and SAT subject tests also write AP tests. More information about the AP tests can be found at www.collegeboard.com.

Other options available to homeschooled students are honors

programs through umbrella schools or enrolling in college-level courses at a local community college. Ignorance is no excuse for allowing your child to miss outstanding opportunities.

## HELPING YOUR STUDENT THROUGH SUMMER SCHOOL

Summer school should not be solely a punishment for students who failed a class. It is a time to take the classes students can't during the semester. Depending on your students' goals, summer courses can be the ideal path to accomplishing their dreams. Encourage your students to work hard during the semester, so that summer time can be a time to learn new things.

If your daughter really enjoys math and hopes someday to be an engineer, then she should take a higher math class at your local community college. Or if your son enjoys history, he should take a history course. Most community colleges open their doors to high school students because they want students to learn. Some schools even offer dual credit that allows students to get high school and college credit for a single class.

If your child happens to fall behind during school, some high schools offer accelerated courses to help him or her catch back up and possibly get ahead for the next year. Ask your guidance counselor about any summer options at your child's school.

## HELP YOUR STUDENT MAKE THE MOST OF SUMMER BREAKS

Contrary to what your son might think, mindlessly wasting school holidays is not the most fun way to spend his breaks. During breaks and holidays you should encourage him to be active, not to just lie around the house or hang out with his friends. Have your child use the summers to help him reach his goals and enrich his life.

Summer time is a great chance for students to learn and explore new areas of interest through classes, experiences, and volunteer opportunities. It is a time to travel and do the things they can't do during the school year. Just as it is important to work toward goals during the semester, it's important to work toward goals during the summer. No other time, other than retirement, will present such blocks of free time to pursue and explore interests and gain an edge. Create a four-year summer plan by deciding what your child wants to accomplish and learn during school and determine what summer opportunities can benefit those goals.

Students can do all kinds of interesting things over the summer, like participate in an independent study, write a novel, enroll in an educational summer campus program, film a documentary, put on a theater presentation, take unaccredited classes, or volunteer. If your daughter decides to do summer college programs, have her diversify and attend multiple campus programs—not just the school she is planning on attending. Also, expensive summer camps are not necessarily impressive to college admission counselors. Here is a website that can help give you ideas of things to do with the summer: www.enrichmentalley.com.

College admissions counselors are also keenly interested in summer breaks, so keep a good record of your student's summer exploits. Make sure you log these activities on the appropriate page in your college and career notebook. **Remember, the Four-Year Summer Plan should begin the summer before ninth grade.**

Students also need their downtime. Students should not burn themselves out during the summer, as they will need time to relax and recuperate before the next semester begins.

## INTERESTS TURNED INTO VOLUNTEER OPPORTUNITIES

Having trouble coming up with summer ideas that fit your child? Why not have your son actively pursue his interests through volunteering or internship programs? This way he can help the community while learning something about potential careers.

1. Counseling – Work at a home for at-risk youth
2. Teaching — Tutor a younger student who needs help
3. Art history — Work in an art museum
4. Theater – Work for local community theaters
5. Accounting — Work for a CPA
6. Public relations — Join a fund-raising campaign for a charity

7. Political science — Volunteer for a local election campaign
8. Nursing — Volunteer for a hospital
9. Choral music — Help out in the church choir
10. Psychology — Volunteer for a Psychology study
11. Astronomy — Volunteer at an observatory
12. Aviation science — Work for a local airport
13. Armed Forces – Join ROTC
14. Linguist – Work with ESL students
15. News anchor— Volunteer at a local news station
16. Radio DJ— Volunteer at a local radio station
17. Child care — Work in church Sunday school programs
18. Journalist — Volunteer at a local newspaper or magazine
19. Zoologist— Volunteer at a local zoo
20. Religious studies— Work at a church

## HELP YOUR STUDENT FIND A REWARDING PART-TIME JOB

Part-time jobs or summer jobs are a great idea for high school students. It helps teach them responsibility and time management. It is also a great way to help them save for college. However, before you let your student settle at the local restaurant as the fry-cook, have her try to find a job that fits in with her future plans or interests.

For example, if your student wants to be a veterinarian, then have him see if the local animal hospital or shelter needs any help. If the student thinks she wants to be a lawyer, then see if any of the lawyers in town need a secretary or even a janitor. Students may not be qualified to do the type of work they eventually want to do, but working in those environments might help them decide if they are on the right track.

Even if your student has no idea what he wants to do, try to find a job that sparks some interest. The high school years are a great time to explore and try new things. There is nothing to lose, so why not try?

## FOSTER A LOVE OF READING

Don't let your students read only for school. Start a family book club with a regular discussion night. Be creative and get your students involved. If you are having trouble encouraging your students to read, set up a reward system. Fostering a love of reading early on will dramatically help your students in the future.

# SPECIAL GUIDE FOR HOMESCHOOLING PARENTS

### PICKING THE RIGHT CURRICULUM

Homeschooling parents have the exciting and terrifying task of choosing their students' high school curriculum. While the state guidelines (if applicable) for homeschool students will create a framework, the job of choosing curriculum is much harder than simply picking out one book for every course that you teach. Homeschooling parents must carefully consider not only what subjects their students will study over the next four years, but also how those subjects will be studied.

Homeschooling by its very nature is flexible. You know your students better than anyone else does, and as long as you meet your state's academic requirements the decision on what and how to teach your students is up to you. You can choose traditional textbook classes, video courses, out-of-the-home classes, on-line classes, or some mixture of these options. Many homeschooling parents spend a lot of time doing research on different curriculum and going to homeschool book fairs to carefully consider their resource options. Some parents leave the educational decisions to their homeschool students, which is a type of homeschool option known as "unschooled homeschooling." Students who are unschooled pick the topics they want to learn, do research on their own, and create their own courses. This type of schooling is similar to self-directed studies in both college and graduate school.

There is no one right way to pick the curriculum for your students, and often if you homeschool more than one student, what works for one student may not work for another student. Many homeschooling parents have their students tested to learn their own unique learning abilities so they can tailor their curriculum to how each student learns best. As a homeschooling parent, you must decide what is right for your individual students.

When making a curriculum guide for your student, look over the three-tier guide (in your college and career notebook) and decide what path is right for your student. You can tailor the curriculum around it. Do as much research as you can on the curriculum and do not be afraid to try something new. Research can be done through reviews, friends' suggestions, and book fairs. Include your students in the discussion process. After all, they are the ones taking the classes.

## PARENTS' HOMEWORK

Having a plan for high school is the best way to succeed. No matter what grade your child is in, he or she will benefit from a personalized high school degree plan. Discuss what classes your son needs, wants, and should take, and then create a four-year academic and four-year summer plan. Make sure you encourage him to take the most rigorous classes he can to help prepare him for college or a career. The section about the college and career notebook provides a step-by-step guide to creating a high school degree plan.

# PART IV:

# Foundation for Future Success

# CHAPTER THIRTEEN: FUTURE DEVELOPMENT

A S HIGH school ends, you will have to make some important decisions about college, career, and possibly your family life. Everything you do in high school should help you prepare for those important decisions.

This section of *High School Prep Genius* will help you plan for the future. Don't put off reading this section until your senior year. You should start thinking about your future in your freshman year to help you establish a plan. Then you should look back at this several times during high school—at least once a year during your sophomore, junior, and senior years—just to make sure you haven't missed anything.

## ESTABLISHING FUTURE GOALS

Before you can have a plan, you have to have a goal. Goals are crucial because they motivate you to accomplish difficult tasks and allow you to work toward something that is important to you. Working for and accomplishing a goal helps give you a sense of pride in your work. You should strive to make big and small goals.

You must recognize your own personal strengths when establishing goals. If you recognize your talents and skills, you can use them when trying to reach your goals. You can also tailor your goals to your specific strengths.

Just as it is important to acknowledge your strengths, it is just as important to acknowledge your weaknesses. You can set yourself up for failure if you try to accomplish goals that are impossible for you. It doesn't mean you should give up on improving your weaknesses; it just means if you are tone deaf, then you probably shouldn't strive to be the next big music star.

## MAKING DREAMS COME TRUE REQUIRES A PLAN

We are all motivated by different dreams, and to obtain those dreams we need a plan of action—whether it is becoming the President of the United States or getting all As in high school. First, identify where you want to go, and then think about the steps it would take to get there. If you don't know where to begin, look at people who have already accomplished a similar goal. This could mean reading about past Presidents and how they got to the White House or speaking to an older sibling or friend who got all As.

Another great thing about goals and plans is that they are both flexible and can be changed. After doing some research and working toward a particular goal, if you find you no longer want to accomplish it, it's OK to change it. Or if a plan you made doesn't work, then toss it out and come up with a new one. Goals and plans aren't permanent and should evolve with you. Just make sure the reason you decide to stop striving for something is that you really don't have any more interest in it, and not that you think it is too hard to do.

## MAKE SMALL GOALS THAT WILL HELP YOU REACH YOUR LARGER GOAL

One problem with having long-term goals is they take a long time to accomplish. It can be very tiring to always work toward a particular goal but never feel as though you are any closer to achieving it. Thus, make short-term goals that help you reach your long-term goal. People get more pleasure from working hard and accomplishing several smaller goals along the way than achieving one big goal alone.

If your goal is to become the President of the United States, to do so you may be considering Harvard (or another prestigious institution). To get into Harvard, you must do well in high school. To do well in high school, you have to get an A in your biology class. To get an A in your biology class, means you have to get a 90 or higher on your test next week. Focus first on studying for your test. It's a small goal that helps you accomplish a much larger one. This will relieve the pressure of becoming President and allow you to concentrate on making the good grade.

There is more than one way to reach a goal.

Things don't always happen the way you want them to happen. Sometimes plans change. Unfortunately, no matter how hard you work toward a goal, sometimes you can come up short. Before a setback discourages you, remember there is more than one way to accomplish something.

Let's say you study very hard for that biology test and you still don't get an A. In fact, you study hard for every test, get tutoring, and try your very best, but you can't seem to break your C test grade average. Perhaps there are other ways to get an A in your biology class than just doing well on the tests. You can always ask your teacher if you can make up the grade with extra credit. Even if you can't get an A in biology no matter how hard you try, you don't have to give up on your ultimate goal. Not succeeding in a short-term goal doesn't automatically mean you can't reach your long-term goal. So, before you kiss Harvard goodbye, think about the situation. Are you certain that if you don't do well in this class you can't get into the college of your dreams? It might make it a little bit harder; perhaps you need to study more for the SAT or PSAT/NMSQT, but one bad grade will probably be insignificant in the admissions process. If you think about it, how many Presidents actually went to Harvard? Only seven. Harry Truman didn't even go to college! To reach your goal, it is OK to have a plan B, C, D, or even Z if necessary.

**GOAL WORKSHEET**

It is time to get those thoughts down on paper. Here is an example goal worksheet to help you stay focused and accomplish the things you want to do.

## Short-Term Goals
Objectives to be accomplished by_____

| Goal | Target Date | Already done toward it | What needs to be done |
|------|-------------|------------------------|------------------------|
| 1. | | | |
| 2. | | | |
| 3. | | | |
| 4. | | | |
| 5. | | | |

## Mid-Term Goals
Objectives to be accomplished by_____

| Goal | Target Date | Already done toward it | What needs to be done |
|------|-------------|------------------------|------------------------|
| 1. | | | |
| 2. | | | |
| 3. | | | |
| 4. | | | |
| 5. | | | |

## Long-Term Goals
Objectives to be accomplished by_____

| Goal | Target Date | Already done toward it | What needs to be done |
|------|-------------|------------------------|------------------------|
| 1. | | | |
| 2. | | | |
| 3. | | | |
| 4. | | | |
| 5. | | | |

## THE CAREER PATH

The word *career* can be a frightening word, especially for high school students who are constantly asked the question, "What do you want to do after school?" During adolescence, you face the monumental task of establishing a personal identity. This identity includes future job and career aspirations.

There are two big mistakes you can make when planning for the future: obsessing about it and ignoring it. The two extremes will either leave you anxious or ignorant when it comes time to take action. You should instead start preparing little by little for the future. This way when the time comes for you to make some crucial life decisions you will be more than ready to take on the responsibility.

The paths after high school are numerous. Today the most common path is some sort of continuing education. You, however, have several options for your post-graduation plans and do not necessarily have to attend a four-year university in order to be successful. You should evaluate your personal goals when deciding what is right for you. You can decide to go to a private or public four-year university, attend a two-year community college, enroll in a technical or vocational school, join the armed forces, take a stint to do volunteer work, or go straight into the workforce. Each post-graduation plan has its own advantages and disadvantages. Typically, the more schooling you have, the higher your income, but that is not always the case. You should look into every option before deciding what is right for you.

Below are some different options that lead toward different career paths. Read over each option carefully, even if you think you already know which path you want to take after high school. Plans change, or you just might discover an option here that is better suited to you. Each option lists possible careers achievable following that path. These lists are by no means comprehensive, but give you a general idea of some career choices available to you. Hopefully these lists will help you think about the steps necessary to achieve your personal goals.

## FOUR-YEAR UNIVERSITY

If you choose a traditional four-year college or university, you will work toward receiving a bachelor's degree in a particular field. You get the opportunity to be involved in a variety of on-campus activities and to take classes outside your major. Many schools also offer students internship opportunities that allow them to get "real world" experience. Four-year schools can cost anywhere from a few thousand dollars to several hundred thousand dollars. The average cost for a public four-year university is $12,804 per year and the average cost for a private four-year university is $32,184 per year.[1] There are scholarships, grants, and loans to help pay for this type of education.

## TYPES OF JOBS FOR BACHELOR'S DEGREE HOLDERS

1. Network systems and data communication analyst
2. Personal financial advisor
3. Newspaper reporter
4. Graphic designer
5. Computer software engineer
6. Forensic science technician
7. Public relations specialist
8. Museum conservator
9. Athletic trainer
10. Environmental engineer
11. School teacher

According to *CNN Money*, as of 2010, students with bachelor's degrees have an average *starting* salary of $48,288. (The actual amount depends on the degree. Students with specialized degrees such as petroleum engineering can make more than $75,000, while students with psychology degrees can make closer to $30,000.) Students who receive their bachelor's degrees can also continue their education by pursuing master's or doctoral degrees or professional certifications.

---

1    According to nces.ed.gov.

## TWO-YEAR COMMUNITY COLLEGE

Many community colleges offer students an inexpensive way to take general education courses in preparation for a larger four-year university. If you decide to get your basics out of the way at a community college, it is important to ensure your classes transfer to your next school. Two websites that can help you determine if your credits transfer are www.collegetransfer.net and www.tranfer.org. If you are seriously considering this option, know that nearly half of the students who attend a community college do not transfer to a larger university. It can be done; you just need to commit to your goals and don't let life sidetrack you.

You can also go to a community college to receive an associate's degrees. Associate's degrees take students an average of two years to complete, and they focus mainly on a chosen field of study. The average cost of attending a two-year community college is $7,629 per year.[2] Similar to four-year universities, community colleges also offer honors programs.

## JOBS FOR ASSOCIATE'S DEGREE HOLDERS

1. Broadcast technician or sound engineering technician
2. Flight attendant
3. Occupational therapist assistant
4. Physical therapist assistant
5. Computer support specialist
6. Dental hygienist
7. Radiation therapist
8. Fashion designer
9. Funeral director
10. Sonographer
11. Nurse

According to *U.S. News and World Report*, as of 2011, students with associate's degrees have an average *starting* salary of $35,000. (The actual amount depends on the degree. Students with high-demand degrees such

---

2    According to nces.ed.gov.

as computer programming can make as much as $60,000 while students who become dental assistants can make as little as $20,000.) Many of the allied health field careers require students only to receive associate's degrees.

## TECHNICAL AND VOCATIONAL SCHOOLS

Technical and vocational schools train students to perform specific types of job. If you want to go rather quickly into the workforce, you should consider attending one of these schools. On average, these schools cost students between $1,000 and $10,000 for the entire program. Students usually receive a license from these schools to perform their jobs.

## JOBS FOR TECHNICAL AND VOCATIONAL SCHOOL PROGRAM GRADUATES

1. Hair dresser
2. Make-up artist
3. Bartender
4. Automobile mechanic
5. Emergency medical technician
6. Electrician
7. Massage therapist
8. HVAC contractor
9. Welder
10. Plumber
11. Farmer

According to *www.TopTenReviews.com*, as of 2012, students who go to a technical or vocational school can have a wide range of starting salaries. The actual amount depends on the degree. While students who become massage therapists can make as little as $17,000, a diesel engine mechanic averages around $40,000.

## THE WORKFORCE

You do not necessarily have to receive any more education beyond high school to find a career. Many jobs offer on-the-job training or apprenticeships. Students who wish to start their careers early should look into this type of job. To begin your job search, use websites like www.careervoyages.com, www.monster.com, and www.snagajob.com to see what is out there for students who graduate from high school and do not pursue further formal education.

Consider looking into apprenticeships. You will be paid to learn essential job skills, and most likely will end up with a job once your training is complete. For more information on apprenticeships, contact the Bureau of Apprenticeship and Training Offices via www.doleta.gov or 877-US-2JOBS. Some of the following jobs may require a licensing test or other qualifications beyond high school.

1. Nanny
2. Home-care aide
3. Postal worker
4. Garbage collector
5. Real estate broker
6. Cable installer
7. Gas plant operator
8. Secretary
9. Store manager
10. Appliance repairman
11. Construction worker

According to the U.S. Census Bureau's 2010 statistics, students who decide to go straight into the workforce have an average *starting* salary of $25,090. (This amount also depends on the job selected. Some jobs offer as much as 40 dollars an hour while others pay as little as 10 dollars an hour.)

## THE MILITARY

Students who are interested in serving their country in a military career should look into the different branches of the armed forces. There are many advantages to pursuing a military career, including diverse career options and possible payment for college education, either through ROTC programs or through education stipends via the GI Bill. Students can enlist in the military when they are 18 or they can join through their colleges' ROTC programs to become officers. If you have no idea where you want to go after high school, the military is a great place to mature, develop leadership skills, learn discipline, gain practical work experience, and receive an education.

Students should examine the different branches and see which ones might be right for them. The length of a student's military contract is different for each branch. Students should discuss their personal questions with the local branch recruiters.

**Possible Military Jobs**
1. Military police
2. Special forces
3. Strategic intelligence officer
4. Military chaplain
5. Psychological operations specialist
6. Air traffic control operator
7. Pilot
8. Public affairs specialist
9. Field surgeon
10. Food safety officer
11. Research psychologist
12. Combat operations

The armed forces offer a variety of pay scales and career benefits. Students should contact recruiters for more information on specific jobs and signing bonuses.

## COLLEGE ALTERNATIVE PROGRAM

College Plus is an alternative college-based program that helps students use CLEP tests to place out of some courses, do distance learning for other courses, and blend work/intern experience to finish their degrees. More info can be found at www.collegeplus.org.

## EDUCATION TRAP

It is important that you don't fall into the trap of thinking only the jobs that require the most amount of schooling and offer the highest paychecks are better and more important. This simply isn't the case. You need to be aware that it isn't the job that makes a career respectable, but the person who performs that job. A janitor who does his job to the best of his ability is more respectable than a president who runs a country through deceitful acts. Remember: Every job is important, from the garbage collector to the Supreme Court judge; both are needed in order for our society to run smoothly. You should not let other people's opinions dictate how you feel about certain career paths. Be open to all sorts of career options. You might find something unglamorous very fulfilling!

## CONTRACT TO MYSELF

No matter what path you decide to take at 18, it is critical that you at least get your high school diploma. Students who fail to finish high school cripple their earning potential. The average starting salary of high school drop-outs is around $18,000, with limited prospects of advancement. Don't give up, and finish strong!

Here's a contract for you.

I_____ promise to complete high school.
_____(date)

## IS COLLEGE RIGHT FOR YOU?

College can be a wonderful experience. It is a great time to discover interests, meet lifelong friends, and grow as an individual. However, college can be a costly endeavor and is not right for every student. You should consider the reasons to go and not to go to college before you make up your mind.

Remember that there are several different ways to reach the same goal. You do not necessarily have to go to college to achieve your dreams. You shouldn't feel forced to go to college right after you finish high school either. While this is the most common time to go, some people just aren't ready for college at 18. That's OK. Do not choose a post-graduation plan based on what your friends have decided for themselves. Be honest with yourself and decide what is best for you.

## REASONS TO GO TO COLLEGE

1. College gives you the ability to continue your education and learn career skills.
2. College opens the doors to new and exciting opportunities like studying abroad.
3. College gives you a chance to explore your interests.
4. College allows you to have a lot of freedom with little responsibilities.
5. College allows you to meet a variety of new people from diverse backgrounds.

## REASONS TO SKIP OR POSTPONE COLLEGE

1. You are not motivated enough to do the work required.
2. You have other career aspirations that don't include college.
3. You have previous family obligations that require immediate attention.
4. You want to take some time off to pursue other passions.
5. You have a once-in–a-lifetime opportunity right after high school.

## LAME EXCUSES THAT SHOULDN'T KEEP YOU FROM GOING TO COLLEGE

1. **It's too expensive:** College can be expensive, but that shouldn't stop you from going. If you really want to go, then you will find a way. Look into scholarships, grants, loans, work-study programs, military stipends, and the possibility of transferring from a community college into a four-year school. Your earning power is so much greater after finishing a university education. Whatever money you spend on receiving a degree should pay itself back by the higher income potential you will gain. Although there is a risk at taking out loans, most students are able to find an option for higher learning that doesn't require an overwhelming loan payment after graduation.

2. **It will be too hard:** College can be a lot of hard work, but it can also be a lot of fun. Sure, you will have to take classes, study, and turn in homework, but schoolwork is only one aspect of college. The college system teaches teamwork, independence, personal initiative, and career preparation. Students who are afraid of the difficult classes should ease themselves into the college life by taking some lighter course loads in the beginning. You can always start at a community college if you're not ready for the big university at first. If easing yourself into the college experience slows you down, feel free to take summer courses to help you graduate in four years.

3. **My grades aren't good enough:** Even if you aren't the best student, there is a college out there for you. After all, grades are only one aspect of the admissions criteria. Colleges are interested in admitting students who will enrich their community, and that doesn't just mean academically. If your grades are extremely low, you can consider starting at a community college. Most community colleges don't have strict admissions requirements, and once you have proven yourself by getting good grades there, you can easily transfer into another school.

4.  **I don't know what I want to study:** Many students come into college without any idea of what subjects to study, much less which career path to choose. That is why schools offer introductory courses. Students can get a taste for many fields of study without declaring a major. Many students change their majors at some point during the college process. Not knowing is all part of the process. There are also different career tests on-line or books that can help you think about what you want to do.

5.  **I have something better to do:** Really? What is so important that you have to put off continuing your education? More likely than not, your other obligations can be continued while going to college.

6.  **None of my family has gone to college before me:** Many students are the first of their immediate family members to go to college. Just because none of your family members have done it before you doesn't mean you can't. In today's workforce, going to college is more important than ever, and it's necessary to be competitive. You should also look into scholarships for first-generation college students.

7.  **None of my friends are going to college:** This excuse is even worse than the one before. Who cares if nobody you know is going to college? Should that stop you? Of course not! Your friends have no real power over your decisions, so don't act like they do. College can be scary if you go alone, but soon enough you will meet many new friends.

## DELAYING COLLEGE

You don't always have to go to college right after high school. Some students choose to delay college for a year or two. You can even apply for college during your senior year of high school, but ask for a deferral after you have been accepted. Most colleges let you delay entering for a year.

Students who choose to wait a year before going to college have what is commonly referred to as a "gap year." This gap of time between high school and college is often spent working a job, traveling abroad, or teaching English in a foreign country. Some students need to take this time for a break from their studies. If you choose to have a gap year, don't waste your time. Use your year to reflect on your future and gain some maturity. Gaining real-life experience not only looks great on future college applications, but can also help you find direction in life.

*Even if you are not considering college right now, you should still take the SAT. The College Board holds your score two years and most colleges will take old test scores. Once out of school, you may forget some basic math and instead of having to restudy these subjects, you will have your score waiting for you.*

 **THINK ABOUT IT**

You don't have to go to college right after high school if you aren't prepared for it or need some time away from the classroom. If you are going to take time off, you should realize that it is harder to get back into the school mode once you have been out for a year or more. If you are serious about considering this path, do your research and still take the critical standardized tests in high school. This allows you to get them out of the way and keeps your options open. Delaying school is just as important a decision as going, so give serious thought to this option and don't just pick it because it sounds easy.

Here are some resources to help you better understand what you can do during your gap year.

www.interimprograms.com
www.leapnow.org
www.takingoff.net
www.timeoutassociates.com

# GUIDE FOR PARENTS HELPING YOUR CHILD ESTABLISH GOALS

Every parent wants their student to be successful. There is no single way, however, to define success. Parents should start by helping their students establish goals.

Beyond encouraging your daughter to make practical goals, have her create lofty ones as well. Imagining she can accomplish something difficult is the first step to her actually accomplishing it. Many students don't let themselves dream big because they are afraid of failing. It is important that your son recognize that if he does not try to achieve big things, he will never reach big goals. Don't let the fear of failure keep him from exploring new interests and working toward something great.

Encourage your daughter to think outside the box and not to just dream of being a rock star, athlete, or movie star. Have her explore her interests and help her come up with goals.

Talk to your child on a regular basis about his or her goals, fears, and plans to reach those dreams. Parents do not necessarily need to push their students toward greatness, but should serve as goal cheerleaders. Your student may not always thank you for the encouragement, but your words go a long way in building your child's self-esteem.

Lastly, parents need to teach their children to be flexible when making their goals. There are many different ways to reach one goal, and sometimes it takes several different attempts before a student can reach it. Don't let your son be discouraged if he tries more than once to accomplish something and fails. Teach him to focus on what is important and decide if the goal is worth pursuing. If it is, then have him try again.

## HELPING YOUR STUDENT DECIDE IF COLLEGE IS RIGHT

In today's society, gaining a college degree is becoming more and more important. Many jobs require at least a bachelor's degree to even apply. College is also a wonderful time for your student to learn and grow. Some of the best memories your child will ever make will most likely be during the college years.

Going to college after high school is very popular, but the reality is that college is not for everyone. According to the National Center for Education statistics, less than 60 percent of college freshmen complete their degree within a 6-year period.[3] Although most students are willing to put in the amount of work needed to succeed in college, some are not. Students who have no intention of working hard should seriously consider whether college is the right choice for them.

College may not be the best option for your child. The worst mistake students can make when planning for their future is blindly picking one option. Encourage your son to seriously consider all the options available to him and talk with people in the various career fields he may be considering in order to understand the expectations and job functions of each different path. Students who thoughtfully consider their options are more likely to choose the path that is right for them.

No matter what, have your daughter prepare as if she were going to a four-year college or university even if she is not sure about it yet. Four-year colleges and universities have strict application processes and require the most out of their applicants. Whether your son chooses to go to college or not, you do not want him to be excluded from the opportunity because of a poor academic record. High school students who adequately prepare for a four-year college or university will also be preparing for all the other possible options. Therefore, make sure your child continues to perform well in his or her high school courses, takes the necessary standardized tests, and continues with volunteer and extracurricular activities.

Your child will learn and grow tremendously during the next several years, and you want to make sure that if college is the best choice, he or she will have a competitive edge in scholarship competitions. More than this, teaching your child to achieve in high school will help him or her learn how to achieve in all other aspects of the future.

---

3    http://nces.ed.gov/datalab/tableslibrary/viewtable.aspx?tableid=3632

## PARENTS' HOMEWORK

The two main reasons students fail to complete college are lack of finances for school and an inability to handle the school workload. On both of these counts, you can help your child be ready for success.

Firstly, paying for college does not need to be a burden. There are many options to help you and your child finance a degree. Read Chapter 17 to help you understand how to help your son pay for education. Once you have read that chapter, make a game plan for financial success. There is a good reason for students to concentrate on obtaining scholarships early.

Secondly, talk with your daughter about the reality of the college workload and discuss whether going to school right after high school is right for her. On average, students should expect to study five to six hours a day on top of their actual class schedule during college. If your child in high school shows little resolve to complete her work, she may not be the best candidate for a full college load.

Nothing needs to be decided right now; there is still time for students to grow and mature academically. If graduation time arrives and your child is still not ready for college but may want to go in the future, talk about the possibilities of taking time off to travel abroad, work for the Peace Corps, or volunteer for humanitarian organizations like Red Cross.

# CHAPTER FOURTEEN: CHOOSING A SCHOOL

I T IS simply not enough to decide to continue your education after high school. Once you have made the decision, you have to decide where you want to go. Not including the military, there are three main educational options after high school: a community college, a four-year university, and a technical or vocational school.

The decision of where to go depends on your goals for education and many factors beyond that. You must decide on what type of school, the price range, the location, potential majors, and so on. There are many different reasons to choose different schools, and you must decide what is best for you.

While family input is a very important factor in this choice, you must remember that this is your journey, and ultimately the decision rests with you.

As you prepare, you must carefully consider all the options in order to make the best choice. Choosing the best college is only the first of many decisions to come. As you consider all your options, talk about the advantages, think about the disadvantages, and look into all the different factors that contribute to this decision.

## COLLEGE SEARCH

When you are looking at schools, you should make a list of personal criteria for your future college. Decide what size school you feel comfortable going to, what type of atmosphere you would like to experience, and any special organizations or classes you want access to. You can make your personal criteria as broad or as specific as you like. More specific information on these criteria is covered later in this chapter.

Many students try to sidestep the difficulty of deciding what schools are right for them by choosing schools that are right for other people. It can be a serious mistake to go to school because a friend, sibling, or boyfriend or girlfriend is going there. Just because a school might be perfect for them does not mean that it will be perfect for you. It would be a shame to be miserable for four years because you didn't want to go to school by yourself or leave a relationship behind. (Plus, with Skype and cheap airfare, long-distance relationships are a lot easier to maintain than they once were.)

### RESEARCH IS KEY

Once you have made a list of things you want out of a college, it is time to start doing research on schools. Great schools exist all across the nation, and around the world, so don't get your sights stuck on just once particular school or type of school. Branch out and see what is available.

Start your college search on the Internet to help you get a good idea of what is out there and to familiarize yourself with college websites. Next you should talk with your family, friends, and mentors about the colleges you are thinking about attending and why you are interested in those particular schools. You can also visit your local college night offered by your school district or homeschool co-op to speak with college recruiters and get more information about schools. Keep all the information in the college and career notebook.

Hopefully, you will research some of the best schools in each particular field. Remember there are *many* great schools all across the nations. Do not settle for just schools with name recognition.

Try to identify ten possible college choices. Request information from those schools and try to contact their admissions counselors if you have any additional questions. (Use your separate college email address.) Remember to print out the colleges' information, including application and any supplemental materials. Also, request to receive information in the mail. School informational packets are great ways to see what the schools like to highlight, as well as to get a broad overview of the schools.

As you look at schools, compare them to the list of personal criteria you made. If you find out that one of your "dream schools" is not for you, then take it off the list and look for another school. There may not be just one perfect fit, but many to choose from.

*Fill out the college comparison worksheet inside your college and career notebook.*

**WHEN LOOKING ON THE INTERNET, TRY THESE SITES FIRST**

You can do all your background work on colleges without ever leaving your own house. You can visit school websites, use college search engines, or just explore your options. When you are first starting out and have no idea what type of school you want to attend or program you want to study, the following websites are all great places to help you begin to identify and narrow down your options. You can start by looking up size, majors, or even school rankings. These websites will also expose you to schools you have never thought about. Once you get an idea of what you are looking for, you can go to particular college websites to request more information concerning the schools.

- www.collegeboard.com
- www.collegematch.com
- www.colleges.usnews.rankingsandreviews.com/best-colleges
- www.ctcl.org/
- www.nces.ed.gov/collegenavigator.

## SCHOOL CRITERIA

There is more to college than just academics. When considering what college is right for you, look at the school as a whole. Think about your personality, spirituality, maturity, as well as your academic and career goals. Also think about the social environment you feel most comfortable in. Search the school's website to find out basic information such as test scores, percentage of graduates, and scholarship opportunities.

You might find that a school fits you perfectly in one area, but not at all in another. No school will be perfect, but there are so many options that you can find one that is pretty close. Do not try to make a school fit just because you want it to, but try to find one that you will get the most out of academically, socially, and emotionally.

## THE SIZE OF THE SCHOOL MATTERS

Colleges come in all different shapes and sizes. You can find schools where you will be just another face in the crowd of thousands of students, or you can find one where your own personality will shine amongst a small group of peers. Bigger schools have more options, but smaller schools are more personal.

You can go to a small college that has fewer than 5,000 students. You can go to a medium college that has between 5,000 and 15,000 students. You can go to a large college that has between 15,000 and 30,000 students. Or you could go to a huge college that has more than 30,000 students.

Which size school you pick depends on your personality and your goals for college. Smaller colleges allow you to get to know many of your fellow students as well as the faculty. These schools tend to be private liberal arts schools. Because of their size, they are often limited in the resources and options that are available to you. Conversely, huge state schools can offer a tremendous number of options in both disciplines to study and extracurricular activities. However, you will not get the same amount of individual attention and guidance as in a smaller school. Medium-sized schools offer a balance between the two extremes: You have more options than a smaller school, but a tight-knit sense of community may be lacking.

Before you decide exactly what size school you want to go to, visit campuses in each size range. This way you can get a feel for what it would be like. You do not have to visit colleges you are seriously considering because all you want to know is if you feel more comfortable on a small, medium, large, or huge campus.

## LARGE SCHOOL VS. SMALL SCHOOL

| | |
|---|---|
| • More areas of specialized study<br>• More courses in each area<br>• More anonymity<br>• Greater range of extracurricular activities and organizations<br>• Larger libraries<br>• More laboratory facilities<br>• Graduate departments | • More personal atmosphere<br>• Small classes with more discussion and interaction<br>• Greater chance for individual participation<br>• Easier access to faculty<br>• More flexible programs |

## ENVIRONMENT IS IMPORTANT

The location of your school can greatly influence your college experience. Things like climate, size of town or city, and distance from home can all influence how much you enjoy being on your college campus. Some location attributes might not bother you at all while others might be deal-breakers.

Think about your personal preferences and decide what is right for you. Think about whether you enjoy cold or hot weather, if you want to be in the hustle and bustle of a city, and whether you will frequently visit your home. Many students forget to consider geographic location when picking a college. It would be unfortunate for a student who really likes city nightlife to end up at a school that is three hours away from the nearest big city. Likewise, students who hate being cold may not want to seriously consider schools that spend six months every year covered in snow.

 **THINK ABOUT IT**

Ask yourself these questions about location for the schools you are seriously considering. Write down your answers in your college and career notebook.

- What is the climate like?
- Is the college located in a city, small town, or rural area?
- What type of outdoor activities will the location offer?
- What is the culture like?
- How far is the college from other major cities or sites of interests?

- How far is the college from my home?
- What changes will I have to get used to so I can live comfortably in this new environment?
- What location factors are most important to me?

## FIELDS AND MAJORS

Schools today offer a diverse selection of programs. Some schools offer broad majors such as English or elementary education while others offer specific majors like American diplomacy and early Middle Eastern history. Which major, or majors, you choose in school will directly influence the career you have after school. Broad majors give you flexibility in your choices while specific ones give you a deeper expertise.

Some majors do not lend themselves to jobs immediately after graduation. Majors like psychology, speech therapy, philosophy, and pre-med typically require some type of post-college education in order to use those degrees in the field. Majors such as accounting, computer science, journalism, and education do not typically require additional school after college graduation. Just because you are in college to help prepare for your career does not mean you need to pick majors that do not require any school afterward—as long as you keep this in mind when thinking about future majors.

Remember: Not all schools have the same majors, so if a specific major is important to you, be sure to apply to schools that offer that major.

Here is a list of popular fields for undergraduate degrees.

- Agriculture
- Computer science
- Education
- Engineering
- English and literature
- Ethnic studies
- Foreign languages
- General and interdisciplinary studies

- Mathematics
- Military science and protective services
- Parks and recreation resources
- Philosophy, religion, and theology
- Public affairs and law
- Biology
- Social sciences
- Visual and performing arts

## ACADEMIC REQUIREMENTS

Always check on the admission requirements when you are researching schools. Some schools have very strict admissions requirements while others are more lenient. Knowing what you need to do to apply will help you plan effectively for the applications. If one school relies heavily on SAT scores, then you know that you need to study extra hard for that test in particular; if another one focuses on volunteer hours, then you can take on a few more community service projects.

Do not spend all of your time trying to be the ideal candidate for one particular school, but do be aware of the different aspects that colleges and universities use to evaluate their candidates.

## PRICE

Going to college can be expensive. Along with the actual tuition, there are many hidden costs that you might not be aware of.

Students who go to schools out of their home states usually pay more than students who go to public universities in their home states. Make sure you check for in-state versus out-of-state tuition rates. Some schools have specific scholarship programs to assist out-of-state students.

Along with tuition, every school requires you to pay a certain amount of fees. These fees are usually included in the overall price on schools' websites or brochures. These fees pay for things like access to the school gym, use of the library, and other resources the school offers.

Your room and board are not typically included in the tuition and fees. This means you will have to add the price of your housing and meal plans into your calculations. The price for room and board varies with the school, housing accommodations, and types of meal plans offered. Most schools will give you an estimate of the price for room and board with information on the price of tuition.

Once you are in school you will also have to purchase your textbooks and school supplies. The cost of a semester's books can range anywhere from $100 to $1,000. Therefore, it is important for you to cut down the cost by trying to find the best deals possible. It is most affordable to purchase used books from other students, the bookstore, or on-line bookstores. Students can now even rent their textbooks for a certain fee.

Another hidden cost is that of transportation to and from the school. Depending on where you decide to go to school, you can have minimal transportation cost— like riding the subway back and forth to your home—or very large transportation costs—like flying halfway around the world to come home. Make sure you include transportation in the overall cost assessment of your schools.

Lastly, you will have personal expenses when you go to school. If you live away from your parents, you will have to pay for everything yourself. This includes dinners out with friends, movie tickets, and all the little extras Mom and Dad usually cover. You also need to consider the cost of dorm room accessories, your computer, or anything else directly related to going to school.

*Don't let the price of college keep you from going. For more information on paying for school, read Chapter 17.*

## THE COLLEGE VISIT

College is too huge a commitment to make blindly. A school might look perfect on its website, but that doesn't always mean that it will feel right in person. Sometimes you can decide a school is right or wrong for you just by being there. It might not be possible to visit every school you want, but try to visit at least your top two schools.

Colleges and universities understand the importance of prospective students' visiting their campuses; throughout the year, they host special preview days so students can get to know the schools better. Even if you can't make it on the special preview days, don't skip out on visiting the campus. Your admissions counselor will be happy to set up a day for you to tour the school. Some colleges even help pay the travel expenses for out-of-town guests. Talk to the admissions department about what options you have when visiting the campus.

Visiting a campus will also allow you to get a sense of the school's ambiance. Ask yourself questions like "Do I feel safe walking around campus at night? Can I live in a dorm room like this? Are these the types of people that I could be friends with?" Every college has a unique atmosphere. Try to use your visit to get a feel for campus life.

## COLLEGE VISIT CHECKLIST

Use this checklist when you decide to visit a college campus.

1. Check the school's website to see if there are any specific college visit dates.
2. Contact your admissions counselor to schedule a visit.
3. Try to go on a weekday to get a feel for the campus.
4. Ask if you can schedule any mandatory interviews on your visit date.
5. Ask if the school you are visiting offers any reimbursement for travel expenses.
6. Make travel arrangements.
7. Tell your high school teachers you will be absent during your travel dates.
8. If possible, speak with the dean, professors, and any important faculty member in your prospective field of study.
9. Sit in on an actual class.
10. Take a tour of the campus.
11. Visit the bookstore, student center, library, and any building of particular interest to you.
12. Try to spend the night in a dorm to get a feel for the housing.
13. Eat at least one meal in a cafeteria.
14. Meet with your admissions counselor face-to-face; after all, this is the person who is helping you through this process. Thank him or her for all the hard work on your behalf.

15. Find time to wander around the campus by yourself.
16. Talk with students, both in and out of your potential department, and ask them about their experiences.
17. Visit the surrounding area of the school to get a feel for the location.

## QUESTIONS FOR THE ADMISSIONS COUNSELOR

Before speaking with your admissions counselor, check out the school's website. Oftentimes this information is readily available. Don't make a fool out of yourself for asking something that you could have easily answered on your own. If you have searched the website and cannot find the answers to the following questions, then ask your admissions counselor.

1. What is the average size of the freshman class?
2. How many of those students return the following year?
3. What makes this college or program special?
4. How easy is it to switch majors?
5. How does this school help students adjust to college life?
6. Is there a Greek life (i.e., sororities and fraternities) at this campus?
7. How important is the Greek system on this campus?
8. What types of organizations are on campus that a student can be involved with?
9. What do the tuition and fees cover?
10. What are some hidden expenses I need to be aware of?
11. Are there work-study jobs available?
12. How is campus safety guaranteed?
13. What are some important housing issues I need to be aware of?
14. Are freshman allowed to live off campus?
15. Are freshman allowed to have a car on campus?
16. What is the campus parking situation?
17. Does the school offer campus-wide tutors?
18. How big is the average class size?

## QUESTIONS FOR CURRENT STUDENTS

1. What is the thing you like best about this college?
2. What is the thing you dislike most?
3. Why did you choose this school?
4. If you had to do it over again, would you pick this school?
5. If I need help, how accessible are the college professors?
6. How much help does your academic advisor give you?
7. What do you like most about your department?
8. Do you like the professors?
9. Are the classes taught mostly by professors or by teaching assistants?
10. How diverse is the student body?
11. How is the cafeteria?
12. What do you do for fun here?
13. How easy is it to make friends here?
14. How close are the local restaurants and shopping centers?
15. How is it living in these dorms?
16. If I go here, which dorm should I apply to get in?
17. What is one thing you wish someone would have told you before you came here?

## OTHER RESOURCES

Depending on your situation, you may have some additional considerations when choosing your school. Here are some supplementary resources for minority and disabled students.

**College Resources for Minority Students**

www.inroads.org
www.nacme.org
www.naacp.org
www.nul.org
www.uncf.org
www.aihec.org

www.gmsp.org
www.hacu.net
www.hsf.net

**College Resources for Disabled Students**
www.ahead.org
www.add.org
www.chadd.org
www.cldinternational.org
www.heath.gwu.edu
www.interdys.org
www.ldanatl.org
www.nichcy.org
www.rfbd.org
*Students with disabilities or diabetes can get priority in registering.*

## CHOOSING TO APPLY

Now that you've considered your options, researched your top schools, and visited campuses, you should have a good feel for the types of things you want out of a college or university. You might have only one school that is perfect for you, or you may have too many. Nonetheless, try to apply to five or six schools. Your list should include a couple of schools that you are pretty sure you can get into, a couple of schools that you may or may not get into, and a couple of dream schools that might be more selective in their admissions process. Having a mixture of safe, realistic, and dream schools will give you security, flexibility, and motivation for school choices.

Do not fall into the trap of applying to only one school. The college admissions process is completely out of your hands, and you want to keep your options open. The probability of acceptance plus financial aid packages varies from school to school. Multiple good options will ensure that you do not get left empty-handed in the spring!

## THINK ABOUT IT

The college search may seem overwhelming, but do not freak out. Chances are you could be happy at any number of places. Solidify this idea by thinking about your top school choices.

Safe Schools

_____
_____
_____

Realistic Schools

_____
_____
_____

Dream Schools

_____
_____
_____

## COLLEGE SEARCH DOS

- Do spend time researching different schools.
- Do request information from each school.
- Do look at each school's admission criteria.
- Do branch out and look at schools you hadn't originally considered.
- Do look at the financial commitment for each school.
- Do be realistic in your expectations.
- Do look at different programs offered by each school.
- Do visit _all_ the schools you are applying to if you can.
- Do speak with actual students at each school you are applying to.
- Do apply to about five or six different schools.
- Do apply to at least one "safe" school where you are almost guaranteed to be accepted.

- Do apply to at least one "realistic" school where you will most likely be accepted.
- Do apply to at least one "dream" school you would like to go to but are uncertain that you will be accepted into.
- Do find out if the college's mission statement or focus fits with your goals and personality.
- Do find out what the college is known for and see if it's a good fit for you.
- Do speak with others who have gone through this process before you.
- Do ask about the overall safety of the campus.

## COLLEGE SEARCH DON'TS

- Don't just look into big-name schools.
- Don't choose a school just because all your friends are going there.
- Don't go to school just to follow a relationship.
- Don't try to make a school a good fit just because you want it to be.
- Don't get your heart set on just one school.
- Don't go blindly to a school without visiting the campus.
- Don't be afraid of taking chances and applying to more selective schools.
- Don't be fooled by websites and brochures; some colleges are a lot different than portrayed.
- Don't get overwhelmed or stressed out. Remember that you can always change your mind later or transfer schools.

 **THINK ABOUT IT**

Finding a school that fits you is critical to your success. Think carefully about the different factors that were brought up in this chapter (size of school, environment, distance from home, etc.). Loneliness or feeling out of place is a key reason many students drop out of college. The college years are some of the best and hardest times of growing up. Be honest with yourself about your personal needs when choosing a school.

Factors that are important to me:

_____

_____

_____

_____

_____

_____

# GUIDE FOR PARENTS HELPING YOUR CHILD PICK THE RIGHT COLLEGE

Trying to pick the right school can be very stressful for students. Teens do not always know what they want and often fool themselves into thinking they want something that isn't a good fit. Your child will spend at least nine months of every school year living in the place he or she picks for college. Nine months is a long time to be miserable. Plus, happier students perform better.

The most important advice you can give your son is to be honest with himself when considering certain schools. He should take an honest look at his likes, dislikes, and preferences before picking a school. If your daughter hates hot weather, then she probably should not go to a school in the desert. Or if your son is a homebody and does not like venturing far from family, then he should probably not go to a school that is several thousand miles from home.

## PARENTS' HOMEWORK

Many high school seniors obsess about finding the perfect school. Students should understand that there may be more than one perfect school for them. While all colleges have some specific aspects that make them unique, similar schools will offer students a similar experience.

When trying to narrow down college choices, make a general guideline for what students do and do not want in a school. Then explore all the schools that fall into those guidelines. General guidelines allow students to identify the type of school they are looking for while still keeping many options open. For example, if your son wants to go to a mid-size, private university located in a warm climate, these general guidelines allow him to narrow down the options without limiting him to specific schools.

This flexibility allows students to compare other aspects of colleges like price or campus atmosphere, and ensure that no matter which school they pick, students will be generally happy with the experience.

## KEEPING TRACK

After your child has narrowed down his or her college search, it is very important to make sure you stay on track with deadlines, applications, scholarship information, etc. Hang up a large poster board (divided into one section per school), include important dates along with the following information, and make sure to put a check box next to each item:

**NAME OF COLLEGE**

    Application-Custom/Common

    Supplemental documents_____

    Resume: Mailed____Emailed_____

    Scholarship Offered_____

    Records Sent_____

    Transcript Sent_____

    SAT Sent_____

    ACT Sent_____

    SAT Subject test required

    Early Action_____

    Money Awarded_____

# CHAPTER FIFTEEN:
# STANDARDIZED TEST PREP

**M**OST STUDENTS are required to take an entrance exam before applying to college. Each of these schools has a minimum score requirement that applicants must meet in order to be considered for admissions and for academic scholarship opportunities. All schools will take either the SAT or the ACT, and if they prefer one, they will convert the score. For example, a 1300 (Math/Critical Reading) on the SAT is equivalent to a 29 on the ACT.

Tests like the PSAT/NMSQT and the PLAN help students prepare for their harder counterparts (i.e., SAT and ACT), and studying for these tests should be a priority in your first couple of years of high school. The PSAT/NMSQT is particularly important because it can qualify you for amazing scholarship offers in your junior year.

Regardless of whether you are planning on going to college, take these important standardized tests while you are in high school and basic skills, such as algebra and grammar, are fresh on your mind. Typically, your scores are good for a few years after high school. This will allow you to have the option of going to the school of your choice later on.

Keep in mind most colleges take just the highest scores, so take the tests as many times as you want. The SAT offers "Score Choice," which allows you to send only your best scores to colleges. However, some schools (like Ivy League) may want to see all your test scores. If you are aiming at a top-tier school, practice long and hard before taking the *real* test. If the cost for these tests is an issue, many high school counselors have fee waivers for students who qualify. These waivers can cover subject tests as well as the PSAT/NMSQT. *Homeschooled families can also apply and be eligible for waivers at their local high schools.*

Some schools are "test-optional," (i.e. no entrance exam required) including many music, technical, and religious schools. For a complete list, go to www.fairtest.org.

## THE PSAT/NMSQT

The PSAT/NMSQT is more than just a "practice" SAT; it is a qualifying test for the National Merit Scholarship Program. It is offered once a year in October. Check the SSS (Student Search Service) box on the answer sheet in your junior year to allow your scores to be available to participating colleges. Do not check this box in other grades or your mailbox may be inundated with junk mail.

This test is similar to the SAT, and the same test-taking strategies can be used. Incredible scholarship offers are available to students who rank in the top one to three percent. Qualifying test scores for scholarships vary by state (e.g., in 2011 students in South Carolina qualified for semi-finalist with a score of 209 out of 240).

Although the PSAT/NMSQT counts toward the scholarship contest only in a student's junior year, freshmen and sophomores should take it for practice. When students takes the test their freshman year (and sometimes in eighth grade), then they would not check off any grade-level boxes since there is only a box for sophomores and juniors. Taking the test early in high school can help students become familiar with the test and identify their strengths and weaknesses early so they will have time to improve their scores since their test booklet will be returned to the school. Homeschooled students can receive their test booklet in the mail if they use the homeschool code for their state. See page 328 for a list.

More information on the PSAT/NMSQT can be found at www.collegeboard.com.

## THE NATIONAL MERIT PROCESS

Once the test has been administered, a total of 50,000 students are originally chosen out of all the students from the top percentage from each state. Then the National Merit Corporation will notify about 16,000 of those students the following August that they have achieved semi-finalist standing. To be named a semifinalist, students must reach a certain qualifying score. This score varies from state to state, but is usually in the top two to three percent of test takers. This score is the sum of the three scores from the critical reading, math, and writing sections of the test. Each section is worth 80 points, with a possible total score of 240.

A list of semifinalists' scores will be available to be sent to all four-year U.S. colleges and universities and the students' local newspapers. Students must check the "student search box" on the PSAT/NMSQT to have their test scores available for participating colleges to see. (Have your student do this only in his or her junior year because tests taken in other years do not count toward the scholarship contest).

## FROM SEMIFINALIST TO FINALIST

The first step to becoming a National Merit finalist is paperwork. If your student is a semifinalist, all he needs to do to qualify for finalist standing is to complete and return the National Merit scholarship application before the appointed deadline. This application will ask for a complete high school transcript, an activities/awards/leadership positions list, letters of recommendations, and a self-descriptive essay. The importance of the application packet cannot be stressed enough. If an application is not received before the deadline, that student will automatically be disqualified from continuation in the program.

Students are also required to take the SAT-1 and earn scores that confirm the PSAT/NMSQT performance. The National Merit Scholarship Corporation wants to ensure that students deserved the PSAT/NMSQT score and did not merely get lucky. Students should take the November SAT right after the October PSAT/NMSQT. Since they will already be primed to take the first test, the second one should be a breeze.

Be prepared with good records of all your student's accomplishments and a list of potential letter-writers. Make a copy of all the information and ask for additional letters of recommendation to store on file. In case something happens to the packet, you want to have a backup. The National Merit Scholarship Corporation is also very considerate of home educators and will send specific information to homeschoolers about how to proceed with completing the paperwork required.

When asking for letters of recommendation, make sure to include the "brag-sheet" (résumé) of the student's accomplishments. This way the person writing the recommendation will easily remember good things about your student. Don't underestimate the importance of this letter; the committee wants to have a broader picture of your students. Homeschooling parents can write the letter for their students; however, it might be wiser to pick more unbiased perspectives, such as an outside teacher, boss, coach, pastor, etc.

Make copies of all the documents and mail the packet on time using a tracking system such as Registered Mail. Once you have sent in the application packet, call the National Merit Scholarship Corporation to confirm the arrival of the packet and that your student has finished all the necessary steps. Make sure to do this in plenty of time before the deadline, so if there is a problem, you will have enough time to send in another packet. You can contact the National Merit Corporation at 847-866-5100.

From 16,000 semifinalists, approximately 15,000 will be named finalists. Certificates of Merit are sent to the finalists in February.

### FINALISTS TO SCHOLAR

From the 15,000 finalists, approximately 7,900 National Merit scholars will be chosen. There are three types of National Merit scholarship awards: National Merit $2,500 scholarships, corporate-sponsored scholarships, and college-sponsored scholarships. All finalists are considered for the 2,500 National Merit $2,500 awards. The 1,200 corporate-sponsored awards are only available to students who meet certain criteria. There are also 4,200 college-sponsored awards for finalists. Students should contact the institutions of their choice to see if they offer specific scholarships for National Merit finalists.

A committee of experienced college admissions officers and high school counselors will meet in late January to choose the winners of the National Merit $2,500 scholarships. The committee members evaluate each finalist's academic record (course load and difficulty level, depth and breadth of subjects studied, and grades earned); scores on PSAT/NMSQT and SAT-1; the student's essay; leadership experience; and the school's recommendation. The following March, the corporation will notify the selected National Merit scholars and corporate-sponsored scholarship recipients. The college-sponsored winners are notified in April through June.

## ALTERNATIVE TESTING METHOD

If your student misses the junior-year PSAT/NMSQT, then check into the alternative testing method, which allows a student to take the SAT in place of the PSAT and the scores will be converted. Contact the National Merit Corporation before March 1 and let them know you missed the test. Students can take the November, December, January, March, May, and June SAT in exchange for the PSAT/NMSQT and the highest scores will be used for the National Merit scholarship contest. Visit www.collegeboard.com for more information. A high school counselor or homeschool parent will need to sign the necessary paperwork for the alternative testing method.

## THE SAT

The SAT is a test of reasoning and critical thinking. Correct answers can be determined using basic logic skills. Offered seven times a year, students can take it as many times as they want. 2400 is a perfect score.

The scores are not averaged, and most colleges usually take the highest score or create what is called a "super score" by combining the highest scores from different sections of multiple tests. Students don't have to send every score to every school—this is called "score choice."

More information on the SAT can be found at www.collegeboard.com.

## THE PSSS

Some schools offer the Preliminary SAT Scoring Service (PSSS), which is an additional service offered by the makers of both the PSAT/NMSQT and the SAT. This service offers a practice test that is similar to the SAT and helps students familiarize themselves with the tests without having the scores go on their record. For more information about the PSSS, go to http://professionals. collegeboard.com/k-12/prepare/psss.

## THE EXPLORE

Created for eighth- and ninth-grade students, EXPLORE is the first of three tests created by the makers of the ACT. This test helps students become familiar with the concepts they will learn in high school and prepare them for the other two tests, the PLAN and the ACT.

Unlike the PSAT/NMSQT, SAT, and ACT, the EXPLORE and PLAN tests are not nationally administered tests. You will need to check with local school districts to find a location that offers these tests.

More information on the EXPLORE can be found at www.actstudent. org/explore/.

## THE PLAN

The PLAN is the second pre-ACT test students can take, this time in their sophomore year of high school, and tests tenth-graders' college readiness. The same people who make the ACT produce this test, and taking it can help students prepare for the ACT. Students who take the PLAN will be tested in English, math, science, and reading. The test also includes a section on career possibilities to help students think about future jobs.

More information about the PLAN can be found at www.actstudent.org/plan/.

## THE ACT

The ACT examines a student's knowledge of English, math (including trigonometry), reading, and science (including physics reasoning). The ACT is offered six times a year. Students who perform better on content-based tests rather than reasoning-based tests should consider taking the ACT as well as the SAT. Thirty-six is a perfect score.

More information on the ACT can be found at www.act.org.

## PRACTICING FOR STANDARDIZED TESTS

You should always take a practice test before you start studying for the actual test. Taking a practice test sets your baseline score and helps you establish which test subjects need improvement.

You can pick up free SAT, PSAT/NMSQT, and ACT practice test booklets from the guidance counselor's office at most local high schools or on-line. These booklets are free to any student, regardless if the student attends the particular high school. Homeschooled students can therefore take advantage of these free materials as well.

As you study for these tests, you should keep records of your progress in the test prep examination inventory of the college and career planning notebook. Every time you take a practice test or actual test, record your score. This way you can chart your progress.

You can learn how to ace standardized tests such as the SAT and PSAT/NMSQT at www.collegeprepgenius.com.

## TEST DAY ID

Students will need to have a picture ID when taking standardized tests. If you don't have a school ID or you are homeschooled, one can be obtained by sources such as the DPS or through the HSLDA.

## TEST SCORES AND SCHOLARSHIPS

Universities use your test scores to determine scholarship eligibility. (The higher the score, the bigger the scholarships.) Students should start test prep as early as ninth grade (seventh grade if they are doing the Duke Talent Identification Program or other talent searches). The longer students wait to learn how to take the test, the less time they will have to improve.

Scholarships could include full ride, full tuition, free room and board, honors dorms, money to study abroad, graduate money, and more.

## TWO MISUNDERSTOOD TESTS

The SAT is a logic-based test and is designed to showcase a student's ability to use critical-thinking and problem-solving skills. The ACT is content-based and reflects more of what was learned during high school. Nonetheless, this contrast isn't exactly airtight. Many questions on the ACT test critical thinking, and the range of material on the SAT is based on basic high school knowledge.

Out of the two, the SAT is the more widely taken. Assessing three sections (math, vocabulary, and reading comprehension), the SAT tries to evaluate the "innate ability" of students. It does so by using tricky and confusing phrasing to determine skill level (i.e., the student's performance under pressure and the ability to identify what's being asked). It isn't necessarily measuring comprehension on a specific subject, but rather how well a student can think through a problem. The SAT has shorter sections and is scored on a scale of 200 to 800 per subject. Improving an SAT score requires a student to understand basic test-taking tricks.

The ACT is designed to test skill levels in English, math, reading, and science reasoning. The ACT focuses on the knowledge acquired during high school, meaning that the test assesses subjects and skills found in a typical student's curriculum. It does contain trigonometry and an optional longer writing section. ACT scores are only two digits, and sometimes a single point can be the difference between getting into college and not. To do well, students must study actual subject matter.

Both the ACT and the SAT ultimately test your ability to think, and both cover the basics of a high school education. Therefore, learning critical thinking skills can benefit both tests and can also help on other standardized exams such as AP tests, CLEP, LSAT, ISEE, etc. More than that, the skills used in preparing for the SAT will also be extremely helpful in preparing for the PSAT/NMSQT.

## DOING WELL ON THE SAT

Many smart students often bomb standardized tests like the SAT and PSAT/NMSQT because they do not understand the structure of the test. It is not content-based, like typical school tests or the ACT, but rather a critical thinking and logic test, and students easily pick the wrong answers. Once a student can learn the hidden recurring patterns found on the SAT, then they will need to make plans to set aside time and practice the correct way using only materials from the College Board, the makers of the test.

By studying the test itself and how the questions are written, students can learn how to ace the test, which in turn will give them higher scores. Students will need to approach the sections of the SAT with these things in mind:

**Critical Reading** – This is an ironic name because this section is not really about reading, but rather about identifying the three question types and where to find them. Students can actually skip 70% of the passages and still get every answer right. Every answer to the questions can be found in the passage by looking at key areas.

**Math** – Outside of knowing basic math, a student does not need to be a genius to ace this section. It is not necessarily testing how smart you are in math, but really testing your critical thinking skills using math problems. By understanding strategies and shortcuts, math questions can generally be answered in 30 seconds or less.

**Writing** – Most students dread the writing essay because they have to write a paper in 25 minutes, not knowing the topic ahead of time, and it is worth 30% of their writing grade. The good news is that the essay is standardized like the rest of the test, and they are looking for a clear, consistent, and concise essay. With the right amount of practice you can get a perfect score of 12 on the essay.

The following chart compares SAT scores with their equivalent ACT scores. Please note, the SAT scores exclude the Writing portion and are based on the Critical Reading and Math sections.

# SAT AND ACT CONVERSION CHART

| SAT RANGE | ACT |
| --- | --- |
| 1600 | 36 |
| 1540-1590 | 35 |
| 1490-1530 | 34 |
| 1440-1480 | 33 |
| 1400-1430 | 32 |
| 1360-1390 | 31 |
| 1330-1350 | 30 |
| 1290-1320 | 29 |
| 1250-1280 | 28 |
| 1210-1240 | 27 |
| 1170-1200 | 26 |
| 1130-1160 | 25 |
| 1090-1120 | 24 |
| 1050-1080 | 23 |
| 1020-1040 | 22 |
| 980-1010 | 21 |
| 940-970 | 20 |
| 900-930 | 19 |
| 860-890 | 18 |
| 820-850 | 17 |
| 770-810 | 16 |
| 720-760 | 15 |
| 670-710 | 14 |
| 620-660 | 13 |
| 560-610 | 12 |
| 510-550 | 11 |

# TWO IMPORTANT TEST SERVICES

## STUDENT ANSWER VERIFICATION SERVICES

A student can find out more about a specific SAT that they took using these services. Students will receive a booklet copy of the SAT questions (not their original) and a report including their answers. They will also receive the correct answers and additional scoring instructions as well as information about the type of test questions and levels of difficulty of the questions.

This service is available for the October and January Saturday tests for the U.S. and Canadian testing centers and the May Saturday and Sunday tests worldwide. Students can order this service during registration or up to five months after the test date. Visit www.collegeboard.com and select Order Verification within My Scores or call 888-728-4357 (United States and Canada) or 212-713-7789 (international). Allow at least six weeks for materials to arrive. There is a fee for this service, and for another additional fee, students can receive a copy of their answer sheet from the Question-and-Answer Service.

## THE PSSS (PRELIMINARY SAT SCORING SERVICE)

This service is offered by many school districts and nonprofit organizations to help younger students identify their weaknesses on the PSAT/NMSQT, get an early assessment of students' academic skills, as well as provide important tools to help students improve. This is a great way students can familiarize themselves with the types of questions, instructions, and format they will encounter on the PSAT/NMSQT and SAT.

A practice PSAT/NMSQT is administered by a facilitator between January 10 and March 30. The score report will provide personalized feedback on students' skills and offer suggestions for areas in which students can improve to better prepare for the test in the future.

This is a great service for younger students such as ninth-graders (especially those whose schools cannot accommodate them during the actual PSAT/NMSQT), ESL students, and SSD students. Scores are not used for the National Merit Scholarship Program. It is not available to juniors, and some restrictions apply to students who have taken prior PSAT/NMSQTs.

This is a great opportunity for homeschool groups to test their students. There is a minimum order of fifty test booklets for a small fee and another fee for scoring reports. Booklets need to be ordered around the end of October. To get started, facilitators need to download the PSSS Brochure and Order Form and fax it to 212-253-4210 For more information, see http://professionals. collegeboard.com/k-12/prepare/psss, call 212-373-8730, or email psss@ collegeboard.com.

 **THINK ABOUT IT**

You probably are not excited about having to study for these standardized tests, but think long-term (i.e., college entrance and scholarships). Working hard now can save you time and money in the end. It is a lot easier to review math concepts, grammar rules, and critical thinking skills when you are studying these subjects in school. It is best to start practicing at least three months before the actual test. Adding in a couple extra hours a week to regular study time can help students become familiar with test questions and how the test itself is set up. Help yourself get through the dreaded tests by having a good attitude and a long-term perspective.

Studying now for these tests can benefit me by…

_____

_____

_____

_____

_____

# GUIDE FOR PARENTS
# HELPING YOUR CHILD PREPARE FOR
# COLLEGE ENTRANCE EXAMS

If your child is an advanced learner in middle school, consider having him or her enroll in a talent search competition. This requires having your student take the SAT or ACT in the seventh grade. Preparing your child to do well on this test is necessary. Although it might seem ridiculous to have young students prepare for these tests, getting your students familiar with standardize tests early has resounding benefits.

Students who score well on the SAT or ACT in middle school are eligible for different types of talent searches, which look good on students' academic résumés and make them eligible for recognitions, awards, camps, and scholarships. (For more information, see Chapter 7.) Each program has its own requirements, and you can find more on-line. While students do not have to be involved in one of these programs to succeed later on, many highly competitive (and not-so-competitive) universities look favorably on students' involvement in talent searches.

Also, getting your students familiar with standardized tests at an early age will help take some of the fear and pressure out of the standardized test process. Many students who wait until their last years in high school to take the test do poorly because they don't feel adequately prepared.

Finally, because the PSAT/NMSQT and SAT are logic-based tests, practicing the question types and learning to look at the test with a critical eye will help your students develop the mindset required to do well. This way, when the time comes to take the tests for college scholarships and entrance exams, your child won't need to cram. Then, the information will only be a refresher when he or she gets ready for the real exam.

There is a great deal of emphasis from colleges on these standardized tests because they put all students on an equal playing field since every high school weighs and calculates their GPAs differently.

## UNDERSTANDING THE IMPORTANCE OF THE PSAT/NMSQT

The PSAT/NMSQT is not just simply a practice SAT. While your students may take the PSAT/NMSQT as a form of practice for the SAT, the test is designed for an entirely different purpose. The PSAT/NMSQT, otherwise known as the Preliminary SAT/National Merit Scholarship Qualifying Test, is a way to find scholarship opportunities. Students all across the nation take the PSAT/NMSQT in hopes of obtaining the title of National Merit Scholar and all the benefits that come with it. National Merit Scholars are more likely to be offered entrance to top colleges and universities and often given full rides to many schools. To qualify for the competition, students must take the PSAT/NMSQT in their junior year of high school.

The PSAT/NMSQT is usually offered the third Wednesday or Saturday in October, depending on the date set by the individual school. Registration must be done through a high school and cannot be done on-line. Schools should allow homeschooled students to participate at their site and students can choose to take the test at any school offering the PSAT/NMSQT. Because the test booklets are pre-ordered, you should register your students as soon as possible to ensure a place on the actual test day. Some school districts have PSAT/NMSQT sign-ups in May.

Test booklets are sent back to the school for evaluation, and each high school has its own code. Homeschooled students have a specific code in each state; you can obtain your state's code at www.collegeboard.com/ student/testing/PSAT/NMSQT/reg/homeschool/state-codes.html. For example, the Texas code for PSAT/NMSQT is 994499. Homeschooled students will receive their booklets at their home, and their scores will not be used to calculate the local high school's average.

Students should start preparing for and taking the PSAT/NMSQT in ninth grade because it is so important. If your student's high school doesn't offer the PSAT/NMSQT, then register with a high school that does. Just speak with the high school guidance counselor to sign up.

Scores for tests taken in freshman and sophomore years will not count for the National Merit competition; however, taking the test early acquaints students with the format of the test and may help reduce test anxiety when it counts. Also, since students will receive their test booklets back and the answers to the test, you can see what your student got right and what he got wrong. This will help students identify their strengths and weaknesses on the test.

Colleges and universities use the PSAT/NMSQT as a way to get information about prospective students. The Student Search Service aspect of the test enables colleges to mail information to students who meet certain criteria and who may be interested in the programs and in majors they offer. Students should check the Student Search Service option on the PSAT/NMSQT exam in their junior year to take advantage of this program. However, the College Board does not report specific scores to schools; specific scores will have to be sent by the individual. Through this process, your mailbox begins to fill up with college materials as these colleges recruit your student.

# PSAT/NMSQT CODES FOR HOME-SCHOOLED STUDENTS

| | | | | |
|---|---|---|---|---|
| 990199 | Alabama | 992899 | Nebraska |
| 990299 | Alaska | 992999 | Nevada |
| 990399 | Arizona | 993099 | New Hampshire |
| 990499 | Arkansas | 993199 | New Jersey |
| 990599 | California | 993299 | New Mexico |
| 990699 | Colorado | 993399 | New York |
| 990799 | Connecticut | 993499 | North Carolina |
| 990899 | Delaware | 993599 | North Dakota |
| 990999 | District of Columbia | 993699 | Ohio |
| 991099 | Florida | 993799 | Oklahoma |
| 991199 | Georgia | 993899 | Oregon |
| 991299 | Hawaii | 993999 | Pennsylvania |
| 991399 | Idaho | 994099 | Rhode Island |
| 991499 | Illinois | 994199 | South Carolina |
| 991599 | Indiana | 994299 | South Dakota |
| 991699 | Iowa | 994399 | Tennessee |
| 991799 | Kansas | 994499 | Texas |
| 991899 | Kentucky | 994599 | Utah |
| 991999 | Louisiana | 994699 | Vermont |
| 992099 | Maine | 994799 | Virginia |
| 992199 | Maryland | 994899 | Washington |
| 992299 | Massachusetts | 994999 | West Virginia |
| 992399 | Michigan | 995099 | Wisconsin |
| 992499 | Minnesota | 995199 | Wyoming |
| 992599 | Mississippi | 995499 | Puerto Rico & U.S. Territories |
| 992699 | Missouri | 995599 | Outside United States |
| 992799 | Montana | | |

## PARENTS' HOMEWORK

Standardized tests are not only the ticket to college entrance but also can yield scholarships from the higher test scores. Find a test prep program that teaches individual test structure, recurring patterns, and shortcuts to success. Start your students early (preferably in ninth grade). For information on how to raise your student's PSAT and SAT scores, visit www.collegeprepgenius.com.

Remember to sign your student up early (at the school) for the PSAT in ninth, tenth, and eleventh grades. Check into the EXPLORE and PLAN tests, and see if any schools in the area administer them. Make sure your students take several SATs and ACTs until they get their desired score. See if your school has the PSSS service for any younger students.

# CHAPTER SIXTEEN: COLLEGE APPLICATIONS

O NCE YOU have done all the research, narrowed your list down to a few top schools, and taken your standardized tests, it is time to start the application process. Applying to schools may seem like an overwhelming task, but with proper planning and adherence to application deadlines, the process can go smoothly. In this section, you will learn how to organize an application checklist, ask for letters of recommendation, write a winning essay, conquer the college interview, and set up a college visit.

When reading applications, the admissions boards are looking for how well-rounded students are. Generally, when making their decisions, they focus on your transcript, GPA, class rank (if applicable), standardized test scores, extracurricular activities, volunteer work, and letters of recommendation. You don't need to be an all-star in every aspect; just make sure you meet all the requirements and you show continued growth in weak areas.

Colleges also keep an eye out for those students who set themselves apart from the rest. Students with mediocre credentials (grades, tests scores, etc.) can make themselves stand out by highlighting extraordinary qualities. Remember: Colleges are looking not only for smart students, but also for students who will diversify and enrich their campuses. Colleges are also looking for students who will make them look good—who will get involved, make good grades, and become successful alumni in the future.

Another way to stand out is by breaking the mold of normal applicants. Try applying to schools where you are the minority. For example, if you are from the West Coast, look into schools on the East Coast. Or if you are a male student, think about applying to a predominately female school or program. Because every college's entrance requirements are different for admissions, be sure to review your top school's "common dataset." This dataset is usually published on the college website, or you can ask your admissions counselor for the information.

So increase your chances of getting into the college of your choice by doing the usual and the unusual.

## ADMISSIONS TERMINOLOGY

Before you start your applications, it is important to familiarize yourself with the application lingo. Different colleges and universities offer different programs and use various application procedures. Understanding some key terms will help you evaluate certain programs and navigate the application process. Familiarize yourself with these terms in Appendix E, and use them as a reference guide to help you through your college applications.

## APPLICATION CHECKLIST

- ☐ Narrow down the colleges you are applying to.
- ☐ Make note of all important deadlines.
- ☐ Contact people for letters of recommendation.
- ☐ Write down all the application requirements for each school.
- ☐ Gather all financial aid applications and information.
- ☐ Type or write neatly if application is not on-line.
- ☐ Leave no blanks; instead, write "not applicable."
- ☐ Write a personal statement/essay for each school.
- ☐ Double-check *all* spelling on application.

- ☐ Send in a picture with any mailed application.
- ☐ Mail all application, supplementary forms, and financial aid paperwork before deadlines.
- ☐ Visit all prospective campuses.
- ☐ Meet with professors and other important faculty members in the departments.
- ☐ Get to know your admissions counselors and talk to them about any additional questions.

Remember: If you start this process early in the high school years, it will save you a lot of stress. If you are not satisfied with your SAT score yet, consider taking the October, November, or December SAT. Many colleges allow a student to turn in better test scores after the initial college application.

## YOUR RÉSUMÉ

This will be a concise compilation of the pertinent information that you have been recording in your college and career notebook. This is your brag-sheet of extra-curricular activities, volunteer work, awards received, job experience, travel experience, club associations, etc. You can use this for your college application, scholarship contests, and intern opportunities. Since the paper will be skimmed through quickly, make it noteworthy and appealing to the reader. Check out the example in the college and career notebook section. *Always make sure you have two to three trusted adults proofread it before you send the final copy.*

Your résumé should display your "well-roundedness"—i.e., good records in several areas: academics, community service, extracurricular activities, honors, awards and achievements, and standardized test scores. A little bit of "lopsidedness" is good too, where at least one area has greater depth than the rest, demonstrating excellence in a particular endeavor— academic, extracurricular, or otherwise. The more selective colleges actually want students who have a particular focus, or passion, in one or two areas.

## ATTENTION-GRABBING ACTIVITIES

1. Start an organization or business
2. Build something big (cars, boat, plane)
3. Run for a prestigious office
4. Write for the local paper
5. Invent something
6. Become a subject matter expert
7. Direct a film
8. Bike across America
9. Raise animals to sell
10. Plant a community garden

When it comes time to apply for colleges, you should enclose something from your attention-grabbing activity (e.g., seeds from your community garden, letters from satisfied customers, or a picture of your boat). This is a great way to impress the admissions boards.

## BEFRIEND YOUR COUNSELORS

Your admissions counselors can be great assets when it comes time to apply for college. In many ways, admissions counselors are the gatekeepers to your ideal schools as they hold many of the answers that can help you make the best application packet possible.

Do not treat your admissions counselors with apathy, but rather get to know them. Ask them questions, be polite, and always express your appreciation. Do not overwhelm them, but don't be afraid to get their advice when you really need it. It never hurts to make friends with the people who know the ins and outs of the schools you are applying to.

## BEST-KEPT SECRET

One of the best-kept secrets to being highly competitive is just being prepared. Knowing what you want and what you need to get there goes a long way in helping you reach your dreams. Organization and preparation, along with a little bit of risk, will help you reach your goals and exceed your expectations. These tips will not only help you in the future when you are applying for college, but will also help you develop skills that you can use in everyday life. Go out, make goals, and don't give up.

To help aid college applications and stand out to more selective colleges, consider inventing something, starting a busines, writing apps, etc.

## ADVANTAGES OF EARLY APPLICATIONS

If you're planning to apply to a competitive university, applying for an early decision may significantly increase your chances of getting in. Early decision deadlines usually start around November and they are a great motivator to get your application turned in and completed. However, by applying for early decision, you are telling that school that if they accept, you will go there for sure. That's a big decision to make, and may not be the right option if financial aid is a factor for you. It may be better to wait to see the financial aid packages of several universities before committing to just one. Nonetheless, if you know for sure you want to go to that university, then apply for early decision.

If applicable, for any university application, see if you can apply for a financial aid "Early Award." Once you get your financial aid package, it is binding until you enroll. Thus, if your grades drop during your final semester, it won't affect your financial aid award.

## ASKING FOR PERSONAL REFERENCES

Asking for personal references is one of the easiest steps in the college application progress. All you have to do is ask your teachers, employers, counselors, or family friends to write letters for you. Make sure they have all the information needed to send out the letters. Here are some important things you need to keep in mind before asking for letters of recommendation. Remember: It is your responsibility to give the people who are writing letters all the necessary information to write and send the letters.

1. Don't wait until the last minute to ask. You want to give your potential recommenders plenty of time (three to four weeks) to write a good letter. This way, if someone can't write a letter, you will have time to find someone else before it is too late.

2. You can't ask people to lie for you; however, you can ask them to focus on a particular trait that might be important to the different schools, such as leadership skills, foreign language proficiency, or moral character.

3. Each school has different criteria for letters of recommendation, so be sure to check the website or speak with your admissions counselors before asking for specific letters of recommendation.

4. Check to see if your schools require a letter of recommendation form. This is a form in which the person who is writing a letter for you will also evaluate your skills in survey form. If one or all of your schools require a form, make sure to include it when you give the other information to your recommenders.

5. Give each recommender stamped envelopes that are already addressed to each of the schools. This way they don't have to do any extra work other than write and send the letters.

6. Give each recommender a "brag-sheet" (i.e. your résumé) listing all your extracurricular activities, honors, and awards so they have enough information to include about you. While this might seem unimportant to you, many of your recommenders do not know all that you are involved in and will appreciate the information to add to your recommendation.

7. Make sure your recommenders understand that these letters are times for them to describe your qualities and not just list off your accomplishments in bullet form. Those reading the letters want to get to know you through stories and the perspectives of those writing the letters about you.

8. Pick different types of recommenders. Most schools like to see letters from people who know you academically, through work settings, personally, or spiritually.

9. Remember that it's OK to ask some people to write for one school and not for another. If there is someone who you think would be

perfect for one school, but someone else who would be perfect for another, it's OK to ask different people to write for you. Just don't overwhelm everyone you know with letter requests.

10. Once the letters are complete, request several <u>signed</u> copies so that you have the letters on file. This way if you apply to an additional school or if a job interviewer needs a letter of recommendation, you don't have to ask your recommenders for additional letters.

11. Do not forget to send all of your recommenders handwritten thank-you cards. Sure, you can thank them verbally once they say yes to write the letters for you, but do not forget to show how much you appreciate their time by sending an actual card.

## WRITING A WINNING COLLEGE ESSAY

Your personal statement or college essay should be a representation of you and should convey who you are, where you are going, and what you have to offer the college or university. Sometimes your essay is the only chance you have to introduce yourself to the admissions committee, so make sure you make a good impression.

Before you sit down to write your personal statement, check each school's application requirements, either on-line or with your admissions counselor. Some schools have a generic essay topic while others ask you to write on a specific idea or concept. You can save yourself a lot of time and frustration by understanding what each institution wants before writing your essays. Make sure you *always* answer the question. If you are unsure about anything, feel free to speak with your admissions counselor.

If a couple or all of the schools you are applying to ask the same type of question, feel free to write just one essay and tweak it for each particular school. Make sure you completely answer any and all elements of the given questions. Once you have answered the specific questions, it is OK to add some additional information about yourself as long as it logically fits with the rest of the essay and does not exceed any word count requirements.

Your personal statement should reflect that you are a leader and a thinker, creative, and analytical. If applicable, talk about your uniqueness and stand-out activities. You might even want to use a personal anecdote to introduce your essay.

This is your time to shine and to *sell* yourself. Be specific about your accomplishments, and stay away from negative topics. Your personal strengths should be conveyed but not compared to someone else's weaknesses. Avoid writing about misfortunes and hard times unless they show how you have grown or help you answer the essay question.

Also, communicate how you can benefit the college and why you want to go there. Explain how studying at this school will help you reach your dreams, perhaps by giving you the chance to study under a great professor or by providing an environment in which you will thrive as a future leader.

You want to show the admissions committee that you have taken the time and effort to write the best possible paper. You want to make a good impression while also grabbing their attention. This can be accomplished by offering a good "hook" at the beginning that will make them want to read on. Remember: These people will be reading hundreds of essays and you want yours to stick out. Good hooks often come in the form of dramatic statements, interesting quotes, personal anecdotes, or intelligent questions that are backed by the rest of your essay. Make sure your hook makes sense and helps you answer the essay question in a unique and intelligent way.

Here is an example of a dramatic statement used as a hook:

> Just call me Superwoman Extraordinaire. Not only have I been president of the Spanish Club, captain of the Drill Team Raiderettes, and secretary of Student Senate, I've maintained a 4.0, was named Volunteer of the Year in my city, and won four local art contests, all while working part-time as a cashier in a grocery store.

Do not forget to have your English teacher or another qualified editor look over your work and help you polish it. The best papers are written and then rewritten. This may be your only chance to impress the admissions committee; don't be lazy and send in the first draft.

## CONQUERING THE COLLEGE OR SCHOLARSHIP INTERVIEW

The interview is often very important for admissions as well as for winning a scholarship. Colleges and universities use this time to get to know prospective students and decide whether they are a good fit for the institution, and sometimes whether they want to offer the students financial aid. Your interview can set you apart from other prospective students.

Even if your school does not require an interview, you can usually request one. This is especially beneficial if your application is not as competitive as other applications (i.e., you are lower in your GPA, ranking, or tests scores).

When interviewing for scholarships named after someone, do your homework: Who was this scholarship named after, and how is he or she associated with the school? Research famous former recipients, how it will be judged, and how you can meet the criteria to receive the scholarship.

Here are some tips on conquering the college/scholarship interview.

## DOS OF THE COLLEGE INTERVIEW

- Do be honest.
- Do be kind and respectful.
- Do dress appropriately (i.e., modest, business attire).
- Do shake the interviewer's hand firmly at the beginning and end of the interview.
- Do introduce yourself.
- Do look the interviewer in the eye.
- Do address the interviewer by name.
- Do be excited.
- Do be confident.
- Do use manners.
- Do stand up when the interviewer stands up.
- Do be prepared.
- Do have confident body language.

- Do be specific (your goals, questions asked, etc.).
- Do be diplomatic and congenial.
- Do be conversational.
- Do speak up for yourself. (No one else will be there with you.)
- Do let the interviewer know how you can fill a need at the school.
- Do be prepared to ask questions.
- Do smile.
- Do own your mistakes.
- Do think before you speak.
- Do find ways to show you are responsible.
- Do be positive.
- Do be attentive.
- Do sell yourself.

## DON'TS OF THE COLLEGE INTERVIEW

- Don't be late.
- Don't interrupt.
- Don't chew gum.
- Don't complain or be negative.
- Don't bring a parent or a friend with you.
- Don't be apathetic.
- Don't look at your watch.
- Don't be prideful.
- Don't speak negatively about other schools.
- Don't expose tattoos or body piercings.
- Don't forget your college and career notebook.
- Don't forget a back-up outfit.
- Don't bring a cell phone.

Come to each interview prepared. This shows not only that you are interested in the institution, but also that you are responsible and ready to take on the college journey. Do some research on the school and the department before your interview. Don't only think about questions they might ask you, but come up with some intelligent questions for your interviewers. Do not just ask about information you could easily find on the college website. Impress the admissions counselors and review board by showing them you care about the school.

Before the interview, consider talking to people who already attend the college. It could be very helpful to know their insights into the college interview as well as their knowledge of the college in general. Make sure you know a brief history of the school and who the current president is. Find what the school is best known for, what unique programs it offers, and who some of its famous alumni are.

Even though the admissions counselor has copies of your transcript, extracurricular information, and letters of recommendation, bring another set for the interviewer just in case he or she asks for it. Be prepared to discuss what you wrote on your application. Also, bring any finished project that could be pertinent to attending this college. Bring up your *best* assets.

Be confident answering questions. Talk as if you *will* be attending this college: "When I go here, I plan to join the debate team and run for student government." If asked about other college interviews you have had, let the interviewer know that his or her school is in your top ranking. Ask what the college is looking for in a student and then show how you fit those criteria.

Usually students are informed of the college's decision by a response letter. Don't forget to send a thank-you note to the interviewer.

 **THINK ABOUT IT**

*Practice, practice, practice* your interview skills with at least two people (one you know well and one you don't know well) in a mock interview. Use the above techniques to answer the following questions confidently, but not mechanically. Treat the mock interview like the real one (e.g., Shake hands before and after, introduce yourself, be attentive and humble, and stand up and thank the interviewer and say his or her name.). Share the aforementioned Dos and Don'ts of the College Interview with your mock interviewer and have him or her rate you on each item. *Send a handwritten thank-you note to the mock interviewers.*

Below are some possible college interview questions. Use them, or get creative and make up your own.

## POSSIBLE COLLEGE OR SCHOLARSHIP CONTEST INTERVIEW QUESTIONS

What is the last book you read? (*Be prepared to talk about it.*)

What is your biggest fear?

Who is the most influential person in your life and why?

Where do you want to be in five years, ten years, etc.?

What do you know about the person for whom this scholarship is named? (*When interviewing for a scholarship, research whom the scholarship is honoring.*)

Whom do you want to be most like?

Do you have a potential major? Why or why not?

Can you describe a turning point in your life?

If you could redo any situation, what would it be?

If you had the chance to spend one year working for a non-profit organization, what would it be?

What is your opinion on (a current event)?

(*Study current events and possible questions that might be asked in this area. Read papers, search the Internet and form your own opinion on each matter.*)

What made you choose this university?

(*Be sure to explain how the interviewer's college is best for what you want to accomplish in life.*)

How would others describe you?

What high school courses did you enjoy most? Which did you dislike most?

Whom do you admire the most?

What's the one thing you will never do?

Can you describe yourself in three words?

What is your favorite pastime or activity?

What is your greatest accomplishment or failure?

Why should we accept you? Why should we give you this scholarship?

What does your perfect day look like?

How would you spend a million dollars?

How has high school prepared you for college?

What are your greatest strengths and weaknesses?

Have you ever broken tradition or gone against the grain?

How would you live your life over again if you could?

Is your room typically clean or messy?

How do you evaluate success?

What motivates you?

What are some recent goals you have achieved?

What do you know about our school and why are you considering it?

(*Do your research, especially the particular field(s) you are interested in, and know how you will contribute to the college's campus.*)

What have you done to prepare for higher education? What has been your greatest experience in high school or in life?

What do you want to do in the future?

(*Let the interviewer know how you will be a world-changer.*)

What is your biggest pet peeve?

Whom would you want to play you in a movie about your life?

What brings you happiness?

What is your favorite book/author/movie/musician?

Which of your accomplishments are you the most proud of?

If you could meet any important person in the past or present, who would it be and what would you ask him or her?

If you could be any animal (fruit, tree, etc.), what would you be and why?

What do you like about your family?

What would be the title of your autobiography?

What's an event that changed your life?

Have you ever failed at anything?

What established leadership skills have you demonstrated?

## COLLEGE AUDITIONS

If you are planning to major in the performing arts, such as music, dance, or theater, an audition may be required for admissions or scholarships. Prepare several diverse arrangements that highlight your particular talents. Variety shows the evaluators your performance prowess. Put together a short DVD with clips of some of your best performances to give to the interviewer and create a YoutTube link as well for easy access. Majoring in the arts may also require that you exhibit some original work; highlight any of your own creations.

Some auditions have very specific requirements while others are more flexible. Be sure to talk with the appropriate person in the department before coming to your audition.

## REJECTION

If you are rejected by a school you really want to go to, don't be discouraged. You can always call your admissions counselor to get any specifics on the reasons you weren't accepted and ask how you can appeal the decision. Be honest with the fact that you really want to go to the school and ask your counselor about the steps needed to accomplish this goal.

Admission boards can *always* change their minds. It may be as easy as asking or as difficult as sitting on a waiting list. Colleges want students who really want to be there, therefore expressing your strong desire to go is beneficial to you.

If you ask for an appeal and are accepted, you must be prepared to honor your college decision. It will reflect very poorly on you to turn down a renewed offer. Therefore, appeal only if you are serious about that school.

If the school rejects your appeal and you really want to go, ask about alternative admission programs. Many large schools have connections with local community colleges, summer programs, or even night and weekend classes. Using an alternative admission route can help get you into the full-time program. If you choose an alternative admission route, be sure to maintain your college GPA to help you get into the program of your choice.

## LATE APPLICATIONS

While most schools have applications that are due at the first of the year, some schools have what is known as rolling admissions or they extend their application deadlines. If you either decide late that you want to go to college or are rejected by all of your schools, you can still get into college. You may have to do some research on what options are still available, but many schools allow for late applications when openings become available. Call the schools you are considering and ask about their policy on late applications.

College application fees can also be waived for students who qualify. Talk with your high school guidance counselor or college admissions counselor for more information concerning fee waivers.

## ADMISSIONS FOR INTERNATIONAL STUDENTS

International students may have additional requirements for attending a college in America. They may have to provide documents from previous schools such as transcripts, courses, and degrees. A certified translation as well as proof of financial responsibility for tuition and fees may be required. These students will probably need to take entrance tests like SAT, ACT, GRE, etc. To prove proficiency, an English test such as the TOEFL (Test of English as a Foreign Language) or the IELTS (International English Language Testing System) is also required.

# GUIDE FOR PARENTS
# HELPING YOUR CHILD PREPARE FOR
# COMPETITIVE APPLICATIONS

A key to helping your student prepare for the application process is having a good record of all your student's activities and accomplishments. Therefore, document everything. Always record when your student gets involved with special programs, activities, and honors. This way, when it is time to fill out applications, your student will be prepared.

Not only will students' résumés aid them when they are applying for college, but their résumés will also make great brag-sheets. Brag-sheets are exactly what they sound like—a list of things worth bragging about. When asking for letters of recommendation for college admissions, you can give the recommenders brag-sheets so they know what to write about. Great recommendations can go a long way in helping your student get into the college of her dreams.

## PARENTS' HOMEWORK

Make a plan to augment your student's applications. If you plan on going on a family vacation this summer, then pick a place that is interesting and educational. This doesn't mean you need to spend the entire trip crammed in museums; just pick a place that has some historical interest. Before you go, have your family read up on the history and discuss the location's significance. You don't have to go far to find places of interest. If your daughter seems hesitant about an educational vacation, pick a place that is interesting to her. If your son is really interested in the Civil War, visit famous battlefields. If she spent a good amount of time learning about the American Revolution, take a trip to Boston to see where it all started. Finding a balance between learning and fun can make your student's education come alive and help him or her have interesting things to write about later on.

If family vacations to educational locations will not work for your family, consider sending your high school student to a rewarding summer camp. Some colleges offer specific programs for qualified students interested in a particular field. If your daughter has grand hopes of getting into MIT, because of the competitive nature of the school, she should consider attending a math or science training camp. If she dreams of becoming a prima ballerina at Juilliard, then perhaps a summer at ballet camp would be beneficial.

If, however, your son does not want to go to a highly competitive school, then when considering what camps and programs are right for him, think about the purpose of the camps. Will there be chances for leadership? What will he learn? Not all camps are created equal. Look into all the options before choosing one.

# CHAPTER SEVENTEEN: PAYING FOR SCHOOL

SOMETIMES IT seems that getting into school is easier than paying for it. Continuing education beyond high school can be an expensive endeavor; however, there are many different options for paying for your school. From scholarships to loans, students have many resources to help with financial needs. Getting financial assistance does not have to be a daunting and intimidating task. This chapter is designed to help you get the most out of your dollars and cents when funding your education.

Before you can fully understand all of the different aspects of financial aid, you must first understand the terminology. Below is a financial aid glossary that should help you through this process.

## FINANCIAL AID GLOSSARY

**Expected family contribution (EFC):** This is the amount of money you or your family is expected to pay based on income and other life circumstances.

**FAFSA:** FAFSA stands for "free application for federal student aid," and is necessary for every student to fill out to receive federal financial aid or federally backed student loans. For more information, go to www.fafsa.

ed.gov and fill out the form. Make sure you type the website in correctly, as www.fafsa.com is a financial service website that will charge you for helping you fill out your FAFSA. You do not need to pay money to fill out the government form.

**Grants:** Non-repayable awards, usually based on need.

**Loans:** Borrowed money that is expected to be repaid, often with interest. Educational loans are available through private lending companies, many colleges, and the federal government. Most student loans have low interest rates with deferred payments. Loan forgiveness is offered in some rare instances like the Texas B-On-Time loan, which does not have to be repaid if the student meets all graduation requirements.

**Merit-based:** Types of grants and scholarships that are awarded for an academic, athletic, or artistic skill.

**Need-based:** Types of grants, scholarships, and loans that are awarded based on financial need.

**Need-blind:** Financial aid that considers all applicants without regard to their financial needs.

**Non-subsidized loan:** A loan that accrues interest while a student is in school.

**Scholarships:** Non-repayable awards based on various criteria like academics, athletics, or special skills. Students will usually need to maintain a minimum GPA to keep a scholarship.

**Student Aid Report (SAR):** A form sent to students after they have completed their FAFSAs. Schools use this form to help determine a student's financial aid packet.

**Subsidized loan:** A loan that does *not* accrue interest while a student is in school.

**Work-study programs:** Jobs that allow students to earn money on campus to apply to their tuition and expenses while they are enrolled in school.

## IMPORTANT NOTE ON FAFSA

Do not miss out on this opportunity! Most people believe the FAFSA is only for low-income families. This isn't the case. The FAFSA determines the allocation of federal grants, loans, and work-study opportunities for all students.

Your parents can set up a pin number for you at any time at www.pin. ed.gov. Be sure to store and save your pin number because you must renew your FAFSA every year you are in college and graduate school. You will need to sign in with your pin number to complete the forms.

The earliest date to actually apply for FAFSA is January 1 of your senior year. All money is awarded on a first-serve basis, so apply early.

It will take you, or your parents, about an hour to complete the FAFSA forms. Make sure you have all the required documents in order to finish the application. You will need both your and your parents' social security numbers, driver's license numbers, birthdates, previous year W-2 forms or record of money earned, previous year's income tax returns (they don't have to be filed and can be estimated until filed), untaxed income records, last three months' bank statements, current investments/farm investments, and alien registration if applicable. Make sure not to leave any section blank; instead, use the number zero for income that is not applicable.

In 2012, the IRS created a new tool that can help make completing the FAFSA simpler. The IRS Data Retrieval Tool will take data directly from a person's e-filed tax return and place it in the correct boxes on the FAFSA application. In order to use this tool, you will need a valid social security number and a filed tax return from the previous year. Once you log onto the FAFSA website, click the IRS link to reach the IRS website. After you complete your security questions, your tax information will be automatically uploaded to the FAFSA form.

Applicants will need to file their taxes on-line first before applying for FAFSA. If you plan to use this option, prepare for a slight delay as it will take about two weeks for your electronic tax return to go through before you can fill out the FAFSA. If you choose not to file your taxes on-line, it will take even longer to use the retrieval tool. Don't be afraid to file your taxes early so you can use the retrieval tool to apply for the FAFSA as soon as possible. Even if you file in January, you can delay paying the IRS any amount due until the April 15 deadline.

While this tool is convenient, not every parent or student will be able to use it. Married FAFSA applicants who filed their taxes separately, those who filed an amended tax return the previous year, and those whose marital status changed after the first of the year are ineligible to use the tool.

After you file for the FAFSA, the government will create a Student Aid Report (SAR), which will indicate if the student is available for financial aid. The SAR is sent to the student and to any colleges the student has expressed an interest in. FAFSA will also calculate and provide an EFC (Expected Family Contribution).

To estimate your potential aid, use the FAFSA4caster on the site.

When you apply for FAFSA, it is a good idea to keep only limited funds in your savings and checking accounts. When your personal assets are counted, your savings and checking accounts can be counted against monies given or awarded to you. Also, keep your resources detached from your parents' assets; otherwise your parents' income can be factored in. For more information call (800) 433-3243 or go to www.fafsa.ed.gov.

**Sources of Financial Aid**

Federal work-study program

State agencies

Federal Perkins Loan Program

Federal Direct Parent Loans for Undergraduate Students

Professional and service organizations

Private foundations

Individual postsecondary schools

Contests

**Types of Federal Grants**

Pell Grant

Supplemental Education Opportunity Grant

Academic Competitiveness Grants

National Science and Mathematics Access to Retain Talent (SMART) Grant

DVA Yellow Ribbon Program

TEACH Grant Program

**Types of Federal Scholarships**

ROTC Scholarships

Scholarships from federal agencies

Robert C. Byrd Honors Scholarship

**Types of Federal Loans**
> Perkins Loan
> FFEL Stafford Loan
> William D. Ford Federal Direct Loans
> PLUS Loans

**Tax Benefits for Continuing Education**
> HOPE Scholarship tax credit
> Lifetime Learning tax credit
> Tuition and fees tax deduction
> *Check with the IRS or your accountant for more information.*

**Special State Scholarships**

Some states have in-state scholarships available for their own qualifying residents. Students will need to meet criteria such as a certain SAT or ACT score, class rank, GPA, etc. (e.g., Palmetto Fellows Scholarship in South Carolina or Bright Future Scholarship in Florida).

**Other Financial Resources**

**Bonner Scholars Network:** Participating colleges give money to students who continue community service throughout college.
> www.bonner.org

**City of College Dreams:** Resource for all types of college information. www.cityofcollegedreams.org

**College Savings Plan Network:** Information about developing a 529 plan.
> www.collegesavings.org

**CSS/Financial Aid PROFILE:** The College Board offers an on-line financial aid application service to help students find and apply for financial aid.
> https://profileonline.collegeboard.com/prf/index.jsp
> Foundation Grants to Individuals Online: Resource for finding grants. www.gtionline.fdncenter.org

**The Gates Millennium Scholars Program:** Scholarship program for minority students who demonstrate financial need.
> www.gmsp.org

**GrantsNet:** Database of searchable grants.
www.grantsnet.org

**Hispanic Scholarship Fund:** Scholarship opportunities for Latino Students.
www.hsf.net

**The Jackie Robinson Foundation:** A scholarship opportunity for underserved populations.
www.jackierobinson.org

**National Achievement Scholarship Program:** This program is a competition for outstanding Black American high school students.
www.nationalmerit.org/nasp.php

**National Association of Student Financial Aid Administrators:** Information regarding laws and regulations of financial aid.
www.nasfaa.org

**Sallie Mae:** Information about student loans.
www.salliemae.com

**Teri:** Financial planning service for low-income students.
www.teri.org

**Upromise:** Earn scholarship money by making everyday restaurant or grocery purchases. You can also get all your friends and family involved, and their purchases can count toward your child's education.
www.upromise.com

**Wall Street Journal Education:** Latest news about university education and financial resources. www.collegejournal.com

## SCHOLARSHIPS

The best way to pay for higher education is scholarships. There are billions of dollars in scholarship money available each year. It may seem like a lot of work, but searching for scholarships now can save you from working during school or paying back school loans once you graduate. The money is out there; all you need to do is search and apply for it.

The search can begin as early as seventh grade, and fourteen-year-olds can set up scholarship profiles at websites such as www.schoolsoup.com and www.scholarships.com, so don't wait until the senior year to start looking and applying.

Many scholarships are based on essay contests, videos, or community service, not necessarily financial need. Many are awarded based on a student's well-roundedness: Academic records, community service, leadership skills/athletic prowess, desire to serve others, integrity, public service, strong family ties, or open-mindedness in learning. Impressing scholarship judges is the key to winning them over.

Once you make sure you are a good fit for the scholarship, apply even if you think the odds are against you. For some scholarships, if you don't win the top money, finalists can often be awarded a smaller award. Big or small, whatever money you receive in scholarships you will not have to pay back later.

The Internet is an amazing tool when searching for scholarships. Here are some ideas that you can include in the search engine for scholarships: adventure, strong academics, leadership abilities, athletic achievements, personal aspirations, community service, parent's employment, world outreach, ethnicity, career-based, military, endowment, trust, foundation, honorarium, fellowship, and donors. Scan the website of your chosen college for internal scholarships offered to incoming students.

Keep your scholarship records organized by keeping a separate file for them. It should contain copies of your résumés and letters of recommendation. Before you mail a completed scholarship application, do the following:

Create a cover letter.
Fill in all blanks.
Include the essay and résumé and any additional forms required.
Double-check for grammar errors.
Make a copy for your own records and file them away.
Mail in a large manila envelope.
Use a tracking service such as Registered Mail.

*For more information on winning scholarship contests, visit www.scholarshipgold.com.*

## OTHER FINANCIAL AID OPTIONS

There are many top-tier schools like Harvard, Duke, Yale, Princeton, Stanford, and Cornell that cover tuition, room, and board for low-income students (usually up to $60,000 annual family income, but some consider $100,000 as low income). For example, Harvard will cap tuition at ten percent of income for a family earning between $120,000 and $180,000. Other selective schools have sliding-scale tuition waivers for families who have up to $200,000 in income. To increase chances of admission, students desiring to attend one of these prestigious universities should focus on obtaining exceptional grades, stellar SAT scores, and noteworthy extra-curricular activities (i.e., demonstrate their "well-roundedness" in the areas of leadership, community service and/ or athletic talent). SAT II subject tests may also be required. Check out www. finaid.org/questions/noloansforlowincome.phtml.

Some colleges will cap their loans at $5,000.
Visit http://projectonstudentdebt.org/pc_institution.php.

Some colleges will substitute grants for loans for those students who apply themselves academically and demonstrate good grades, high test scores (1400-1600 on the SAT math and critical reading tests), community service, leadership skills, subject tests, etc., while other colleges will accept students need-blind and create a financial packet for them afterward.

## YOUR SCHOLARSHIP PROFILE

Did you know you can get scholarships just because you are you? Seriously! Different organizations and companies put aside money for different types of students to help them pay for college. Anything can make you eligible, from your ethnicity to the type of cereal you eat in the mornings. Consider everything that helps make up you and your family to make your very own scholarship profile, a list of things that may help you win scholarships.

Think about what organizations you and your family have been involved in. Think about you and your family's personal interests. Remember to store your scholarship profile in the scholarship section of your college and career notebook in the section for tracking your scholarship applications.

## EXAMPLE: JANE SMITH'S SCHOLARSHIP PROFILE

Gender: Female
Age: 18
Plays volleyball
Plans on studying theater in college
Church intern
National Merit Scholar
Dad works at the United States Post Office and is a union member
Mom works for Dr. Pepper
Mom's side of the family is German
Dad's side of the family is English
Parents use both Visa and Discover cards
Eats Special K for breakfast
Plays the piano
Used to be a Girl Scout
Volunteers at the local hospital
Mother is a member of the Daughters of the American Revolution
Family shops at Wal-mart

Now Jane has a list of things to help her search for possible scholarship opportunities. Start brainstorming today what opportunities might await you.

## WEBSITES TO GET YOU STARTED

www.adventuresineducation.org
www.campustours.com
www.collegeanswer.com
www.collegeconfidential.com
www.collegeexpress.com
www.collegeispossible.org
www.collegenet.com
www.collegesportsscholarships.com
www.collegetoolkit.com

www.fastaid.com

www.fastweb.com

www.fedmoney.org

www.finaid.org

www.financialaidofficer.com

www.findtuition.com

www.freshinfo.com

www.gocollege.com

www.guaranteed-scholarships.com

www.go4college.com

www.iefa.org

www.jkcf.org

www.iesabroad.org

www.internationalscholarships.com

www.internationalstudent.com

www.military.com

www.naacp.org

www.petersons.com

www.scholaraid.org

www.scholarshipexperts.com

www.scholarshipmonkey.com

www.scholarship-page.com

www.scholarships.com

www.scholarshipsearch.com

www.students.gov

www.studentaid.ed.gov

www.studyabroadfunding.org

www.studentawards.com

www.supercollege.com

www.wiredscholar.com

www.xap.com

## OTHER PLACES TO FIND SCHOLARSHIPS

High school guidance counselor
High school teachers and coaches
High school and elementary school PTA
Local libraries
College and university academic departments
Parents' alma maters
Parents' employers
Your employer
Community and civic organizations
Your state's higher education assistance agency
Athletic clubs
Performing arts organizations
Military

Never *ever* pay anyone to search for scholarships for you or join organizations that guarantee awards. Do not give any such organization your social security number or any of your financial information! No one, except colleges and universities themselves, can guarantee scholarships. If you have any questions about possible fraud, visit www.fraud.org.

## TEST SCORES AND BIG SCHOLARSHIPS

Students who have been studying hard for standardized tests are often rewarded not only with great test scores but also with great scholarships. A substantial portion of scholarship money is usually awarded to a student based on academic merit.

As discussed earlier, students who do well on their PSAT/NMSQT are eligible for the National Merit Scholarship Program and thus are eligible for many great scholarship opportunities. Scoring well on the PSAT/NMSQT, however, is not the only chance for students to receive scholarships from their test scores. Many colleges and universities offer scholarship opportunities based simply on a student's SAT or ACT score combined with his or her high school GPA. Many colleges give full-ride scholarships to students with SAT scores starting around 1400 (math plus critical reading scores) or ACT scores starting at 31. Check with each college's website as test score scholarship requirements are usually posted. If you receive scholarship money directly from the school, here are some tips to help get *more* scholarship money after they've decided your financial award. First, you can appeal to the financial aid department for more money. (Do this after you have received an award letter.) You can also apply for re-awards, by asking to be considered for any extra scholarship money that was awarded to students who decided not to attend the school. See if your school will let you raise your SAT or ACT score after you are already enrolled to try to up your scholarship money.

*Remember you should stay on friendly terms with the financial aid advisor during this process. Be sure to send him or her a thank-you note for working on your behalf.*

## TIPS ON APPLYING FOR FINANCIAL AID

1. Start looking into scholarship opportunities during your freshman year of high school.
2. Don't forget to look into contests that offer awards.
3. Search the Internet for possible scholarships that fit your profile.
4. Apply to every scholarship you are eligible for; you cannot expect to receive all of them, but every little bit helps.
5. Keep things organized and plan ahead. Make sure you have enough time to send in all of the necessary documents.
6. Always follow the directions. You might be perfect for a scholarship, but if you ignore the deadlines and rules then you will be out of luck. Make sure to fill out all the appropriate forms and answer any questions.

## ATHLETIC SCHOLARSHIPS

Athletic scholarships make up a large portion of the scholarship money pool. Most universities set aside a substantial portion of their financial aid for recruiting athletes. Before banking on an athletic scholarship to fund your way through school, there are some things you must consider.

First, realize there are not as many full-ride athletic scholarships available to college freshmen as you might think, and typically only football, basketball, and volleyball offer those scholarships. Most schools offer partial scholarships with renewable contracts. This means if things don't go well your freshman year, you might not be offered the same financial packet the next year. Or if you do very well your freshman year, you might be offered more scholarship money the next. Keep in mind athletic scholarships are based on your performance and skill in your sport, so when playing your sport, you can't slack off.

The next thing to consider is the commitment you make when accepting an athletic scholarship. There will be meetings with coaches, training sessions, practices, and games at school and away, which will cut into your study and social time. Most colleges and universities have a GPA requirement for their athletes as well as performance criteria, so you will have to be prepared to take on both responsibilities while at school.

Don't be discouraged if getting an athletic scholarship is your dream. Just realize it might not be an easy ride to school as you might once have thought.

Also, realize that while schools might not be recruiting you for your athletic ability, you may still find a school that is willing to offer you some scholarship money to play for its team. Opportunities do not always come knocking at your door; sometimes you have to go out and look for them. If going to school on an athletic scholarship is something you want or need, go out and pursue it. Sometimes all you need to do is show a coach what you have to offer to get the financial assistance you need.

If you want to pursue an athletic scholarship, the certification process must be started before a student's senior year. Start in your junior year, or earlier! Talk with your guidance counselor to make sure you have the right academic credits and SAT or ACT score to qualify for college sports. When you take either the SAT or ACT, be sure to mark down the official NCAA code (9999) to have the test results sent directly to the organization. You must also be certified by the NCAA Eligibility Center before you can play Division I or II college sports.

For official rules and regulations, visit www.eligibilitycenter.org. You also can download the NCAA student guide *College-Bound Student-Athlete* from www.ncaa.org.

You can also play sports through the National Association of Intercollegiate Athletics (NAIA). High school students need a minimum 2.0 GPA and an ACT score of 18 or an SAT score of 860 (math plus critical reading). For more information on the NAIA, go to www.naia.org, call 816-595-8000, or visit the National Junior College Athletic Association (NJCAA) at www.njcaa.org.

To find specifics about being recruited for each different sport, visit www. athleticscholarships.net. For more detailed info, download the FREE e-book *How to Get an Athletic Scholarship* from www.college-athletic-scholarship. com/free-ebook.

Remember: Even the most talented athlete will not be eligible to accept a full-ride, or any scholarship, if he or she does not have the academics or college entrance exam score to back it up. Colleges are looking for students who can thrive both athletically and academically. Therefore, when you are looking for your athletic scholarship, do not neglect studying for those important standardized tests.

## DOS OF ATHLETIC SCHOLARSHIPS

1.  Do search for colleges and universities that offer your sport.
2.  Do contact the institutions and see if they offer scholarships in your sport.
3.  Do make a list of schools you are interested in applying to.
4.  Do contact the head coaches and write letters requesting consideration for recruitment. You should send an e-mail to introduce yourself to coaches. Be sure to include information about yourself like your positions, sport statistics, and high school coach contacts.
5.  Do send the coaches both athletic and academic résumés. Be sure to include any news articles, statistics, records, honors, and clippings that highlight your athletic performance.
6.  Do put together a video highlight of your athletic abilities. You can also make this a YouTube video that you can send as a link to all the coaches.
7.  Do send the coaches letters of recommendation from your high school coaches.

8. Do ask for a formal interview.

9. Once in the interview, do ask intelligent questions.

10. Do send thank-you notes to the coaches and recruiters for taking time to interview you.

11. Do be persistent and follow up.

## DON'TS OF ATHLETIC SCHOLARSHIPS

1. Don't wait until your senior year to start the process. You must begin the NCAA application before the end of your junior year.

2. Don't bank solely on getting an athletic scholarship for paying for school.

3. Don't wait for college coaches to contact you.

4. Don't wait for your high school coaches to contact colleges on your behalf.

5. Don't neglect your grades or your SAT/ACT scores.

## QUESTIONS FOR THE ATHLETIC INTERVIEW

Like any interview, you want to come prepared not only to answer the questions that are asked of you, but also to have your own intelligent questions. Remember: Interviews are a two-way street, and you need to know if the team will be a good fit for you just as much as the coach wants to know if you will be a good fit for the team. Below are some questions you might want to consider asking when you are in an athletic scholarship interview.

1. What position will I play on your team?

2. Have you personally watched me play? If so, why do you think my skills fit into your program?

3. Describe the current players competing at the same position. What skills do they possess?

4. How many freshmen are being recruited for my position?

5. Where do you see me fitting in the program this year? Over the next four years?

6. What chance do I have to win playing time as a freshman?

7. I know you have a list of potential recruits for this position. Where am I on that list?

8. Can I "redshirt" my first year? Under what conditions do you typically redshirt players?

9. What are the physical requirements (training commitments, weight, etc.) each year?

10. Will I receive a written contract or tender?

11. What are your expectations of me as a player? As a person?

## THINK ABOUT IT

When trying to be recruited, you need to view yourself with the expectations of the coaches. They want to create a winning team, so you need to show them that you will provide a good return on their investment. Before seeking your scholarships, make sure you do a thorough self-evaluation. Think about your overall strengths and weaknesses and what improvements you need to make. Examine your GPA, SAT scores, and your place on the team. Are you the leader, follower, or encourager? Knowing yourself will help you appropriately sell yourself to potential coaches.

# GUIDE FOR PARENTS HELPING YOUR CHILD PAY FOR COLLEGE

One of the best ways for students to get scholarships is through earning a high test score on college entrance exams. Students who receive high test scores can generally expect anywhere from a couple thousand dollars in scholarship money to full-rides to the colleges of their dreams. Success on college entrance exams, however, does not happen overnight. Some of the brightest and most determined students do poorly on these tests because they do not understand how to properly study for them.

The best way to help your students prepare for college entrance exams is to find a test prep program that teaches the formula of the tests. Standardized tests such as the PSAT/NMSQT and the SAT are reasoning tests that can be figured out if the students can understand the recurring patterns and strategies. Students should start early, learn how to take these tests, and practice using official test materials. Spending extra time on studying for these tests can help reduce the financial burden of college through high test scores and great scholarships.

## PARENTS' HOMEWORK

Almost every student who wants financial aid for college must fill out the FAFSA. Before you and your students complete these forms, you must get each student a pin number. Go to www.pin.ed.gov now and sign students up. Save this information in a safe place because you must use it every year your students are in school.

Be sure to apply for the FAFSA as early as January 1 of your student's senior year.

In the meantime, with your students, fill out the college money chart at the end of this chapter. This will not only help you when it comes time to fill out the FAFSA, but it can also keep you and your students on track financially for college.

Also, one of the best ways to save for college is to plan for a 529 account. This is not a custodial account. Make sure to add your child as beneficiary. Keep in mind this does not affect financial aid qualifications, and you can often get state tax benefits as well.

Paying for college is easier than you think. For many good tips on helping you through this process, go to www.collegeprepgenius.com to download the e-book 15 Secrets to Free College. Regularly priced at $9.95, you can download the e-book for a penny using the code "HSPG."

## COLLEGE MONEY CHART

| COLLEGE FUNDS | 9TH GRADE | 10TH GRADE | 11TH GRADE | 12TH GRADE |
|---|---|---|---|---|
| | | | | |
| Student Resources | | | | |
| Savings account | | | | |
| Summer job earnings | | | | |
| Part-time school-year job | | | | |
| Scholarships earned | | | | |
| Scholarship name | | | | |
| Scholarship name | | | | |
| Scholarship name | | | | |
| Scholarship name | | | | |
| Scholarship name | | | | |
| Scholarship name | | | | |
| Scholarship name | | | | |
| Other | | | | |
| Other | | | | |
| Parent Resources | | | | |
| Income contribution | | | | |
| College savings fund | | | | |
| Insurance | | | | |
| Sales of land/stocks | | | | |
| Cash in 401K/mutual funds | | | | |
| Home equity | | | | |
| Other | | | | |
| Other | | | | |

# CHAPTER EIGHTEEN: COLLEGE ESSENTIALS

ALTHOUGH YOU might be excited about ending high school, chances are the thought of beginning college is a little bit overwhelming. Soon you will be starting new classes, making new friends, and possibly moving far away from your family. In college you will experience more freedom as well as more responsibility. Whether you are moving across the nation to a four-year university or staying home and going to a community college, there are some things you should do to prepare yourself for your first year of college. Success in college comes from discipline, organization, and commitment.

## SUMMER BEFORE COLLEGE BEGINS

You probably have less than three months before your new adventure begins, so start by taking time to prepare yourself for what's ahead. Remember to spend the summer with your family and friends. Enjoy activities that give you one-on-one time with the people you value.

1.  Relax and have fun with family and friends.
2.  If you haven't already, schedule your classes for the upcoming semester.

3. Make sure you have your room and roommate assignment.

4. Contact your new roommate and make plans to meet before school starts.

5. Go to the new student orientation if offered by your school.

6. Sit down and make goals for your college freshman year.

7. Purchase things you need for your dorm room.

8. Make sure your medical records are up to date, and get any necessary immunizations.

9. Get your car inspected before you leave.

10. Make sure your personal bank account is set up.

11. Work at least part-time to save money for the upcoming semester.

12. Get your first-semester book list and purchase your books early to save money. (You can usually purchase used books on-line. Try www.bookfinder.com or www.amazon.com.)

13. Use social networks to locate other incoming freshmen. Start networking now so that you know people when you start in the fall.

14. **Let your family and friends know how important they are to you!**

## CHOOSING YOUR CLASSES

Picking a major, choosing your classes, and making sure you get the most out of your college experience can be very daunting tasks. Luckily, every college assigns an academic advisor to each incoming student. Your advisor will be your best friend when you are navigating a course schedule.

Consider signing up for honors classes in college. These may be a little harder, but they have some of the benefits: Priority registering, smaller classes, your own personal honors counselor, and being able to graduate with honors.

If you have already declared a major or two, then your advisor will most likely be in the department where you will spend the most time. If you haven't decided on a major yet, which is typical for incoming freshmen, than a general advisor will be given to you. Often students will change academic advisors when they change majors.

After you have accepted a college's offer of admission, find out who is assigned as your academic advisor. Schedule a time to speak with him or her and register for classes. Some colleges have a preregistration day for incoming freshmen when students come to the campus, meet with their advisors, and make their fall schedules. If you cannot make the preregistration day or your college doesn't offer one, then it is up to you to find time to talk with your advisor and set your schedule.

Think about what classes you need to take and what classes you want to take. One path that works well is taking several basic courses the first year, so you can take the harder classes later.

College is a great time to explore several different options, so don't lose out by not taking diverse classes. Don't be afraid to branch out and try new things. Even if you know what you want to major in, explore different fields of study and take several introductory classes. You might be surprised to find something you want to minor in. It may also lead to adding another major or changing majors altogether.

Also, think about the things you wish to accomplish while you are at school. Although four years might seem like a long time, the years have a funny way of flying past you. Think ahead, and set several goals for yourself. Plan ahead, so you can make those goals a reality. See what your school has to offer, and see if you want to be a part of it.

Please note: Not every professor will be a good professor. Before you sign up for a class, make sure to do your research. You can talk with other students who have taken the class or go on-line to see what others are saying about your next potential professor. See if the professors are on www.ratemyprofessor. com and www.pickaprof.com. Take people's words with a grain of salt; some people may have bitter reviews because of childish reasons. Nonetheless, this will help you find classes that better suit your learning style.

Before you schedule classes, think about what you can and can't handle. Don't get too ambitious and don't sell yourself short when registering for your classes.

## PICKING A MAJOR

Don't worry if you haven't picked a major yet. Most students don't know what they are going to study until later. There is also nothing wrong with coming to college with a major in mind. If you already know what you want to do and have your future career path all planned, that's great. If, however, you come to college having very little idea of what you want to do, that's great too.

No matter what position you find yourself in, take time to explore different fields of study. Think about what you would want to do even if you weren't going to get paid for it, and follow your passions. Branching out is a great way to reveal hidden interests and possible career choices.

Having an "undecided" major for your first year is OK, and sometimes helpful, but realize the longer it takes after that to declare a major, the less likely it is you will graduate in four years.

## PICKING SCHOOL HOUSING

School housing policies depend on individual schools. Some schools require students to spend all four years on campus while others let freshmen live in off-campus apartments. When deciding what type of housing is right for you, consider what type of housing would be most beneficial at this point in time.

Although an off-campus apartment might seem like a good idea, chances are living off campus as a freshman could be a terrible mistake. You would have to commute to school and you would miss many opportunities to get to know your classmates.

Dorm rooms might seem unappealing, but there are many unseen benefits of living in on-campus housing. First, being on campus is a great way to get plugged in and start making friends. Second, having a roommate can be very nice because it means you don't have to experience your first semester completely alone. You always have someone that you can spend time with or talk to.

When picking student housing, it is best to pick a place where other freshmen will be. This way you can develop friendships and get to know your incoming classmates better.

## LIVING WITH A ROOMMATE

To be honest, even in some of the best dorm rooms across the nation, a freshman's room is not terribly big. Every year students from diverse backgrounds are forced to live peacefully in close proximity to utter strangers.

This might seems like an impossible task, but here are a few tips that will make living with a roommate a whole lot easier.

1.  Try not to make move-in day the first time you speak with your new roommate.

2.  Decide on ground rules for the room; consider privacy, quiet time, room chores, and borrowing.

3.  Make sure to give each other space; make your personal time outside of the room. Find somewhere you can go and make it your own.

4.  Get to know your roommate like you would any other friend. Just because you are living with the person doesn't mean he or she will instantly be your best friend. Take time to get to know your roommate and try to build a lasting friendship.

5.  If you have a problem with your roommate, talk to him or her first. Try to keep major problems from happening by communicating about the minor ones. Don't be afraid of confrontation because not dealing with a small problem will almost guarantee a larger one later on.

6.  Talk to your residence staff if you are having major roommate problems. Dorm parents, resident advisors (RAs), and the housing staff are there to make sure you live as comfortably as possibly. If you are having trouble working out issues with your roommate, talk to them about possible solutions.

7.  If things don't work out, don't be afraid to switch rooms and roommates. Chances are after the first semester or two you will find someone you will want to live with other than your current roommate.

8.  It's OK to change rooms and roommates—even if you don't have any real problems with your roommate and you simply want to live with someone else. Just make sure you are upfront about it with your current roommate. Be considerate of his or her feelings, and tell your roommate you are planning on changing in enough time for him or her to find someone else.

9.  Seriously consider whether or not you want to purchase matching dorm room accessories; 75 percent of freshmen change roommates after their first year.

## TIPS ON LIVING WITH YOUR BEST FRIEND OR OTHER CLOSE FRIENDS

It may seem like a dream come true, going off to college and living with your friend who always felt like more like a sibling. You two get along perfectly. You are used to staying over multiple days at each other's houses. There is no one else you would rather room with in college. So while everyone will be dealing with pesky roommate problems, you two will have it all figured out.

Unfortunately, that usually isn't the case. Even the best of friends will get on each other's nerves when living in such close proximity to each other. You will learn things about your best friend you never knew, and it will either strengthen your friendship or weaken it. Before you get your heart set on living with any good friends, think about the things that annoy you about that person, your habits, and your likes and dislikes. Living with your best friend can be a good or bad thing, so give it a lot of thought before move-in day.

If you do decide to live with your best friend, here are some tips to help it go smoothly.

1. Be honest with yourself. At some point you both will annoy each other.
2. Before you move in, talk to your friend about some ground rules.
3. Give each other space. This might be particularly hard if your roommate is the only person you know at college, but don't stay tied at the hip. Branch out and meet new people.
4. Make time to have personal time. Find a quiet place on campus to do something you like to do by yourself. Try to avoid using the bedroom for alone time since it is your shared space. Find a place that can be all your own.
5. Don't judge your friend or try to play his or her parent. College is a time when people try new things and search for independence. If your friend decides to stay up until five in the morning and skip his or her homework, that is not your problem. Or if your friend starts hanging out with people you don't like, it is not your place to

tell him or her not to see those people. You have to let your friend make mistakes. If you feel like your friend is making bad choices, you should talk to him or her about it—but only as a friend and not as someone who knows everything. It is OK to express care and concern and even tell your friend you don't agree with his or her choices, but then you have to let it go.

6. If your friend is putting himself or herself into dangerous situations, it is your responsibility to tell someone who can help. Don't let the idea of "privacy" keep you from helping your friend. Getting help might just save your friend's life.

7. Don't assume your friend is OK with all of your habits. Be respectful and considerate of your friend as you would a stranger. Ask before you borrow things, clean up your space, and don't take your friendship for granted.

## LEAVING HOME

It can be hard to deal with the separation from your family and friends back home, especially if you have really close ties. Chances are you have never lived away from your family before and moving out on your own will be an adjustment.

The summer before students leave for college can be difficult on their parents too. Tension can build, and it might seem like all you do with your parents is fight. Before you get mad at your parents for not understanding you, recognize some, if not all, of this tension is building because you are leaving home and your parents are going to miss you.

If you find yourself feeling uneasy and easily upset, recognize that it might have something to do with the fact you are scared because of the upcoming changes too. If you and your best friend or girl/boyfriend start fighting, it might be because things are about to become very difficult. Even if you are extremely excited about the future, don't take for granted the feelings of those who are closest to you.

## TIPS TO HELP WITH SEPARATION ANXIETY

1. Realize that everyone will be dealing with his or her own fears and anxieties about your leaving. Don't just assume your parents or friends are being mean or don't want you to go to college; they are probably just sad you are leaving.

2. Take time to talk to your family and friends individually about how they are feeling. Give them your full attention and just listen to what they have to say.

3. Make time to spend with your family and friends individually. The summer isn't very long, but don't try to lump everyone together at a going-away party. Make the effort to have one-on-one time with the people who are closest to you.

4. Include your parents in some of the decisions you are making about college. Parents probably feel sad because you are now an adult and will be making most, if not all, of your own choices. They may feel that you don't need or want their guidance anymore. Make them feel included by asking their advice on things you are thinking about. Take your mom shopping for dorm room stuff and ask her what she thinks, or ask your dad about different classes or extracurricular activities you are thinking about joining. Let them know you still value their input.

5. Spend time with the friends whose friendships you want to keep throughout the college years. Things change once you leave for college. Whether your friends leave for another school or stay home, your relationships will change. Take time to spend with those whom you want to keep in touch with over the years.

6. Hug your mom at least once a day (preferably ten times) and tell her that you love her. Moms usually are hit with separation anxiety the most. Most moms hate the idea of their children leaving home and want you to stay with them for at least a little bit longer. Show your mom that you understand how she is feeling and let her know you care. Going out of your way to hug her and tell her you love her at least once a day for the entire summer will go a very long way (even after you leave) in showing her you care for her!

## HOMESICKNESS

Freshman year can be one of the loneliest times in students' lives. That's because they have just left everything they have known and have not had enough time to make the new place feel like home.

First, it is OK to miss home. It is completely normal to miss your family and friends, and it's OK to let them know that you miss them. When you feel sad and miss people close to you, write them an email, give them a call, or text to say hi. The instant connection will make you feel better.

However, know that the longer you dwell on your home and the way things used to be, the longer it will take for you to establish a new home. So often freshmen never let themselves grow accustomed to their new homes, and many change schools after their first year because the school wasn't the right fit. It is OK to transfer schools if you really don't like the school you are attending. Just make sure you give the school a fair chance before you decide it isn't the place for you.

Here are some tips on combating homesickness.

1. **If you feel like you have no friends**, go out and meet some. Everyone is trying to meet people and find friends; you are not alone. Meet people in your class, at the local coffee shop, in your dorm, or through different organizations.

2. **If the campus feels large and unfamiliar**, spend a day or two walking around campus and look for your new favorite spots. Don't make the mistake of going straight from your dorm room, to your class, and back to your dorm room. Explore your new surroundings. Take a book and look for a great study spot. Walking around and learning the area will make it feel more like home.

3. **If you feel that you spend too much time by yourself**, join a club or organization. Getting involved is one of the best ways to rid yourself of homesickness. Joining a group will instantly connect you with other students on campus, give you something to do at least once a week, and help you make the campus feel like home. Once you start making friends, forming a new schedule, and getting familiar with the campus, you will start to feel that you belong.

4. **If you feel that you can't handle all of the changes**, first let yourself admit that change can be difficult, and it doesn't matter if everyone else seems to be handling it better than you. Chances are you just aren't there when your new friends freak out. Most campuses have a counselor on staff to help students adjust to the changes of college life. The services are usually free and covered by your tuition. If you feel very homesick and in need of help, seek someone who is trained to guide you through this time.

5. **If you feel that home is very far away**, realize no matter where you go to school, if it's an hour from home or across the ocean, you can always go home. This doesn't mean you should hop in the car or a plane every time you feel homesick, but don't get trapped into thinking home is so far away that you can't go back. Once you realize you have the freedom to go back if you *really* need to, chances are you won't feel so desperate to go back.

## COMMON FRESHMAN MISCONCEPTIONS AND HOW TO AVOID THEM

While every student's freshman year will be different, there are several common mistakes that first-time college students often make. Although most of these begin as minor mistakes, if left unchecked many can turn into serious bad habits. The best way to stop bad habits from forming is to avoid starting them in the first place. Here is a list of several things you should avoid not only your first year, but throughout your college experience.

**Misconception #1: Because you are out of the house, you can eat anything you want and not worry about gaining a pound.**

Have you ever heard of the "freshman fifteen"? While it is not true that every freshman student will gain fifteen pounds of fat during his or her first year, there is a reason why people talk about the freshman fifteen. Students often find great liberation knowing they can eat anything they want at any time, and a lot of them suffer the consequences of it.

Think about it. If it is four in the morning and your friends want to go to a late-night drive-through, you can and probably will go. The great thing is it's OK to do so. Every once in a while, it is fun to get out and do crazy things with your friends. Sometimes a dollar taco can be irresistible. However, if you combine that four-in-the-morning taco run with a skipped breakfast, a hamburger at the cafeteria for lunch, a couple cookies in the afternoon for a snack, pizza for dinner, and Pop-Tarts for a study break earlier that evening, you can see where the pounds start to add up.

College students, especially freshmen, are notorious for eating unhealthy food. It's partly due to the lack of meal structure; after all Mom or Dad isn't cooking dinner anymore. And it's partly due to the fact that unhealthy snacks are cheaper and more easily accessible in dorm rooms. Snacking becomes a mindless endeavor that most students don't think about, and if the food is there, you'll probably eat it.

The best way to avoid the freshman fifteen and mindless snacking is simply to watch what you eat and make time to exercise. These are habits to start now, before college even begins. Getting in the right mindset before leaving home is the goal. Here are a few more tips to help fight off any extra weight.

- If you are having trouble knowing your own food habits, keep a food journal and write down everything you eat for a week. This way you can see your own habits.
- When you buy snacks, check the labels and know what you are eating.
- Try to get up in enough time to eat a balanced meal for breakfast.
- When eating lunch or dinner, make sure to add portions of fruits and vegetables.
- Limit soft drink and coffee consumption.
- Plan ahead, and eat several small meals throughout the day.
- Avoid things you know are bad for you.
- Allow yourself some "yummy" food; just make sure you know when and how much you consume.
- Make sure to exercise at least three times a week to stay in shape.

Getting into the habit of healthy eating will help you keep off any additional weight and help avoid any crash or extreme diets in the future. Remember that it's not about living on any specific weight-loss diet; it's about making wise choices, so you live a healthy lifestyle.

**Misconception #2: You can stay up all hours of the night and still make it to your eight a.m. lecture.**

OK, you probably can stay up all night talking with friends or playing videogames and still make it to your early morning class the next day. However, how awake will you really be and how much will you learn in that class?

Even if you can handle a late-night schedule for the first couple of weeks, or first part of the semester, sooner or later your lack of sleep will catch up with you. Your quality of work will slip, you'll have trouble staying focused, and you might stop being a very nice person.

Avoid these problems by getting a healthy amount of sleep every night. Start this in high school! Try to establish a sleeping schedule that allows you to get at least seven to eight hours of sleep each night during the week. Reserve staying up late for the weekends and nights you don't have anything pressing early the next morning. In the long run you'll be happy you did.

If you know you are a night owl and won't be getting to bed early, consider having your first class start at ten instead of eight.

**Misconception #3: Drinking and partying throughout the week won't affect you or your academic life.**

First off, as a freshman you are probably underage and you shouldn't be drinking. That said, if you do go to parties and there is alcohol, you need to know how drinking will affect you. Students think they can be both good students during the day and good drinkers at night. That simply is not true. Students who spend the majority of their nights out partying during the week will suffer for it. There is simply not enough time in the day to do both. Eventually students who party all the time probably lower their moral standards, falter in their grades, and lose valuable friendships.

**Misconception #4: It's OK—or maybe even kind or romantic—to let others get your drinks (alcoholic or otherwise).**

The second big mistake students make when it comes to partying is feeling protected by their newfound friends. If you are at a party, never assume you are safe. Never accept a drink from a stranger or a new acquaintance. You don't know everyone at the party, or at least you don't know everyone there very well. You never know what might happen when you are not looking. There is always a chance that someone may try to put a drug like Rohypnol into your drink.

While it might seem paranoid to assume that your new friends might want to harm you, it is still best to be on your guard and take precautions to keep yourself safe. Some people are wicked, some people are selfish, and some people are just plain stupid. Regardless of a person's intentions toward you, his or her mistakes can be devastating to you.

The idea of "date rape" may sound like an impossible scenario, but it can happen. More than 60 percent of women sexually assaulted in their 20s are acquainted with their attackers before the incidents occur. Don't blindly trust your wellbeing to people at parties, not even friends.

You are the only one who has your best interests at heart. As an adult, it is your responsibility to make wise choices. If you do plan to frequent college parties, it's best that you leave it to the weekends and always take a friend whom you know you can trust.

**Misconception #5: You don't know anyone, so you won't make any friends.**

You might end up going to a school where you don't know anyone else. It's a scary, but very real possibility. Just because none of your high school buddies came to college with you, however, doesn't mean you are doomed to a friendless existence. Making friends takes time and effort. You will be starting from scratch and have to get to know a whole bunch of new people. The great news is, so will everyone else.

Don't let yourself be shy. You don't have to be the life of the party, but don't settle on staying a loner because you don't know anyone. Realize your next best friend is probably out there; you just haven't met him or her yet.

For more help on making friends, go back to Chapter 6.

**Misconception #6: You have to be the same person you were in high school.**

Chances are you knew your classmates in high school for a very long time (maybe since kindergarten). Since you have grown up with most of your fellow students, you have probably grown accustomed to being a certain type of person around them. Whether you were captain of the football team or a self-professed loner, you don't have to carry those titles with you into college. College is a blank slate with new people and new experiences. If you didn't like the person you were in high school, you don't have to stay that person. Now is the time to develop who you are and who you want to be. Take this opportunity to grow and change.

**Misconception #7: You have to be a completely different person than who you were in high school.**

Likewise, just because college is a fresh start, it doesn't mean you have to automatically reinvent yourself. You don't have to come in with a new attitude, style, or personality. You can if you want to, but if you are happy with the person you are, then take time in college to continue to work on your personal strengths and weaknesses.

**Misconception #8: Everyone is smarter, more attractive, or more talented than you are.**

Most colleges are a lot bigger than a student's high school, and therefore there are a lot more students to interact with. You might have come from a school where you were the best at something, but when you come to college, you find yourself behind everyone else. This can be very discouraging.

Realize your first mistake is comparing yourself to other people. No matter where you go or what you do, there will always be someone else in the world better than you, so stop comparing.

Second, realize that you will never be happy with your performance until you learn to accept your personal best. Focusing on doing your best and being happy with it will make you a lot more satisfied than trying to outdo everyone else. So stop worrying about other people and start working on your personal best.

**Misconception #9: Your dorm room is the best place to spend most of your free hours.**
Your dorm room is probably the most natural place to hang out. You will inevitably gravitate to it because it's familiar in a time of crazy change. It is your home, it has your stuff, and it can be really safe. If, however, you spend all of your free time in your dorm room, then you will never feel safe on the rest of the campus. Don't rush back to your room after class; walk around, mingle with new friends, and jump right into the college experience.

**Misconception #10: Being a gentleman means you always have to pay.**
Many young men are taught that it is polite to pay for female friends, even if it is not a date, when out for a meal. However, college is a time when tons of friends go out together often. While it is a sweet thought, male students will likely go broke if they try to stick to this philosophy. It is perfectly gentlemanly to have everyone go Dutch when out, and don't let girls take advantage of your kindness.

Ladies, don't allow your male friends to insist on paying for your meals. Try to always pay your own way. The rules change a bit if you plan on seeing somebody romantically, but more likely than not, your boyfriend will be an unemployed college student, so help him out by sharing the financial weight of going out.

**Misconception #11: You can do it all…or you can't do anything.**
No one has super powers and can do it all. Don't try to outdo every other student on campus by taking eighteen credit hours, joining a dozen organizations, making friends with everyone on your hall, and trying to keep a 4.0 GPA. It's just impossible, and it will leave you feeling discontent and worn out.

Instead of playing superman or superwoman, set realistic goals for yourself and work to accomplish them. Decide what is important to you and set your priorities accordingly. If you have to maintain a certain GPA to keep a scholarship, then focus more time on your studies. If you want to adjust to college slowly, take an easier first-semester load of classes and add some extracurricular activities.

Learning how to say "no" is a skill. Likewise, learning how to say "yes" can be a very important skill as well. Do not get so focused on one aspect of the college experience that you miss other great opportunities. You know yourself best: Decide whether you need to learn to say "no" or "yes" to the opportunities that present themselves.

**Misconception #11: Bad things won't happen to you.**
Don't fall into the trap thinking that something perfectly reasonable for everyone else is ridiculous when it comes to you. No one is immune to making mistakes, so don't pretend otherwise. When it comes to making decisions and weighing consequences, be realistic. It is so easy to think of yourself as invincible.

Let's say your roommate flunks Spanish because he or she didn't study for the tests or didn't turn in the homework. Do you feel it would be impossible for you to flunk it for doing the same things? You will face the consequences of your actions. Thus, don't believe you can defy the need for sleep or drive safely after drinking. Thinking like this can cost you and your family everything.

Every action has some sort of consequence, either good or bad. Don't be foolish and tell yourself it won't happen to you.

## MAKING THE MOST OUT OF THE NEXT FOUR YEARS

College is a wonderful time for students to learn, grow, and gain independence. Don't take this time for granted. Think about what you want to accomplish during these next four years. Make goals and work to achieve them.

Don't be afraid to challenge yourself and to broaden your interests. There is so much to discover inside and outside of the classroom. Visit and join different organizations. Think about getting involved in student government, the school newspaper, or an intramural team. Make new friends and listen to the wisdom of your professors. Make sure to take advantage of college movie nights, campus speakers, and concerts, especially if they are a part of your tuition.

Many students look back at their time in college with at least some regret about not doing more. Make sure you take pictures, get involved, and treasure every moment. Do not let the stress of all your responsibilities overshadow your college experience.

**STUDYING ABROAD**

Studying abroad during college is often a once-in-a-lifetime opportunity. Students who go abroad get to live in a foreign country, learn about a new culture and language, and receive college credit. Many American colleges have programs with foreign colleges or universities that allow students to apply credits received overseas to their graduation requirements. Some schools even offer study-abroad stipends or scholarships to students who wish to take advantage of these opportunities.

Many students miss the opportunity to study abroad because they don't think about it until it is too late, or they can't seem to plan it into their schedules. Start thinking about these opportunities now and look into what scholarships are available, through either your school or other organizations. Talk with the international department of your prospective schools to see if they have any special arrangements with other schools across the world. Decide where you want to study and think about when it will be best for you to go. Time abroad can yield a wealth of experience as well as give you an international edge on your résumé after you graduate.

Still not convinced? You have the fortunate advantage of going to college in a highly globalized economy. This means the job market expands beyond the boundaries of the United States. However, this also means the job market is highly competitive. One of the best things you can do to set yourself apart from your peers is to seriously learn a second language. Many employers will jump at the chance to hire you if you possess the ability to speak multiple languages.

You will not achieve language proficiency simply in a college classroom or through self-study. These methods will give you a foundation, but to be truly fluent in another language you must have immersion in both the country and culture in which the language is spoken. This is another reason studying abroad during your college years is important.

If you cannot study in another country during the school year, think about going over the summer. It is possible to obtain college credits for language schools or cultural experiences.

Do not settle for a common foreign language (German, French, etc.), but challenge yourself and learn an in-demand tongue. According to the FBI the list of language skills that are currently deemed critical are Arabic, Chinese (all dialects),

Farsi, Hebrew, Hindi, Japanese, Korean, Pashtu, Punjabi, Russian, Spanish, Urdu, and Vietnamese. While knowing one of these languages cannot guarantee that you will have a job after college, your chances for immediate employment after college dramatically increase with the ability to speak one fluently.

### INTERNSHIPS

Now more than ever students need real-world experience before they get their first job. Internships are great because they help you become familiar with the types of jobs you hope to pursue in the future. They give you the opportunity to use the skills you have learned in the classroom inside the workforce. You should make every effort to obtain at least one type of internship when you are in college. Contact your academic advisors for help. Most internships are unpaid; however, you can find some that pay a modest wage.

High school students can also look into internships to help them decide what types of jobs they would like to have someday.

### CLEP CREDITS

Students can take fewer classes in college by getting college credit for information you already know. If you have already studied a particular subject, you can turn that knowledge into college hours and therefore take a lighter load in college. CLEP (College Level Examination Program) allows you to earn college credit by taking qualified CLEP tests in a particular subject. The tests are designed to correspond to a one-semester class, but they sometimes cover up to a two-year course. The exams are generally ninety minutes long and cover specific knowledge and skills about a certain subject.

You can take these exams in high school or once you're already in college. The exams are administered once a month at more than fourteen hundred testing centers around the nation. Like AP exams, there are several advantages to doing well on CLEP tests. Ask a local school advisor or go to www.collegeboard.com for more information on the CLEP program. CLEP is not necessarily a substitution for taking college courses, but it can help you prepare and enhance your college experience.

It is also cheaper to take some CLEP tests. CLEP exams cost roughly $65, which is minor when compared to the cost of tuition. CLEP exams are also free to those who are serving in the military. Or you can finish your degree. If you are missing some courses for graduation, CLEP exams are a great way of getting those last few college hours.

One word of warning: Too many college credits (via CLEP, AP or dual credit) can also nullify freshman scholarships. Many students have lost out on scholarship money because they were no longer considered incoming freshmen but instead transfer students because of their "earned college credit."

To find out more, visit www.collegeboard.com/student/testing/clep/about.html.

## CAMPUS LIFE

### GREEK LIFE

Joining a sorority, fraternity, or social club on campus is a great way to get connected and involved at your new school. Many students find that joining a club gives them a sense of belonging and fellowship. These clubs are not for everyone, and they do take up a lot of a student's time throughout the semester.

If a school's having a Greek Life is something that weighs heavily on your college decision, make sure you understand the ins and outs of the fraternity or sorority lifestyle. While clubs can be tons of fun, they can also be tons of work. Students who join are required to go through rush and pledge weeks, pay club dues, and be actively involved in campus activities.

Before you make a decision, talk with older students who have done it and those who did not. Make sure a prospective club will help you become the person you want to be in college. Never join out of peer pressure. The reputation of the club will reflect on you, even if you don't participate in the activities that earn the club any particular reputation.

If you can't wait to join a fraternity or sorority, and then you find that the club is not right for you, you can always quit or become an inactive member.

### WORKING WITH PROFESSORS

The size of the school you attend will influence how much interaction you will have with your college professors. It is very unlikely that you will know or even speak with your professors at huge universities while it is very likely you will at small private colleges. Regardless of the size of the campus you attend, getting a good reputation with your professors will greatly enrich your academic experience. Professors know which students are hardworking, and they delight in teaching students who really want to learn.

Gaining a distinguished reputation with your college professors can also help you when it is time for graduation. If you decide to go to graduate school or apply for jobs, you will need people to recommend you. Who better than a professor who has known you for four years?

Even if you have a large class, try to meet with your professor once to introduce yourself. Tell your professor that you want to get the most out of the class and ask for advice to help you learn the materials. Be attentive to the syllabus and if you are unclear about anything, ask your professor. If you sit in the front couple of rows, your professors will see that you are actively participating and care about learning. Do not be a sycophant, but show a genuine interest in your professor and the subject. This will help you develop a good reputation among the faculty.

If you are fortunate enough to go to a smaller school, getting to know your professors can lead to great benefits. Not only can you learn from their wisdom outside of the classroom, but you can also count on them to help you out when you are struggling in their subjects.

## SCHOOL RESOURCES

Going to college will have its ups and downs, not only during your freshman year but also throughout your college experience. This is natural and all a part of growing up. This is a transitional time during your life, and it will be both fun and challenging. Realize that everyone will have a difficult time at one point or another; there is no shame in feeling overwhelmed. Instead, use campus resources to help keep you feeling both mentally and physically prepared to tackle the challenges ahead.

Most schools have campus counselors if you need them. This is usually a free service offered by your school. If you find yourself struggling with any aspect of college life, make an appointment with a counselor. Even if you think you can handle the situation, make an appointment. This may be the only time in your life that you won't have to pay additional fees for counseling.

Just as schools offer you a means to take care of your mental well-being, they also have resources to help with your physical well-being. Campus clinics are there to help you when you are sick. Schools also have campus security to help keep you safe. Get familiar with the safety measures of your school, and make sure to have a friend when you walk alone at night.

*Warning signs that warrant a visit to a counselor: long periods of sadness, staying away from friends, constant incomplete work, frequent exhaustion that leaves you unable to go to class, dramatic changes in appetite or weight, long bouts of insomnia, consuming feelings of hopelessness or loss, compulsive need to have something (drugs, alcohol, porn), suicidal thoughts, or thoughts of extreme violence.*

## LOOKING FORWARD

College is an adventure, so give yourself time to get used to all of the changes. It takes approximately three months to feel settled and to relax, so stick it out for the first semester. Realize that college will require a lot of hard work, and most of your freshman peers will not be prepared to handle the amount of outside class work. Use this time to work on your discipline, and understand that adulthood is reached when your decisions reflect a higher level of maturity and strong character. Treat school as if it is a full-time job and don't begrudge the amount of work that is expected of you. Remember that playtime should be a reward for studying, not a substitution.

Be careful not to complain to your parents about how difficult the college experience is, as they have likely made several sacrifices for you to attend. Do not be flippant about money, and always be grateful for the help of your mom and dad. Even though you may feel that you have the right to do whatever you want in college, that does not mean you have the right to keep your parents out of your experience. If they are paying for all or part of your school, you should be respectful and keep them updated on your progress. You are their investment, and they have a right to know what you are doing with their money.

## BEFORE-YOU-LEAVE-HOME CHECKLIST

Knowing what you need to pack and what you don't can be tricky. Incoming freshman usually make the mistake of bringing too much stuff to school and have a hard time finding a place to put everything. Plan for the everyday situations and not the worst-case scenarios. When packing for college, remember less usually is more. Ideally, everything you bring should fit inside a Kia Soul, because that's about how much space you will have in your dorm room.

## FOR YOUR CAR

Bringing your vehicle to college is something you need to consider. Many colleges and universities do not accommodate student parking or there may be a fee. In big cities, like New York or Boston, having a car may be more of a hassle than it's worth. Don't just expect to take your car with you. Try to make the right decision for your campus.

Make sure your car has been inspected and is ready for the semester before leaving home. It would be a major inconvenience to worry about your car breaking down at school. Also make sure to learn how to change a tire and check your oil. If simple car maintenance has always been handled by your parents, it's now time to take on the responsibility.

Things to bring:

1. Car insurance card and proof of registration
2. Driver's license
3. Emergency roadside kit with flashlight, flares, and first aid kit
4. Change of housework clothes and walking shoes
5. Something warm like a jacket or fleece
6. Bottle of water for a leaking radiator
7. Jumper cables (and the knowledge to use them)
8. Spare car key to keep in the dorm room
9. Five dollars in quarters and one $20 bill
10. Maps for every state you will be driving through
11. Roadside assistance program membership card (enroll now if you haven't already)
12. Navigation system for your car (physically in your car or on your smartphone)
13. Towing insurance/auto club membership card for breakdowns*

*\*Some states have an 800 number on the driver's license for stranded motorists, which are for calls of a non-emergency nature. Cell phone companies often have similar numbers. Do not accept help from strangers, but contact a trusted source and stay in your car until help arrives.*

## PERSONAL CARE

Before leaving home is also a great time to get a regular checkup. Personal maintenance may take a backseat to your rigorous studies and increased social schedule. Take the opportunity to go to the dentist. Get your teeth cleaned and protect yourself against cavities. The last thing you want is a root canal during finals week!

Bring with you:
1. Medical records
2. Immunization records
3. Refills for personal medications
4. Information on how to transfer existing prescriptions
5. Valid, up-to-date medical insurance card

## FOR THE DORM

Before you start packing for your dorm, be sure to check and see what your college provides and prohibits. Some dorms have irons and vacuums for the halls to use. Others might have rules against bringing certain items such as candles or hanging things on the walls with nails. Your roommate probably has plans to bring some of these things already, so please check with him or her before packing. The following is a list of suggestions for items that may be able to enhance your dorm room. Be aware: Dorms are very small; having too much stuff may make it crowded and cluttered.

Items to consider:
1. Pillow, bedding, and mattress protector
2. Radio/CD player and CDs/MP3 player
3. Alarm clock

4.  Pictures and other decorations
5.  Towels
6.  Small refrigerator
7.  Rug for floor
8.  Broom or vacuum
9.  Garbage container and bags
10. Computer chair
11. Reading lamp
12. Clothes drying rack
13. Computer with wireless internet capability (laptops are generally best)
14. External hard-drive
15. Printer
16. Printer paper
17. Cups/mugs/silverware/plates/bowls
18. Dish soap/dish rag
19. Basic cleaning supplies
20. Fan
21. Handi-Tak to hang posters
22. Hangers
23. Iron
24. Ironing board
25. Laundry bag
26. Laundry detergent
27. Medicine/first aid kit
28. Microwave (one cubic foot)
29. Rolls of quarters for laundry (if necessary)
30. Small sewing kit
31. Shower caddy
32. Toiletry items/soap dish/tooth brush holder
33. TV/DVD player
34. Computer camera/microphone (so you can use Skype or FaceTime to talk to parents and friends)
35. Keychain flash drive (may help eliminate the need for a printer)

36. Headphones (for TV, MP3 player, or computer)
37. Duct tape
38. Small toolbox with basic tools
39. Power strip with surge protection
40. Bookshelf
41. Fireproof safe for important documents
42. Curtains and curtain rods
43. A list of email and/or regular addresses for people back home

## MISCELLANEOUS

1. Cell phone
2. Telephone for land line
3. School supplies and backpack
4. Cash/checks/credit card
5. Camera
6. Umbrella
7. Favorite books and movies
8. Sports equipment
9. White board
10. Dry and wet erase markers
11. Stationary
12. Stamps

The question of whether to bring important documents (birth certificate, social security card, passport, etc.) is not easily answered. Some students will need these for work-study programs or for acceptance to study-abroad programs. However, college dorms are not known for impeccable security. You should decide for yourself if you need to have these documents with you at college. If you do bring them, keep them locked in a safe place and do not let others know that you have them.

Remember candles, hot plates, and toasters are not allowed in most dorms; make sure you check before buying these. Also, due to the high rate of freshmen (especially girls) who switch roommates after the first semester, it is best not to purchase matching bedding or especially expensive versions of the items on this list. Your next roommate may have the same things you do, and few people need two microwaves!

Make sure that whatever cell phone provider you use offers coverage at your college. You may have to switch providers.

# GUIDE TO PARENTS HELPING YOUR CHILD SURVIVE THEIR FIRST YEAR OF COLLEGE

## GETTING READY FOR THEIR DEPARTURE

The best way to cope with having a child leave for college is by finding other parents who are going through the same thing and form a support group. Also, don't neglect other children who are still at home and aren't going to school yet.

Remember to express to your college-bound student how proud you are of him for graduating from high school and going to college. Try to be patient with students, especially male students, as they try to assert their independence. This can cause family tension, which might make it seem like you are fighting more than usual. Recognize everyone is dealing with excitement and fear. Try your best to understand your son.

Once your daughter leaves, allow at least the first couple of months for her to adjust to college—do not call all the time even though the urge will be very strong. Let her know you are there for her but you know she will be busy and needs her independence. *Students need a chance to adjust and cope with the changes without feeling pulled back home.*

## IMPORTANCE OF BANK ACCOUNTS, CREDIT CARDS, AND CASH

Hopefully your child has already set up a checking and savings account (per Chapter 5) at the beginning of high school. If your son has not, or if the bank is not near his college, then consider setting up a new account. Try finding a bank that has branches in both his hometown and the town of his school.

If there are several great bank account options, then find the bank that has the best deals for students. Many banks offer student accounts with no minimum balance or monthly fees. Make sure your daughter understands all the rules and requirements of her banking accounts before she leaves for school. See if the bank has mail-in deposit options and low or no ATM fees.

Also consider having your child get an account that is in the same bank as yours. This should allow you the opportunity to electronically transfer money if needed.

Students should also make sure they order a box of checks before they leave for school, although with debit and credit cards available, check use is a rarity. Nonetheless, having at least one box on hand is wise. Some places don't take cards, and checks will come in handy if students need to repay a friend.

Credit cards are another important thing to consider for students before they leave for school. Although it might seem dangerous to get an eighteen-year-old who is just moving out of the house a personal credit card, having one for emergency situations can be a lifesaver.

Look into student credit cards with low credit limits. Make sure to read all of the fine print on any credit card contract. Some offer low fees at first, but if a student misses a payment or goes over a certain balance, the fees will shoot straight up. Make sure your student understands the importance of paying off credit cards and not keeping a balance.

Get your child into the habit of carrying at least twenty dollars in cash. Twenty dollars is enough to get some gas or pay for a meal if ever your student is caught in a tight spot. Make sure students understand the cash is there to use when places don't accept either a card or a check.

## PARENTS' HOMEWORK

Let yourself get used to the idea that your child will be leaving soon, and don't try to hold onto your son, but ease him into his new freedom. Plan a weekly family night or a family vacation to take before he leaves for school. If you are driving your child to the school, make it a family road trip.

Before your daughter leaves for college, have her schedule doctor and dentist appointments for any check-ups. Also make sure she has a copy of all insurance documents, medical records, and important phone numbers.

## JUDAH'S CLOSING THOUGHTS

The journey from high school to college is one full of many adventures, tasks, and learning experiences. Both students and parents grow tremendously during this time. Although it is not always easy to prepare for the future, taking each step one at a time is the best way to ensure a smooth transition. Hopefully after reading *High School Prep Genius* you are both encouraged and motivated to take the reins for this next stage of life. So many wonderful experiences, in high school, college, and beyond, await you. Take each day as it comes and try to not only enjoy your plans for the future, but also embrace your moments in the present. These next four years will go by faster than you can imagine, but with the right amount of planning, you can adequately prepare for what comes next.

## JEAN'S CLOSING THOUGHTS

A secure home life is a necessary element of ensuring high school success. The home should be a refuge for escape from negative outside influences regardless of whether your child attends a public, private, charter, or even homeschool. This starts with the bond between parent and child. Let your goal be one of raising a child that you will want to spend time with when they are an adult.

Prioritize building and maintaining open communication between you and your teen. Life's distractions can pull each member of your family in different directions. Be proactive to spend time with your son or daughter. Make a point to sit beside your child's bed every night just to talk with him or her. Ask about his or her questions and listen to his or her thoughts. Be sensitive and do not be critical. Your child will respond to your attitude.

Have no taboos in conversation with your teen. When your son asks a frank question, give him a frank answer. Allow your daughter to trust your word by refusing to lie or soft-sell the truth. Keep in mind, to be able to talk to your child about the "big" issues, you must be willing to start early, long before he or she encounters them, and be committed to open, truthful dialogue.

As a parent, you may have to give the unpopular answer of "no," but convey that your response is motivated by your love and your desire for best his or her's possible future. Pick your battles wisely! Dyeing her hair blue or wearing his ugly sweater to school—if a decision is immature but without permanent negative consequences, cut your teen some slack. Part of growing up is learning from one's mistakes.

In conclusion, most teenagers really want their parents' approval and they want to know you care. Allow your son or daughter to see you are not perfect. Seek to always be genuine and transparent. This may mean admitting your mistakes and asking your child for forgiveness. This opens the door for your teen to reciprocate the behavior.

The intricate relationship between a parent and a teenager can be a very special one. It does not have to be difficult or strained in the midst of all the many changes that seem to be happening all at once for the teen.

Thank you for helping your child through this process.

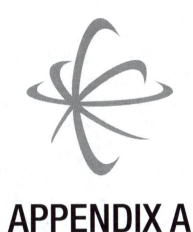

# APPENDIX A

## HOW TO BUILD A HOMESCHOOL TRANSCRIPT

Every student needs a high school transcript to apply for colleges. Today, most colleges and universities are open to and excited about having homeschooled students apply. Although some colleges might ask homeschooled students to include additional application requirements that are not asked of public or private school students (GED scores, SAT subject tests, etc.), most schools require only the basics, which include college entrance exam scores, letters of recommendation, and high school transcripts.

As a homeschooling parent, it is your responsibility to keep a record of your student's academic progress throughout the high school years. Homeschooling parents should start working on their student's transcripts in the student's ninth grade. Although it usually does not matter when your student takes particular courses, it is important to ensure your student completes the minimum requirement of courses to graduate from high school.

Creating transcripts does not have to be a daunting task. Keeping up with a student's transcript is not difficult as long as you're consistent. All you need is a transcript template and the discipline to write down the course material, credits, and dates of completion. Simply include every class and record his or her grades consistently over the next four years. It's as simple as that.

It is also a good idea to save schoolwork samples using the most important assignments or projects. This allows your student the ability to showcase his or her best work and reference examples when applying for college or a job.

Don't allow people/companies to give you fear by trying to sabotage your homeschooling with statements such as "students need their classes accredited" in order for them to be legitimate.

## TRANSCRIPT FORMAT

There is no wrong way to format a transcript. Colleges and universities expect to see a variety of transcript styles because every school uses a different style. As the homeschool administrator, you can choose whatever format works best for you. Transcripts can be created on any computer program, including Word. Some homeschool parents prefer a traditional transcript format (one that is broken up by semesters) while other parents prefer an unconventional transcript format (one that is broken up by class content or subject matter). Either will work as long as you are consistent throughout the transcript.

*Transcript examples can be found at the end of this appendix.*

## BIOGRAPHY INFORMATION

All transcripts should have identifying information including a student's name, address, phone number, date of birth, email address, gender, and social security number. Schools use this information as a quick reference to identify applicants and to organize a student's information. If your student's transcript is more than one page long, ensure that there is enough biographical information on every page to properly identify the student. This way if the pages get separated, the information can easily be put back together.

## COURSE TITLES AND DESCRIPTIONS

When filling out a transcript, you need to use specific course titles such as English I, II, and III; algebra; biology; American history; and so on. While it is perfectly acceptable to give your student's courses generic titles such as English I, it is also okay to give their courses more specific titles such as comprehensive essay writing. Specific course titles give colleges and universities an idea of the material your student focused on in that particular class. Specific titles also add variety and flare to your student's transcripts. If you are having trouble coming up with creative course titles, look at a local college course catalog to get some ideas. You can also go to your state's educational agency's website to help you name your classes.

**Examples of How to Turn Generic Course Titles into Specific Course Titles**
- Computer Skills: Web Design
- Home Economics: Cake Decorating
- History I: The Rise and Fall of Great Nations
- Speech: The Art of Great Presentations
- English II: Great American Novels

## CURRICULUM INFORMATION

Not all subjects that you include in your student's transcript have to fall into traditional classroom subjects. Students who do independent studies, such as career training, computer skills, or home skills, can receive academic credit. Students just need to put enough hours into these subjects to warrant credit and their work needs some sort of evaluation scale. You can also choose to give your students pass/fail grades on such courses. Independent studies are great ways to turn your student's extracurricular interests into high school electives. Test prep can also be considered an elective, as well as Bible studies.

When you are planning what subjects your student will take during the semester or year, it is a good idea to fill out a curriculum information sheet and save it with your student's records. This sheet has an outline of each class a student is taking that semester/year and the general overview of the subject that is being covered. (See the example curriculum record sheet at the end of this appendix.) You can include the books and materials used in class, the outline of projects and grading rubrics, along with a general description of the course.

## GRADING SCALES

Make sure to include a grading scale on your student's transcript. It does not matter what particular grading scale you choose as long as you are consistent. Colleges and universities like to see grading scales along with the grades your students received in order to help evaluate the type of grades recorded on the transcript. (For examples of grading scales, see Chapter 10.)

## CREDITS

While every state's requirements are different, students typically need to complete an average of 24 credits in order to graduate from high school. What is a high school credit? A high school credit is a unit of measure to record class time.

Typically, students receive one credit once he or she has completed between 120 and 150 hours of class time in a particular subject (not including homework, which should be an extra 50 to 65 hours). Credits are generally given in halves for 60 to 75 hours of class work and wholes for 120 to 150 hours of class work. Credits can also be based on finishing a particular curriculum or book, which for some students will take less or more time.

Credit can also be given for students who have reached the level of mastery required for a particular course. Mastery in a course should not be left up to subjective judgment but should be proven through some objective means like a test, writing sample, or evaluation by an outside person. If you feel that your student has mastered a subject through independent study, even though he may not have an actual classroom time on that subject, have him prove his ability in a way that is appropriate for that topic. If you have a student who has done a lot of reading on Ancient Greece and you want to count it as credit toward his or her high school transcript, have your student write a ten- to fifteen-page research paper on the topic. Likewise if your student has a special talent for math and has the ability to skip algebra 1 to go straight into algebra 2, have that student take a test that proves he or she understands and can do all of the concepts in algebra 1.

Homeschooling parents need to document their student's work. Even if you know that your student has mastered subjects without formal classes, have something that proves it.

### Things to Include on Transcripts

1. Name and address of the homeschool
2. Parents' contact information
3. Student's personal information: gender, grade level, birth date, and social security number
4. List of courses and grades for ninth, tenth, eleventh, and twelfth grades
5. A course description key and grading scale
6. Cumulative GPA
7. Standardized test scores (SAT, ACT)
8. Dual enrollment, AP, CLEP and honors courses

### Things to Keep in Mind for a Finalized Transcript

1. Always type the transcript
2. Make it no more than two pages (put extra info in college and career notebook)
3. Complete it in full
4. Specify course titles
5. Include best standardized test scores
6. Note an asterisk (*) with an explanatory footnote if a course is an alternative to a state equivalent
7. Include a graduation date
8. Sign and notarize

| (Your Homeschool Name) OFFICIAL HIGH SCHOOL TRANSCRIPT | |
|---|---|
| STUDENT INFORMATION<br>FULL NAME:<br>ADDRESS:<br>CITY, STATE, ZIP:<br>PHONE NUMBER:<br>EMAIL ADDRESS:<br>DATE OF BIRTH:<br>SOCIAL SECURITY:<br><br>PSAT SCORE:            SAT/ACT SCORE:<br>PARENT/GUARDIAN: | SCHOOL INFORMATION<br>NAME:<br>ADDRESS:<br>CITY, STATE, ZIP:<br>PHONE NUMBER:<br>EMAIL ADDRESS<br>DIRECTOR:<br>PRINCIPAL:<br>SCHOOL YEARS: |

**ACADEMIC RECORD**

| SCHOOL YEAR: | GRADE LEVEL | SCHOOL YEAR: | GRADE LEVEL |
|---|---|---|---|
| Course Title | Credit     Final<br>Earned   Grade | Course Title | Credit     Final<br>Earned   Grade |
| SCHOOL YEAR: | GRADE LEVEL | SCHOOL YEAR: | GRADE LEVEL |
| Course Title | Credit     Final<br>Earned   Grade | Course Title | Credit     Final<br>Earned   Grade |

| ACADEMIC SUMMARY<br>Cumulative GPA:<br>Credits Earned:<br>Diploma Earned:<br>Graduation Date: | GRADING SCALE<br>90 – 100 = A<br>80 – 89 = B<br>70 – 79 = C<br>60 – 69 = D<br>59 – below = F | NOTES<br>Dual credit, AP, CLEP or honors class information can be put in this section. |
|---|---|---|

*I do hereby self-certify and affirm that this is the official transcript of _____ for the school years of*

Signature:                              Title:                         Date:

**Oakley Christian Academy**

David Charles Oakley National Merit Scholar
Soc. Sec:    XXX-XX-XXXX  SAT, best score: Verbal 790, Math 750
Sex: M  Advanced Placement Tests: English and Literature- 4, English and Lan-
guage-5
Address:  123 Main St.  GPA-4.0
Anytown, USA

| High School Curriculum | Mark | Credit |
|---|---|---|
| **Grade 8 (Honors)** | | |
| Algebra 1 | A | 1 |
| Classical Music Survey | Pass | 1/2 |
| **Grade 9** | | |
| Bible | A+ | 1 |
| Algebra 2 | A+ | 1 |
| English Literature | A | 1 |
| Civics/Government | A | 1 |
| Biology with Lab | A | 1 |
| Expository Writing | A+ | 1 |
| Logic | A | 1/2 |
| Typing | A | 1/2 |
| Theater Arts | A | 1/2 |
| Music (Piano) | A | 1 |
| Physical Education (Self-defense) | Pass | 1/2 |
| **Grade 10** | | |
| Bible | A+ | 1 |
| Physical Science w/ Lab | A | 1 |
| English—honors | A | 1 |
| Geometry | A+ | 1 |
| Vocabulary | A | 1 |
| Advanced Math | A+ | 1 |
| Typing | A | 1/2 |
| Music (Piano, Guitar) | A | 1/2 |
| Foreign Language (Latin 1) | A+ | 1 |
| Physical Education (Square Dancing} | Pass | 1/2 |
| **Grade 11** | | |
| Bible | A+ | 1 |
| English—Advanced Placement | A+ | 1 |
| Geography (Mapping the World by Heart) | A | 1 |
| Foreign Language (Latin 2) | A+ | 1 |
| Church History | A+ | 1 |
| Social Studies (Worldviews in Focus) | A | 1/2 |

| | | |
|---|---|---|
| World History I | A+ | 1 |
| Literature | A+ | 1 |
| Music (Drums) | A | 1/2 |
| Health | A | 1/2 |
| Beginning German | Pass | 1/2 |
| Homemaking (Cake Decorating) | Pass | 1/2 |
| Analytical Games | Pass | 1/2 |
| Physical Education (Volleyball) | Pass | 1/2 |

**Grade 12**

| | | |
|---|---|---|
| Physics | A+ | 1 |
| Chemistry | Pass | 1 |
| English—Advanced Placement | A+ | 1 |
| A+ Computer Certification | A | 1 |
| Language Arts | Pass | 1/2 |
| Speech | A+ | 1 |
| Music (Drums) | Pass | 1/2 |
| Foreign Language (Latin 3) | A+ | 1 |
| Foreign Language (Spanish 1) | W | |
| World History 2 | Pass | 1/2 |
| Social Studies (Understanding the Times) | A | 1 |
| Yearbook Staff | A | 1/2 |
| Bible (How Firm a Foundation) | Pass | 1 |

**Grading System**
A+=98-100+
A=90-97
B=80-89
C=70-79
D=65-69
F= 64-Below
W=withdrawn

**Curriculum Information Sheet**

# HIGH SCHOOL CLASSES AND TRANSCRIPT INFORMATION

This section is especially important for homeschooled students, but any student can use it to keep track of classes taken. You do not need to go into exacting detail about everything you studied, but having a good overview is helpful. Keeping a list of your classes will also help you when it is time to make your transcript or when you are checking over one that was made for you. Make one for each grade.

_____ **Grade**

| CLASS NAME | COURSE DESCRIPTION | BOOKS/ MATERIALS USED | AUTHOR | TEACHER | PROJECT/ GRADING DETAILS |
|---|---|---|---|---|---|
|  |  |  |  |  |  |
|  |  |  |  |  |  |
|  |  |  |  |  |  |
|  |  |  |  |  |  |
|  |  |  |  |  |  |
|  |  |  |  |  |  |

# APPENDIX B

## Talent Searches

### HISTORY OF TALENT SEARCHES

The idea of a talent search was developed by Dr. Julian Stanley, a psychology professor at Johns Hopkins University. Starting in 1971, Stanley studied a number of exceptionally talented youngsters. He found that standardized tests they took in school, such as the Stanford Achievement Test or Iowa Tests of Basic Skills, simply didn't provide enough information about the students' abilities. To test his theory, Stanley gave a large group of seventh-graders a test designed for older students, the Scholastic Aptitude Test—otherwise known as the SAT. This is the same test high school juniors and seniors take each year as part of the college admissions process. Stanley found that the SAT did an excellent job of identifying exceptionally talented youngsters. Wanting to encourage more seventh-graders to take the SAT for talent identification, Stanley created the Johns Hopkins Center for Talented Youth (CTY). There he designed and developed specific educational opportunities for students that the SAT identified as gifted students. Such opportunities include fast-paced summer classes, weekend programs, and on-line classes.

Stanley's talent search concept has grown over the last 27 years. Now students from all 50 states have the opportunity to participate in regional talent searches that service their states. Some of the more prominent programs include talent searches from Johns Hopkins University, Duke University, Northwestern University, and the University of Denver. Over 150,000 students participate in talent searches each year. To qualify for the seventh-grade talent search, students must score in the 97th percentile of a grade-level standardized achievement test (e.g., Iowa Tests of Basic Skills). If applicable, homeschool parents can nominate their own student.

Another outgrowth of Stanley's work with the seventh-grade talent searches has been the Elementary Student Talent Search (third- through sixth-graders), offered by Carnegie Mellon University, Northwestern University, the University of Iowa, and Duke University, as well as the Young Students Talent Search (fifth- and sixth-graders) offered by Johns Hopkins University. The requirements for participation include scoring at the 95th percentile on a grade-level standardized test. Qualifications are usually done around August after a student's sixth-grade year. Students are usually qualified through various programs (e.g., Iowa/Stanford tests tip.duke.edu/node/966), and parents can even nominate their students for some talent searches (see: http://tip.duke.edu/node/539)

For more detailed information about Talent Searches, including research findings, see the Spring 1998 issue of The Journal of Secondary Gifted Education, available from Prufrock Press at 800-998-2208

**Regional Talent Searches**

Many states or regions offer different opportunities for talent searches. States along the Rocky Mountains (Colorado, Utah, Nevada, etc.) can take advantage of the Western Academic Talent Search. Southern states (Texas, Florida, Alabama, etc.) should look into the Duke Talent Identification Program. Northwestern's CTD is for students in the Great Lakes areas and Johns Hopkins' CTY is designed for New England states and the Pacific Coast. However, many of these programs offer cross-enrollment programs because each has different opportunities.

For example, Carnegie Mellon University and Johns Hopkins University offer different opportunities for students in Pennsylvania. Carnegie Mellon University offers the C-MITES Talent Search for third- through sixth-graders.

Those who are involved in the C-MITES have the opportunity to participate in the specialized educational testing (EXPLORE), summer programs, weekend workshops, scholarships, newsletters, and resources booklets. Johns Hopkins University's Institute for the Academic Advancement of Youth (IAAY) offers two talent searches: the seventh-grade talent search, which offers programs, career seminars, newsletters, scholarships, and educational counseling, and the Young Students Talent Search (fifth- and sixth-graders), which offers special educational testing (PLUS), summer programs, educational mailings, and scholarships.

Parents should research for talent searches in their region and take advantage of all the opportunities available. For example, Pennsylvania residents might consider the EXPLORE test through Carnegie Mellon in one grade and the PLUS test through Johns Hopkins in another grade.

**Talent Search Process**

It all begins with academically talented students taking an above-level test. Usually a student can sign up for these on-line or at a local school. Parents should check with talent programs to see which tests they accept. Sometimes this will be the SAT or another regional aptitude exam. Then detailed score reports are mailed to the students and their families. These test scores help parents learn more about their student's abilities, and help experts tailor educational advice to the individual student. Once students are enrolled in a talent search, they will receive booklets, handbooks, newsletters, parent meetings, and career education sessions to improve their educational experience. Students may then be given the opportunity to participate in academic summer programs. These courses may enrich students' educational experience and/or allow them to accelerate their academic programs in middle school and high school. This could result in early entrance to college or more time to pursue in-depth study of topics of interest. Also, some students receive scholarships because of their participation or state recognition.

## SOME WELL-KNOWN TALENT SEARCHES

**Duke Talent Identification Program**

www.tip.duke.edu

Benefits for those who participate:

- Improved test-taking skills through experience
- Receipt of "Educational Resource Handbook"
- Receipt of "Educational Opportunity Guide Online"
- Four-year subscription to Insights magazine
- Certificate of merit
- Receipt of My College Guide annual magazine for high achievers
- Talent search results summary
- Duke TIP scholar weekends

**Johns Hopkins Center for Talented Youth (CTY) and Center for Academic Advancement (CAA)**

http://cty.jhu.edu

Benefits for those who participate:

- Affirmation of academic abilities
- Statistical data to evaluate a student's score compared to his or her national peers
- Certificate of participation
- Award ceremonies
- Access to family academic programs such as language immersion programs and Civic Leadership Institute
- Chance to qualify for summer and on-line enrichment programs

**Northwestern's Center for Talent Development (CTD)**

www.ctd.northwestern.edu

Benefits for those who participate:

- Gathering of gifted students
- Inclusion of parental involvement
- Program inspired by success research

- Programs for pre-K through twelfth grades
- Scholarships for programs
- Diverse academic enrichment programs

**Education Program for Gifted Youth (EPGY)**
http://epgy.stanford.edu
Benefits for those who participate:
- Opportunities to take advanced courses
- On-line classes
- Classes for kindergarten through twelfth grade
- Diverse course opportunities to fit students' abilities and interests

**The Center for Bright Kids (CBK)**
www.centerforbrightkids.org
Benefits for those who participate:
- Western Academic Talent Search
- Regional Recognition Ceremony
- Scholarship opportunities
- CBK Summer Programs

# APPENDIX C

## Great Books to Get You Started

This list is by no means comprehensive; however, these books are considered to be some of the best books of all time. This extensive list is in alphabetical order by last name of the authors, and in no way intended to be exhaustive. A selection of great books is inherently subjective, so feel free to check out other great book lists from Time, the Modern Library, the New York Times, the World Library, the National Endowment for Humanities Suggested Reading List, etc. Not every book will be interesting to or appropriate for every student. Parents should either read the book first or research reviews to make sure it is suitable for their student. For more tailored literature suggestions, talk with your local librarians, parents, teachers, and guidance counselors.

- Agee, James: *A Death in the Family*
- Anderson, Sherwood: *Winesburg, Ohio*
- Austen, Jane
    - *Emma*
    - *Northanger Abbey*
    - *Pride and Prejudice*
    - *Sense and Sensibility*

- Bakeless, John: *Daniel Boone*
- Baldwin, James: *Go Tell It on the Mountain*
- Balzac, Honoré de: *Père Goriot*
- Beckett, Samuel: *Waiting for Godot*
- *The Bible*
  - *Old Testament*
  - *New Testament*
- Bolt, Robert: *A Man for All Seasons*
- Bradbury, Ray: *Fahrenheit 451*
- Brontë, Charlotte: *Jane Eyre*
- Brontë, Emily: *Wuthering Heights*
- Browning, Robert: poems
- Buck, Pearl: *The Good Earth*
- Bucks, Frank: *On the Jungle Trails*
- Butler, Samuel: *The Way of All Flesh*
- Camus, Albert
  - *The Plague*
  - *The Stranger*
- Card, Orson Scott: *Ender's Game*
- Carroll, Lewis: *Alice in Wonderland*
- Cather, Willa
  - *Death Comes for the Archbishop*
  - *My Antonia*
- Cervantes, Miguel de: *Don Quixote*
- Chaucer, Geoffrey: *The Canterbury Tales*
- Chekhov, Anton: *The Cherry Orchard*
- Chopin, Kate: *The Awakening*
- Collins, Wilkie: *The Moonstone*
- Conrad, Joseph
  - *Heart of Darkness*
  - *Lord Jim*
  - *The Secret Sharer*
  - *Victory*
- Cooper, James Fenimore

- - *The Last of the Mohicans*
  - *The Spy*
- Crane, Stephen: *The Red Badge of Courage*
- Dante: *The Divine Comedy*
- Defoe, Daniel
  - *Moll Flanders*
  - *Robinson Crusoe*
- Dickens, Charles
  - *Bleak House*
  - *David Copperfield*
  - *Great Expectations*
  - *Hard Times*
  - *Oliver Twist*
  - *A Tale of Two Cities*
- Dickinson, Emily: poems
- Dinesen, Isak: *Out of Africa*
- Dostoyevsky, Fyodor
  - *Brothers Karamazov*
  - *Crime and Punishment*
- Doyle, Sir Arthur Conan: Sherlock Holmes stories
- Dreiser, Theodore
  - *An American Tragedy*
  - *Sister Carrie*
- Dumas, Alexandre
  - *The Three Musketeers*
  - *The Count of Monte Cristo*
  - *The Queen's Necklace*
- Eliot, George
  - *Adam Bede*
  - *Middlemarch*
  - *Mill on the Floss*
  - *Silas Marner*
- Eliot, T.S.: *Murder in the Cathedral*
- Ellison, Ralph: *Invisible Man*

- Emerson, Ralph Waldo: essays
- Faulkner, William
  - *Absalom, Absalom!*
  - *As I Lay Dying*
  - *Intruder in the Dust*
  - *Light in August*
  - *The Sound and the Fury*
- Fielding, Henry
  - *Joseph Andrews*
  - *Tom Jones*
- Fitzgerald, F. Scott
  - *The Great Gatsby*
  - *Tender Is the Night*
- Flaubert, Gustave: *Madame Bovary*
- Forster, E.M.
  - *A Passage to India*
  - *A Room with a View*
- Franklin, Benjamin: *The Autobiography of Benjamin Franklin*
- Galland, Antoine: *Tales from the Arabian Nights*
- Galsworthy, John: *The Forsyte Saga*
- Gogol, Nikolai: *The Cossack Chief*
- Golding, William: *Lord of the Flies*
- Goldsmith, Oliver: *She Stoops to Conquer*
- Graves, Robert: *I, Claudius*
- Greene, Graham
  - *The Heart of the Matter*
  - *The Power and the Glory*
- Hamilton, Edith: *Mythology*
- Hardy, Thomas
  - *Far From the Madding Crowd*
  - *Jude the Obscure*
  - *The Mayor of Casterbridge*
  - *The Return of the Native*
  - *Tess of the D'Urbervilles*

- Hawthorne, Nathaniel
  - *The House of the Seven Gables*
  - *The Scarlet Letter*
- Heggard, H. Rider: *King Solomon's Mines*
- Hemingway, Ernest
  - *A Farewell to Arms*
  - *For Whom the Bell Tolls*
  - *The Sun Also Rises*
- Henry, O.: stories
- Henty, G.A.: *In the Reign of Terror*
- Hersey, John: *A Single Pebble*
- Hesse, Hermann
  - *Demian*
  - *Siddhartha*
  - *Steppenwolf*
- Homer
  - *The Iliad*
  - *The Odyssey*
- Hughes, Langston: poems
- Hugo, Victor: *Les Misérables*
- Huxley, Aldous: *Brave New World*
- Ibsen, Henrik
  - *A Doll's House*
  - *An Enemy of the People*
  - *Ghosts*
  - *Hedda Gabler*
  - *The Master Builder*
  - *The Wild Duck*
- Irving, Washington
  - *Rip Van Winkle*
  - *The Headless Horseman*
- James, Henry
  - *The American*
  - *Daisy Miller*

- - *Portrait of a Lady*
  - *The Turn of the Screw*
- Joyce, James
  - *Portrait of the Artist As a Young Man*
  - *Dubliners*
- Kafka, Franz
  - *The Castle*
  - *Metamorphosis*
  - *The Trial*
- Keats, John: poems
- Kerouac, Jack: *On the Road*
- Koestler, Arthur: *Darkness at Noon*
- Lawrence, D.H.: *Sons and Lovers*
- Lawrence, Jerome, and Robert Edwin Lee: *Inherit the Wind*
- Lee, Harper: *To Kill a Mockingbird*
- Lewis, Sinclair
  - *Arrowsmith*
  - *Babbitt*
  - *Main Street*
- Llewellyn, Richard: *How Green Was My Valley*
- Machiavelli: *The Prince*
- MacLeish, Archibald: *J.B.*
- Mann, Thomas
  - *Buddenbrooks*
  - *The Magic Mountain*
- Marlowe, Christopher: *Dr. Faustus*
- Maugham, Somerset: *Of Human Bondage*
- McCullers, Carson: *The Heart Is a Lonely Hunter*
- Melville, Herman
  - *Billy Budd*
  - *Moby Dick*
  - *Typee*
- Miller, Arthur
  - *The Crucible*

- *Death of a Salesman*
- Monsarrat, Nicholas: *The Cruel Sea*
- O'Neill, Eugene
  - *The Emperor Jones*
  - *A Long Day's Journey into Night*
  - *Mourning Becomes Electra*
- Orwell, George
  - *Animal Farm*
  - *1984*
- Paton, Alan: *Cry, the Beloved Country*
- Pasternak, Boris: *Doctor Zhivago*
- Poe, Edgar Allan: short stories
- Porter, Jane: *The Scottish Chiefs*
- Pyle, Howard: *Robin Hood*
- Reade, Charles: *The Cloister and the Hearth*
- Remarque, Erich Maria: *All Quiet on the Western Front*
- Rolvaag, O.E.: *Giants in the Earth*
- Rostand, Edmond: *Cyrano de Bergerac*
- Salinger, J.D.: *The Catcher in the Rye*
- Sandburg, Carl
  - *Abraham Lincoln: The Prairie Years*
  - *Abraham Lincoln: The War Years*
- Saroyan, William: *The Human Comedy*
- Sayers, Dorothy: *The Nine Tailors*
- Schiller, Frederick: *Joan of Arc*
- Scott, Sir Walter: *Ivanhoe*
- Shakespeare, William: plays and sonnets
- Shaw, George Bernard
  - *Arms and the Man*
  - *Major Barbara*
  - *Pygmalion*
  - *Saint Joan*
- Shelley, Mary: *Frankenstein*
- Sheridan, Richard B.: *The School for Scandal*

- Shute, Nevil: *On the Beach*
- Sinclair, Upton: *The Jungle*
- Sophocles
  - *Antigone*
  - *Oedipus Rex*
- Steinbeck, John
  - *East of Eden*
  - *The Grapes of Wrath*
  - *Of Mice and Men*
- Stevenson, Robert Louis
  - *Dr. Jekyll and Mr. Hyde*
  - *Treasure Island*
- Stowe, Harriet Beecher: *Uncle Tom's Cabin*
- Swift, Jonathan: *Gulliver's Travels*
- Thackeray, William M.: *Vanity Fair*
- Thoreau, Henry David: *Walden*
- Tolstoy, Leo
  - *Anna Karenina*
  - *War and Peace*
- Trollope, Anthony: *Barchester Towers*
- Turgenev, Ivan: *Fathers and Sons*
- Twain, Mark
  - *Pudd'nhead Wilson*
  - *The Adventures of Tom Sawyer*
  - *Adventures of Huckleberry Finn*
- Updike, John: *Rabbit Run*
- Verne, Jules
  - *A Journey to the Center of the Earth*
  - *Masters of the World*
- Virgil: *The Aeneid*
- Voltaire: *Candide*
- Warren, Robert Penn: *All the King's Men*
- Waugh, Evelyn
  - *Brideshead Revisited*

- *A Handful of Dust*
- Wharton, Edith: *The Age of Innocence*
- White, T.H.
  - *The Once and Future King*
- Wilde, Oscar
  - *The Importance of Being Earnest*
  - *The Picture of Dorian Gray*
- Wilder, Thornton: *Our Town*
- Williams, Tennessee
  - *The Glass Menagerie*
  - *A Streetcar Named Desire*
  - *Cat on a Hot Tin Roof*
- Wolfe, Thomas: *Look Homeward, Angel*
- Woolf, Virginia
  - *Mrs. Dalloway*
  - *To the Lighthouse*
- Wouk, Herman: *The Caine Mutiny*
- Wright, Richard
  - *Black Boy*
  - *Native Son*

# APPENDIX D

## Reduce Test Anxiety Through Relaxation Techniques

Sometimes people have a very difficult time overcoming anxiety. Here are some helpful techniques that can help you reduce the mental and physical effects of anxiety. When you feel your body starting to tense up, try one or more of these techniques.

These tips and suggestions are meant to help you think through your anxiety. If you find these techniques aren't helping, you might want to think seriously about speaking with a professional counselor to come up with a system that will help you conquer your stress.

### DEEP BREATHS METHOD

Often your physical state has a huge impact on your mental state. If your body feels tense, then your mind will feel tense. Learning to breathe deeply is another great way to help relax your body. This simple technique can have profound effects on reducing your overall stress level.

1.  Whether you are sitting or standing, your posture will affect your ability to breathe deeply. Always sit or stand straight up with good posture.

2. Inhale slowly through your nose. Your nose has a natural filtration system and will help keep pollutants out of your lungs.

3. The goal is to breathe from your diaphragm. You may already be familiar with using your diaphragm if you play a wind instrument in the band or are a singer. For those of you who aren't familiar with the diaphragm, it is the big muscle under your lungs that helps you expand your chest. A way to know if you are breathing from your diaphragm is to look at your stomach. Does it push out when you take a deep breath? If it does, then great! If it doesn't, then you aren't breathing from your diaphragm. If you are having trouble, focus on pushing your stomach out when you breathe; this action will cause your diaphragm to expand.

4. Hold your breath, and your stomach out, for a couple of seconds.

5. Exhale slowly, letting the air come out of your mouth. When you first start, you should exhale to the count of five. Keep every breath slow and steady; otherwise, it won't help you calm down.

6. After you have exhaled, wait a few seconds and repeat.

7. Repeat as necessary until you feel your body relax.

## THE TENSE AND RELEASE RELAXATION METHOD

People tend to tense their bodies when they feel anxious. This tension causes them to feel even more stressed, which in turn causes them to further tighten their muscles. Obviously this cycle can continuously compound stress. Try this technique when you are feeling tense, especially when sitting at your desk right before a test.

1. Sit straight up in your chair.

2. Put your feet firmly on the floor.

3. Grab the underneath of your chair with the palms of your hands.

4. Push your feet into the floor while you are pulling your hands up against the chair. You should be pushing and pulling in opposite directions. As you do this, take a deep breath in. Hold your muscles tight and your breath in for about four or five seconds.

5. Exhale slowly as you relax your hands and your feet. Your exhale should take about five seconds.

6. Repeat this process as many times as necessary.

## VISUALIZATION METHOD

Sometimes when you're feeling anxious, it's a good idea to visualize something that is calming. Your calming image could be anything; it could be a place, an item, or a person. Just make sure it is something that relaxes you. Here is a technique that can help you focus on what you are visualizing.

1. Curve your hands to make a cup out of each of your hands.
2. Close your eyes.
3. Put your palms on your cheekbones and your fingers on your forehead, covering your closed eyes with the cups you have made. Make sure you do not touch your eyes directly; you just want to cover them.
4. Think about your relaxing image. It can be a real or an imaginary scene. Make the picture more vivid by adding as much detail as you can. If you are visualizing a place, what does it look like? What does it feel like? How is the weather? What kind of sounds can you hear? If it's an item, what does it look like? How does it feel? If it is person, what does the person look like? What would he or she be saying to you? Why does he or she help calm you?
5. Visualize this calming image for a couple of minutes.

## THE HERE-AND-NOW RELAXATION METHOD

Sometimes when people start to feel anxious they suffer from what is known as a panic attack. Many panic attacks are brought on because the person is overwhelmed by some future situation or task. He or she feels like there isn't enough time to accomplish this particular task, or this person is afraid of what might happen in the future. Many times the fear of the future causes a person to freeze up and feel even more afraid.

A good way to tackle the feeling of being overwhelmed by the future is to remind yourself that you are not in the future. Instead you are living in the here and now, and there is still time to address whatever it is that is stressing you out. With some practice you can help your mind focus on the here and now.

If you are feeling the effects of a panic attack or are simply overcome by anxiety about the future, try this technique:

1.  Sit in a chair. Make sure you have good posture; it will help you breathe better.
2.  Remove your socks and shoes, and place your bare feet on the floor.
3.  Close your eyes.
4.  With your feet planted firmly on the ground, rub your feet against the floor. The contact of your feet on the floor helps your mind focus on your surroundings. This contact helps remind your brain that you are in the present.
5.  Once your mind is focused, tighten your toes for a couple of seconds and then relax them. As you tighten, take a deep breath; as you relax, let out your deep breath.
6.  Bring awareness to your ankles by keeping your feet firmly pressed to the ground. Tighten your muscles and release. As you tighten and relax, breathe in deeply and exhale deeply.
7.  Move up your body bit by bit, continuing all the way to your face. Each time, bring your attention to the muscles on that part of the body. Always breathe as you tighten and relax. Go slowly and make sure you concentrate on every part of your body. Release any tension in that part of the body.
8.  Remind yourself you are living in the present. If you have to, rub your feet against the ground again. Tell yourself whatever you are worrying about is in the future and you can't do anything to change it at the present time.
9.  Tell yourself you are going to do your best on whatever it is you're worrying about.
10. Continue to take deep breaths.
11. Once you have calmed your body and your mind, you can make a plan of attack for your situation. If you find you are always getting ahead of yourself and focusing too much on the future, get into the habit of stopping your thoughts and reminding yourself that you are living in the present. A good way to do that is to carry a water bottle around with you and whenever you start to focus on the future, take a drink. Taking a drink is an easy way to trick your mind to focus back on the here and now.

## POSITIVE SELF-TALK METHOD

What you say to yourself has a huge effect on how you feel. While at first you might think that positive self-talk is silly, you must realize that your mind talks to itself all the time. The question isn't whether you talk to yourself, but whether you are positive or negative.

If you are suffering from anxiety, there's a really good chance you're also suffering from negative self-talk. Whenever you are about to take a test or even think about a test, what do you hear in your mind? Do you think, "No matter what I do, I'm going to fail this test"? Or do you think, "If I put enough effort into studying, I'm going to do great!"? That's the difference between positive and negative self-talk. Learn to change the way you react to tests, and your performance will follow.

Here are some examples of negative self-talk and how to change them into positive thoughts.

**"No matter how hard I work, I am never going to pass."**
"With the right amount of effort I can do well."

**"If I fail this test, I'm doomed to repeat this class."**
"If I try my best and still fail this test, I can talk to my teacher and see what I need to do better. I bet she'll let me do some extra-credit work to help make up some points."

**"No matter how much I study, when it comes to test time, I always forget the answers."**
"I forget the answers because I let myself get freaked out by the test. If I learn not to worry about forgetting the answers, then I won't forget them."

**"There is no way I can study enough to do well on this test."**
"I have done my best and studied the material. I am confident in how well I studied."

**"If I do badly on this test, it means I'm a stupid person."**
"Not everyone is good at every subject. All I can do is my best, and if I still don't get it, then maybe this subject isn't my strength."

If you are having trouble controlling your negative thoughts, then you might want to come up with a positive word or phrase to repeat to yourself every time a negative thought comes into your head. It can be as simple as "I can do well on this test." Repeat your positive phrase to yourself the whole time you are studying and throughout the test. This positive reinforcement will help shut out your negative thoughts.

Make sure to monitor what you say to yourself. When you are thinking about a test, try to look at it as realistically as possible. Your thoughts must accurately reflect the situation; otherwise, they will do you great harm. Just as overly negative thoughts can hurt you, so can overly positive thoughts. It will do you no good to tell yourself that you have prepared for a test if in fact you know you haven't. If you tell yourself you have prepared and then do poorly, it will only reinforce your test anxiety. You can't do well just because you tell yourself you will do well; you must also put in the effort needed to perform well. Likewise you won't do well if you put in the effort to do well but don't tell yourself you can do well. To succeed you must have both.

# APPENDIX E

## Admissions Terminology

**3-2 program:** This is a program in which students spend three years studying liberal arts, then two years in professional training. Upon completion a student will receive two degrees.

**Accreditation:** This is the official recognition that a college, university, or trade school has met the regional or national association standards.

## ADMISSIONS DECISIONS:

- **Admit**: This means you were accepted into the college, university, or trade school to which you applied. You, and sometimes your high school, will receive an official notification with your acceptance status.
- **Admit/deny**: This is both good news and bad news. First you have been offered admission into the school to which you applied. However, you have been denied any financial aid. If you wish to study at this school, you will have to find other means of paying for your education.
- **Deferred acceptance**: This means the admissions decision has been moved to a later date. You will find out then if you are admitted or denied admission.

- **Deny**: Unfortunately you have not been accepted into the school to which you applied.
- **Wait list:** At this point you have been neither accepted nor denied. You have been placed on a waiting list in case an opening becomes available. If you have been waitlisted, make sure to continue to contact the school and check on your status. Admission counselors like persistence and knowing that you really want to be admitted into their respective schools.

**Academic common market:** Students can **study a specialized field at an out-of-state college while paying in-state tuition rates** at members of the Southern Region Education Board (SREB). States stretch from Kentucky down through the Southeast and across to Texas. North Carolina, Texas, and Florida restrict their participation to the graduate school level only. For a list of participating schools and programs, visit www.sreb.org/acm.

**Articulation:** This is an agreement between a two-year and a four-year school within the same state that allows students from the two-year college automatic admissions into the four-year college. This is a great second option of admissions if you weren't admitted directly into the four-year college. It is also a great way to save money for the first couple of years before transferring into a more expensive school.

**Associate degree:** This is a degree granted by a college or university after a student completes a two-year full-time program or its part-time equivalent. Such degrees include an Associate of Arts or Associate of Science, awarded after the first two years of a four-year program, and the Associate in Applied Science, which is usually awarded after the completion of a technical or vocational program.

**Award letter (or award package): Letter notifying a** student about the financial aid that the school is offering to him or her, if he or she chooses that particular college. The package may include grants, scholarships, loans, and work-study opportunities. He or she may not meet all of the financial obligations and that is referred to as the "gap." Some select private universities do promise to meet 100 percent of demonstrated financial need.

**Bachelor's or baccalaureate degree:** This is the degree awarded after the completion of a four-year study at a college or university. The most common degrees are the Bachelor of Arts and the Bachelor of Science.

**Candidates' reply date agreement (CRDA):** This allows students to defer attendance decisions until May 1. Students will have time to get the responses from most of the other colleges they have applied to before making a final decision.

**Common application:** This is the standard application form that is accepted by almost four hundred colleges. In many cases you can use this application instead of using a specific college's or university's application. For more information, visit www.commonapp.org.

**Consortium:** This is when a group of college or universities offers joint programs or allows students from the different schools to share facilities, course offerings, and organizational memberships. Consortiums allow students to diversify their schedules. Joint programs are often made up by neighboring schools.

**Cooperative education:** These co-op programs are offered by some of the larger state schools for students who want to alternate classroom training with practical work experience in their desired field.

**Cost of education:** Total cost including tuition, room and board (if living on campus), student fees, books, school supplies, lab fees, transportation costs, computer costs, club dues parking, and various other expenses.

**Credit hours:** A college-level course is assigned a number of credit hours that it is worth. Most classes count for three credit hours because they meet three times per week for one hour each time. Courses that require extra lab time, such as biology and chemistry, typically count for four hours. Less than twelve hours in a term will qualify the student as a part-time student. Twelve hours or more per semester will qualify the student as full-time. The average course load per semester for a full-time student is fifteen to sixteen hours.

**Double major:** This is when a student chooses to graduate with more than one degree and study for both simultaneously. Both degrees can be accomplished in four years by forfeiting many of their non-major electives in order to pursue the requirements for the other major.

**Early action (EA):** Students apply to a school of their choice early in their senior year and ask for an early application review and notification of admissions. Deadlines for early action are usually between October 30 and January 15. Students typically receive an admissions decision three to four weeks after sending in their applications. An advantage of early action is that if accepted the student *does not* have to attend this institution; however, that student knows he or she has secured admissions into at least one school. Students can still apply to other schools during the regular admissions cycle.

**Early action single option:** This is when a college wants to know how serious the early action applicants are about attending their school. It is not legally binding for the student, but the single option applicant is allowed to apply early action to only one school. He or she may still apply for general admission to other schools.

**Early admission:** Some schools will admit students who have not completed high school. These students are usually exceptional juniors who, if they enroll in the college or university full-time, do not complete their senior year in high school. Once a student has completed a certain number of college hours, the institution will award the student his or her high school diploma.

**Early decision (ED):** The early decision plan allows students to apply to colleges and universities early in a student's senior year and request for an early notification of admissions. If a student has been accepted with the early decision, he or she is obligated to withdraw any other applications to other colleges or universities. He or she must accept admission to the ED school. **Students should not apply for early decision unless they are absolutely sure they want to attend that institution.** Some colleges and universities offer both the early action and early decision options; be careful not to confuse them.

**Emphasis:** This is an area of concentration within a major or a minor. Some colleges and universities require students to pick an emphasis in their field of study. An example of an emphasis is broadcast journalism in the field of mass communications.

**Greek life:** Schools with an active Greek community are schools with a busy campus presence of fraternities or sororities, sometimes known as social clubs.

**Honors program**: Top-performing students often attend the larger colleges who offer these rigorous programs. They require high SAT scores, but they usually receive separate, nicer housing, special advisors, smaller classes, advance registration for their course choices, and other perks. Most colleges require that students complete a separate, additional application in order to be considered for admission.

**Internship:** Students can choose to seek unpaid experience in their future careers and perhaps earn college credit in the process. Colleges will often help students find and arrange for summer internships.

**Major:** This is the subject which a student wishes to focus on during school. Each major will require a certain number of credit hours and defined classes in order to qualify. A major may earn the student a Bachelor of Arts degree or a Bachelor of Science degree, depending on the nature of the subject. Students at four-year colleges will typically declare a major by their junior year, if not before.

**Minor**:  A minor is a subject in which the student takes extra courses, but not enough to qualify as a major. They can be related or unrelated to a student's major. It is optional for students at a four-year school to select a minor.

**Need-blind admissions policy:** This is when the college's application focuses only on the student's academic merit without any knowledge of the student's financial ability to pay for college. Once admitted, the university constructs a financial aid package that addresses the student's financial need. Selective and well-funded universities and colleges do this to attract the top-performing students from all economic backgrounds.

**Open admissions**: Any student with a high school diploma or its equivalent is admitted without review of his or her academic qualifications. Many junior or community colleges admit students under this policy.

**Personal statement**: A personal statement is required for most college application packets. This is an essay written about oneself which may describe career goals, personal challenges, or successes, depending on the prompt. Admission committees use students' personal statements to learn more about all candidates and to see if they are good fits for the college or university. This is a student's chance to shine.

**Quarter system:** The quarter system is an academic calendar that divides the nine months of school into four equal parts. Each part is approximately twelve weeks long. Summer sessions, if offered, are usually about the same length of time.

**Regular admissions:** The regular admissions process is what students typically think of as applying for college. Students typically hear back about their application status between March and April of their senior year.

**Residency requirements:** This is the length of time stipulated by the different colleges or universities that enrolled students must spend on campus taking courses. This term can also refer to how long students and families must reside in a state before being considered for in-state tuition or state aid. **Public colleges in state** may provide a much lower tuition rate for students who are residents of the same state.

**Retention rate:** The number of students who return for the sophomore year. This basically means how many students return after spending one year at the institution.

**Rolling admissions:** This is the admissions policy in which there is no deadline for filing out a college application. This guideline is used most often by state universities. Responses are usually received within three to four weeks after the application has been submitted. Students should try to send in their applications as soon as possible.

**SASE:** A self-addressed stamped envelope, which may need to be included with your application.

**Semester system:** The semester system divides the academic calendar into two equal parts. Each part is approximately eighteen weeks. Summer sessions are often shorter but require more intensive study.

**Test of English as a Foreign Language (TOEFL):** TOEFL is an exam required by almost all U.S. colleges and universities for students whose principal language is not English. The TOEFL is made up of three multiple-choice sections: listening comprehension, structure and written expression, and reading comprehension.

**Transcript:** This is the official record of a student's coursework at a school. Students must send in an unofficial high school transcript as a part of the application progress. Once a student has graduated from high school, he or she is often required to send a final or official transcript to the institution. Remember some schools only accept transcripts that are in sealed envelopes and have either the seal of the school or the administrator's signature across the back.

**Transfer program**: This allows students to continue with his or her studies at four-year colleges by maintaining certain criteria. Such programs are usually found at colleges or universities that offer Associate's degrees.

**Transfer student**: This is a student who transfers from one college or university to another. Credits received from one school will be evaluated. Schools will decide how many credit hours will be accepted as credit. Each school sets different transfer policies. It is best to speak with an advisor before transferring into different schools.

**Trimesters:** This is the academic calendar that divides the school year into three equal terms.

**Yield**: This is the percentage of accepted students who will enter a college or university in the freshman class.

**Wait List**: This is where students are put on a waiting list for admission; they may still be admitted if other students who were admitted decide not to attend. Students on this list will need to follow the instructions given by the school to indicate their willingness to stay on the wait list.

## JEAN BURK

Jean Burk is the author of *College Prep Genius* and has written numerous articles about the SAT and PSAT/NMSQT, college prep, and scholarship search techniques. She has been featured as an SAT expert on Fox, CBS, NBC, TXA/21, and The Homeschool Channel. She homeschooled both her children and they each received incredible scholarships because of their PSAT and SAT scores. As instructor of the College Prep Genius curriculum, she has helped coach students to find scholarships for full tuition, room and board, unlimited laundry and lunchroom passes, study abroad stipends, and more!

She currently travels and speaks about the importance of college preparation at conventions, book fairs, schools, and libraries. She has taught her "Master the SAT" prep class all over the United States as well as China. Her company, Maven of Memory Publishing, has a new book series called VocabCafé that helps teenagers and younger children increase their knowledge of SAT-level vocabulary words through fun, wholesome books.

## JUDAH BURK

Judah Burk is the daughter of veteran homeschooling mom and test prep guru Jean Burk. In 2009, she graduated *summa cum laude* at Ouachita Baptist University with a B.A. in mass communications. She went on to receive her master's degree in international relations at Texas A&M with a 4.0 in 2012. She is one of the authors of the VocabCafé book series and coauthor of *High School Prep Genius*. She has also taught numerous students how to emulate her SAT success in the "Master the SAT" prep class all across the United States and has been a featured speaker. A published journalist since 2005, she has also worked as a freelance writer.